Synonyms and Antonyms

The Ultimate Thesaurus

READERS CHOICE
New Delhi - 110002

Synonyms and Antonyms

The Ultimate Thesaurus

Puneet Kumar

READERS CHOICE
New Delhi - 110002

Synonyms and Antonyms

The Ultimate Thesaurus

ISBN 978-81-922292-7-0

Published by:

Readers Choice

103, 4787/23, Ansari Road,

Daryaganj, New Delhi - 110002

Ph: 9654444181

Laser typesetting by: Naissance Books, New Delhi.

Printed at: Navprabhat Printing Press, Delhi

Preface

In today's world there is immense amount of competition for achieving success and reaching to the topmost level. There is a one factor which plays a very vital role in the world today — conversation skills. Through an appealing conversation one can present himself more firmly and confidently. One of the most important things, which should be kept in mind while conversing or speaking, is the usage of words. However, sometimes the usage of similar words again and again makes the speech monotonous and dry. So, at this point of time the use of antonyms and synonyms becomes important.

A thesaurus or a dictionary of synonyms and antonyms makes a handy composing tool when you need to find another word to keep from sounding repetitious or boring. Of all the books in the world that aid the learning process, a thesaurus is one of the most useful. Like dictionaries, a thesaurus is one of the most common reference works found in schools and libraries. Not only can it help school children and college students, but it serves a useful purpose for people who write business letters, articles, or stories.

The present book contains an amazing collection of synonyms and antonyms. Antonyms refer to the words that are opposite in meaning for a given word. On the other hand, synonyms refer to the words having the same or nearly the same meaning in one or more senses as another word, i.e. many more different words with same meaning of a word.

Usage of antonyms and synonyms of a particular word makes an individual's speech powerful and attractive to the listener. Learning so many different words is also useful in improving the vocabulary which ultimately enriches the person's conversation.

This book performs the same function. It will make you familiar with various antonyms and synonyms of different words. The language is simple and moreover, antonyms and synonyms are arranged in an alphabetical order so as to make the study more interesting. This book will prove helpful at both introductory and professional level.

–Author

Contents

1

Why Use Synonyms and Antonyms?

Synonyms

A synonym is a word or a phrase that means exactly or nearly the same as another word or phrase in the same language, for example, accept is a synonym of abide.

Synonyms are different words with almost identical or similar meanings. Words that are synonyms are said to be synonymous, and the state of being a synonym is called synonymy.

Why use them?

Just imagine how monotonous our communication would be if we always used the same words when speaking, reading and writing! Indeed, everything (person, place, object…) in the world had only one word to refer to it, the world would be a very boring place.

Well, in order to make language a lot more expressive and interesting, we should try to vary the words we use as often as we can (but not too often).

That's where synonyms come into the picture! The word synonym is a composite of two Greek words: The prefix 'syn' means 'together' and 'onym' is 'name.' Synonyms— naming the same thing. In other words, synonyms are words or phrases which share the exact same meaning or a very similar meaning.

For example:

- Calamity : Adversity
- Big : Bulky
- Dad : Father
- Celebrity : Big gun
- Worker : Employee

Words from any part of speech (e.g. nouns, verbs, adjectives, adverbs or prepositions) can have synonyms, as long as they both have the same part of speech.

For example:

- Amazing, awesome, incredible, astonishing (adjectives)
- Car, auto, automobile, motorcar (nouns)
- Participate, take part, join (verbs)
- Quickly, fast, promptly (adverbs)
- On, upon (prepositions)

When replacing a word with its synonym, make sure the meaning of the sentence in the specific context is maintained as well. Synonyms are defined according to certain senses of words.

For example:

This will be Raghu's senior year at the University.

Senior in this sentence cannot be replaced with the words elder or older, since the meaning of the sentence will change and will make less sense.

However, senior in the sense of fourth year can be replaced with the word last and the meaning will remain the same as in the original sentence.

Good speakers and writers often vary their vocabulary and so can you! The best way to expand your vocabulary is to use a thesaurus. A thesaurus is a source that provides you with a listing of similar or related words you can choose from in order to vary your word choice in your text.

A Word of Caution

When you're learning words, they can't help but be spots where things get a little murky. English vocabulary is especially full of pitfalls since the language is so vast.

In English, there are several words that share one meaning or nuances of one meaning. Then there are tiny words like 'set' and 'get' that have so many meaning that their definitions take up multiple dictionary pages.

Then, just to make it more daunting, the English language has over a million words. As far as word banks, English is massive.

But don't let the enormousness of the language turn you off. Antonyms and synonyms can be used to learn new words and add a great deal to your diction and the way you talk about language in particular.

Knowing what words are similar or opposites helps people to understand the same when it comes to ideas. Ideas are impossible without words, and words are impossible without ideas. The more you think about the interrelationships of one, the better you are able to think about the interrelationships of the other.

Finally, Antonyms!!!

Antonyms are words that mean the opposite of other words. The antonym of big is small, for example.

English language lets its speakers make its own antonyms just by adding a prefix. The ability to make up one's own words and have them be real words is something truly lovable about English.

Mis, dis, dys, mal, in, and unare all prefixes one can affix to words to create antonyms.

Examples:

- Official becomes unofficial
- Flexible becomes inflexible
- Adroit becomes maladroit
- Functional becomes dysfunctional
- Peptic becomes dyspeptic
- Philanthropist becomes misanthropist

However, Be Careful: changing prefixes doesn't always work, like flammable and inflammable pretty much mean the same thing—they're synonyms—but usually prefix juggling works like water on fire.

2

List of Synonyms and Antonyms?

A

- **Word:** Abandon (Synonym denoting Meaning: disregard)

  Other Synonyms: Carelessness, free-spiritedness, impulse, impulsiveness, intemperance, recklessness, spontaneity, thoughtlessness, unrestraint, wantonness, wildness.

  Antonyms: Attention, canniness, care, carefulness, circumspection, deliberation, discreetness, discretion, foresight, forethought, heed, heedfulness, providence, prudence, vigilance, watchfulness.

- **Word:** Abate (Synonym denoting Meaning: lessen)

  Other Synonyms: Allay, cool, decline, decrease, die away, diminish, dull, dwindle, ebb, lay back, lessen, let up, mellow out, moderate, quell, recede, reduce, slack off, slacken, slow, subdue, subside, taper, taper off, wane, weaken.

  Antonyms: Actualize, advance, amplify, augment, beautify, broaden, build-up, cultivate, deepen, dilate, elaborate, enlarge, enrich, evolve, exploit, extend, finish,, heighten, improve, intensify, lengthen, magnify, materialize, perfect, polish, promote, realize, refine, spread, strengthen, stretch, unfold, widen, work out.

- **Word:** Abbreviate (Synonym denoting Meaning: shorten)

  Other Synonyms: Abridge, abstract, boil down, clip, compress, condense, contract, curtail, cut, cut back, cut down, cut off, cut out, cutback, digest, nutshell, pare, prune, reduce, shorten, summarize, synopsize, take out, trim, truncate.

  Antonyms: Add, augment, beef up, boost, build-up, deepen, develop, elaborate, enlarge, exaggerate, expand, expatiate, extend, flesh out, heighten, hike up, inflate, intensify, jack up, lengthen, magnify, pad, pyramid, raise, soup up, strengthen, stretch, supplement, swell, widen.

- **Word:** Abide (Synonym denoting Meaning: stand)

  Other Synonyms: Accept, acknowledge, bear, bear with, concede, consent, defer, endure, hang in, hang tough, live with, put up with, receive, sit tight, stand, stand for, stomach, submit to, suffer, swallow, take, tolerate, withstand.

  Antonyms: Abstain, avert, bypass, circumvent, deflect, desist, ditch, divert, dodge, duck, elude, escape, eschew, evade, fake out, fend off, flee, hide, hold off, jump, keep clear, lay low, obviate, recoil, shake, shake off, shirk, shrink from, shuffle off, shun, shy, sidestep, skip, skip town, skirt, stay away, stay out, stutter step, turn aside, ward off, weave, withdraw.

- **Word:** Ability (Synonym denoting Meaning: adeptness)

  Other Synonyms: Adeptness, aptitude, bent, capability, capacity, command, competence, comprehension, dexterity, endowment, expertise, facility, faculty, intelligence, knack, know-how, might, potentiality, power, proficiency, qualification, resourcefulness, skill, strength, talent, understanding.

  Antonyms: Benightedness, bewilderment, blindness, callowness, creeping, crudeness, denseness, disregard, dumbness, empty-headedness, fog, greenness, half-knowledge, illiteracy, incapacity, incomprehension, innocence, insensitivity, mental incapacity, naïveté, nescience, oblivion, obtuseness, philistinism, rawness.

- **Word:** Abnormal (Synonym denoting Meaning: different)

  Other Synonyms: Aberrant, anomalistic, anomalous, atypical, bizarre, curious, deviant, deviate, deviating, different, divergent, eccentric, exceptional, extraordinary, funny, gross, heteroclite, irregular, mutant, odd, off-base, off-colour, offbeat, peculiar.

  Antonyms: Accepted, average, banal, bourgeois, casual, characteristic, colloquial, commonplace, conventional, current, customary, daily, everyday, familiar, frequent, general, habitual, hackneyed, homely, humdrum, informal, mediocre, monotonous, natural, obscure, passable, plain, prevailing, prevalent, probably, prosaic, regular, routine.

- **Word:** Absence (Synonym denoting Meaning: gone)

  Other Synonyms: Absenteeism, AWOL, cut, hooky, no show, non-appearance, non-attendance, truancy, vacancy.

  Antonyms: Admittance, attendance, attention, audience, audit, audition, chance, conference, congress, consultation, council, discussion, inquiry, interview, investigation, meeting, negotiation, notice, parley, performance, presentation, reception, review, test, trial, tryout.

- **Word:** Absent-minded (Synonym denoting Meaning: unaware)

  Other Synonyms: Absent, absorbed, abstracted, bemused, day dreaming, distracted, distrait, dreaming, dreamy, engrossed, faraway, forgetful, goofing off, heedless, inattentive, lost, mooning, moony, oblivious, pipe dreaming, preoccupied, remote, removed, spacey, unconscious, unheeding, unmindful, unobservant, unthinking, withdrawn, wool-gathering.

  Antonyms: Active, bright, cagey, careful, circumspect, clever, good hands, heads up, heedful, hip, hopped up, intelligent, jazzed, lively, looking, observant, on guard, perceptive, psyched up, quick, ready, sharp, spirited, switched on, vigilant, wary, watchful, wide-awake, wired, wise, with it.

- **Word:** Abuse (Synonym denoting Meaning: exploit)

  Other Synonyms: Exploit, impose on, use, wrong.

  Antonyms: Admire, adore, appreciate, apprise, care for, clasp, cleave to, cling to, coddle, comfort, cosset, cultivate, defend, dote on, embrace, encourage, enshrine, entertain, fancy, fondle, foster, guard, harbour, hold dear, honour, hug, idolise, imagine, like, love, nourish, nurse, nurture, pet, preserve, prize, revere, reverence, safeguard, shelter, shield, support, sustain, treasure, value, venerate, worship.

- **Word:** Academic (Synonym denoting Meaning: scholarly)

  Other Synonyms: Bookish, college, collegiate, erudite, intellectual, learned, pedantic, scholarly, scholastic, studious, university.

  Antonyms: Apprenticed, benighted, bird-brained, blind to, dense, green, illiterate, imbecilic, inexperienced, innocent, insensible, mindless, misinformed, moronic, naive, oblivious, obtuse, sappy, shallow, thick, unaware, unconscious, uncultivated, uncultured, uneducated, unenlightened, uninformed, uninitiated, unknowledgeable, unlearned, unlettered, unmindful, unread, unschooled, unsuspecting, untaught, untrained, unwitting, witless.

- **Word:** Accept (Synonym denoting Meaning: receive)

  Other Synonyms: Acquire, gain, get, obtain, secure, take, welcome.

  Antonyms: Abate, backslide, cheapen, decay, decrease, degenerate, depreciate, deteriorate, diminish, disintegrate, droop, drop, dwindle, ebb, fade, fail, fall, fall off, flag, go downhill, languish, lapse, lose value, lower, pine, recede, relapse, retrograde, return, revert, rot, sag, settle, shrink, sink, slide, subside, wane, weaken, worsen.

- **Word:** Accompany (Synonym denoting Meaning: escort)

  Other Synonyms: Associate with, attend, chaperon, come along, conduct, consort, convoy, date, draft, drag, escort, follow, go along, guard, guide, hang out, keep company, lead, look after, shadow, show about, show around, squire, stick to, string along, tag along, tailgate, take out, usher.

Antonyms: Abdicate, back out, bail out, bow out, cast off, chicken out, cop out, cut loose, deep six, desert, discard, discontinue, disown, ditch, drift away, drop, drop out, duck, dump, dust, forsake, give up, kiss goodbye, lay aside, leave, leave behind, let go, pull out, quit, reject, relinquish, renounce, ship out, slide, stop, storm out, strand, surrender, throw over, throw overboard, toss over, vacate, walk, withdraw, yield.

- **Word:** Accord (Synonym denoting Meaning: approve)

  Other Synonyms: Accede, acquiesce, admit, allow, award, bestow, concede, confer, endow, give, grant, present, render, tender, vouchsafe.

  Antonyms: Altercate, bandy, battle, bicker, buck, bump heads, contend, cross, cross swords, disagree, dispute, face down, face off, feud, hammer, hammer away, hash, hash over, hassle, jump, jump on, kick around, knock around, lock horns, pettifog, quarrel, quibble, rehash, row, sass, set to, squabble, talk back, wrangle.

- **Word:** Accuse (Synonym denoting Meaning: blame)

  Other Synonyms: Allege, apprehend, arraign, arrest, attack, attribute, betray, blame, brand, bring charges, censure, charge, cite, complain, criminate, denounce, finger, frame, hold accountable, impeach, implicate, impute, incriminate, inculpate, indict, libel, litigate, lodge complaint, name, pin on, prosecute, recriminate, slander, slur, sue, summon, tax.

  Antonyms: Acquit, bleach, blink at, clear, clear excuse, discharge, exculpate, exempt, exonerate, forgive, free, launder, let go, let off, liberate, lifeboat, loose, pardon, release, relieve, sanitise, set free, spare, spring, vindicate, whitewash, wink at, write off.

- **Word:** Achieve (Synonym denoting Meaning: accomplish)

  Other Synonyms: Accomplish, acquire, actualise, adjust,

attain, bring about, bring off, carry off, carry out, carry through, close, complete, conclude, consummate, deliver, discharge, dispatch, do, earn, effect, effectuate, enact, end, execute, finish, follow through, fulfil, gain, get, get done, manage, negotiate, obtain, perfect, perform, procure, produce, rack up, reach, realize, resolve, score, seal, see through, settle, sign, solve, win.

Antonyms: abate, aid, allay, alleviate, ameliorate, assist, assuage, bolster, buck up, calm, cheer, commiserate with, compose, condole, confirm, console, delight, divert, ease, encourage, enliven, free, gladden, grant respite, hearten, help, inspirit, invigorate, make well, mitigate, nourish, quiet fears, reanimate, reassure, refresh, relieve, remedy, revitalise, revive, salve, soften, solace, soothe, strengthen, stroke, succour, support, sustain, sympathize, uphold.

- **Word:** Acid (Synonym denoting Meaning: bitter)

  Other Synonyms: Acerbic, acidulous, biting, piquant, pungent, sharp, tart, vinegary.

  Antonyms: banal, blah, boring, dull, flat, flavourless, ho-hum, humdrum, insipid, milk-and-water, monotonous, nerdy, nothing, sapless, tame, tedious, unexciting, uninspiring, uninteresting, vanilla, vapid, waterish, watery, weak, wimpy, wishy-washy, zero.

- **Word:** Acquire (Synonym denoting Meaning: receive)

  Other Synonyms: Access, achieve, amass, annex, attain, bring in, buy, catch, collect, cop, corral, earn, gain, gather, get, grab, have, hustle, land, lock up, obtain, pick up, procure, promote, rack up, scare up, secure, snag, take, take possession, wangle, win.

  Antonyms: Cost, damages, fine, forfeiture, loss, mulct, penalty, relinquishment.

- **Word:** Adaptable (Synonym denoting Meaning: alterable)

  Other Synonyms: Adjustable, all around, alterable, can do, changeable, compliant, conformable, convertible, ductile, easy-going, flexible, malleable, modifiable, plastic, pliable, pliant, putty, resilient, supple, switch hitting, tractable, variable, versatile.

Antonyms: Adamant, adamantine, determined, dogged, dyed-in-the-wool, firm, fixed, hard, immovable, immutable, implacable, indomitable, inexorable, intractable, iron, obdurate, obstinate, relentless, resolute, rigid, rigorous, set, single-minded, staunch, steadfast, steely, stiff, strict, stringent, inadaptable, unbending, unchangeable, incompliant, uncompromising, unrelenting, unswayable, unyielding.

- **Word:** Addition (Synonym denoting Meaning: totaling)

  Other Synonyms: Accretion, accrual, computing, counting, enlarging, expanding, increasing, reckoning, sum, summation, summing, tabulating, toting.

  Antonyms: Answer, assumption, cogitation, consequence, consideration, contemplation, corollary, deliberation, derivation, finding, illation, inference, inferring, judgement, meditation, mulling, musing, opinion, pondering, ratiocination, reasoning, reflection, result, rumination, sequitur, speculation, thinking, thought, understanding.

- **Word:** Address (Synonym denoting Meaning: focus)

  Other Synonyms: Apply, attend to, concentrate, devote, dig, direct, engage in, focus on, give, go at, go for, hammer away, have at, peg away, pitch into, plug, take up, throw, to, try, turn, turn to, undertake.

  Antonyms: Abstain, avert, bypass, circumlocute, circumvent, deflect, desist, ditch, divert, dodge, duck, elude, escape, eschew, evade, fake out, fend off, flee, hide, hold off, jump, keep clear, lay low, obviate, recoil, shake, shake off, shirk, shrink from, shuffle off, shun, shy, sidestep, skip, skip town, skirt, stay away, stay out, stutter step, turn aside, ward off, weave, withdraw.

- **Word:** Admirable (Synonym denoting Meaning: respected)

  Other Synonyms: Ace, attractive, best ever, cat's pajamas, choice, commendable, cool, copacetic, crack, crackerjack, daisy, deadly, deserving, dilly, dream, estimable, excellent, exquisite, fine, gnarly, good, great, greatest, groovy, heavy, hunky dory, keen, laudable, mean, meritorious, neat, peachy, praiseworthy, rare, smashing, solid, spiffy, super, super-duper, superior, unreal, valuable, wicked, wonderful, worthy.

Antonyms: Abhorrent, abject, abominable, bad, base, beggarly, cheap, currish, degenerate, despicable, despicable, detestable, dirty, disgusting, fink, hateful, heel, ignoble, ignominious, inferior, low, low-down, lowest, mean, odious, outcast, paltry, pitiable, pitiful, poor, rat, sad, scummy, scurvy, shabby, shameful, sordid, sorry, swinish, unworthy, vile, worthless, wretched.

- **Word:** Admission (Synonym denoting Meaning: entrance)

  Other Synonyms: Acceptance, access, admittance, certification, confirmation, designation, door, entrance, entree, ingress, initiation, introduction, permission, reception, recognition, way, welcome.

  Antonyms: Barricade, blank wall, block, clog, deterrent, encumbrance, fence, hindrance, hurdle, impediment, obstacle, obstruction, pale, rail, railing, restraint, road block, snag, stop, stumbling block, traverse, wall.

- **Word:** Admonish (Synonym denoting Meaning: warn)

  Other Synonyms: Advise, berate, call down, caveat, censure, check, chide, counsel, ding, enjoin, exhort, exhortation, forewarn, give comeuppance, glue, growl, hoist, jack up, monition, notice, rap, rebuke, reprimand, reproof, reprove, scold, sit on, speak to, talk to, tell off, upbraiding, warning.

  Antonyms: Accept, acclaim, admire, applaud, appreciate, approbate, commend, cope, countenance, esteem, face it, favour, handle, like, live with, lump it, praise, regard highly, respect, stomach.

- **Word:** Adolescent (Synonym denoting Meaning: pre-adult)

  Other Synonyms: Boyish, girlish, growing, immature,

juvenile, pubescent, puerile, teen, teenage, young, youthful.

Antonyms: Developed, fully grown, grown, grown-up, of age, ripe, ripened.

- **Word:** Advertise (Synonym denoting Meaning: publicise)

  Other Synonyms: Acquaint, advance, advise, announce, apprise, ballyhoo, bill, blazon, boost, build-up, circularize, communicate, declare, disclose, display, divulge, drum, endorse, exhibit, expose, flaunt, hard sell, herald, hype, inform, make known, notify, pitch, plug, press agent, proclaim, promote, promulgate, puff, push, reveal, show, soft sell, splash, sponsor, spot, tout, uncover, unmask.

  Antonyms: Adumbrate, blot out, bury, cache, camouflage, cloak, cover, curtain, disguise, dissemble, ditch, duck, eclipse, ensconce, go underground, harbour, hold back, hole up, hush up, keep from, keep secret, lie low, lock up, mask, not tell, obscure, plant, protect, reserve, salt away, screen, secrete, shadow, shelter, shield, shroud, smuggle, squirrel, stash, stifle, stow away, suppress, take cover, tuck away, veil, with.

- **Word:** Advice (Synonym denoting Meaning: recommendation)

  Other Synonyms: Admonition, advisement, advocacy, aid, bum steer, caution, charge, consultation, counsel, directions, dissuasion, encouragement, exhortation, forewarning, guidance, help, information, injunction, input, instruction, judgement, kibitz, lesson, news, opinion, persuasion, prescription, proposal, proposition, recommendation, steer, suggestion, teaching, telltale, tidings, tip, tip-off, view, warning, word.

  Antonyms: Deception, dishonesty, double-cross, double-dealing, duplicity, falseness, giveaway, Judas kiss, letdown, perfidy, sell-out, treachery, treason, trickery, unfaithfulness.

- **Word:** Aesthetic (Synonym denoting Meaning: beautiful)

  Other Synonyms: Artful, artistic, creative, esthetic, gorgeous, inventive.

Antonyms: Adverse, disagreeable, discouraged, discouraging, displeasing, distressed, gloomy, grim, melancholy, troubled, troubling, unfavourable, unfortunate, unhappy, unpleasant.

- **Word:** Affirm (Synonym denoting Meaning: declare)

  Other Synonyms: Assert, asseverate, attest, aver, avouch, avow, certify, cinch, clinch, confirm, cross heart, declare, guarantee, ice, insist, lock up, maintain, nail down, okay, predicate, profess, pronounce, ratify, repeat, rubber-stamp, set, state, swear, testify, vouch, witness.

  Antonyms: Abjure, abnegate, ban, begrudge, call on, contradict, contravene, controvert, curb, decline, disallow, disavow, disbelieve, discard, disclaim, discredit, disown, disprove, doubt, enjoin from, eschew, exclude, forbid, forgo, forsake, gainsay, hold back, keep back, negate, negative, not buy, nullify, oppose, rebuff, rebut, recant, refuse, refute, reject, repudiate, restrain, revoke, sacrifice, spurn, taboo, turn down, veto, withhold.

- **Word:** Agent (Synonym denoting Meaning: representative)

  Other Synonyms: Abettor, actor, advocate, ambassador, assignee, assistant, attorney, broker, commissioner, delegate, deputy, doer, emissary, envoy, executor, factor, factotum, functionary, go-between, handler, intermediary, lawyer, middleman, minister, mover, negotiator, officer, operative, operator, proctor, promoter, proxy, representative, salesman, servant, steward, substitute, surrogate, worker.

  Antonyms: Arch, capital, cardinal, champion, chief, controlling, crowning, dominant, essential, first, foremost, greatest, head, highest, incomparable, key, leading, main, mainline, major, matchless, maximum, outstanding, paramount, peerless, pre-eminent, predominant, premier, prevailing, primary, prime, prominent, sovereign, star, stellar, strongest, superior, supreme, transcendent, unapproachable, unequalled, unparalleled, unrivalled.

- **Word:** Aggression (Synonym denoting Meaning: hostility)

  Other Synonyms: Aggressiveness, antagonism, belligerence, combativeness, destructiveness, dirty deed, fight, hostility, pugnacity, push.

Antonyms: Attrition, battle, blocking, check, combat, contention, copying, counteraction, cover, defiance, detention, fight, fighting, friction, halting, hindrance, holding, impedance, impediment, impeding, intransigence, obstruction, parrying, protecting, protection, rebuff, refusal, retardation, safeguard, screen, shield, stand, striking back, struggle, support, warding off, watch, withstanding.

- **Word:** Alert (Synonym denoting Meaning: attentive)

  Other Synonyms: Active, bright, cagey, careful, circumspect, clever, good hands, heads up, heedful, hip, hopped up, intelligent, jazzed, lively, looking, observant, on guard, perceptive, psyched up, quick, ready, sharp, spirited, switched on, vigilant, wary, watchful, wide-awake, wired, wise, with it.

  Antonyms: Comatose, conked, crashed, dead, dormant, dozing, dreaming, flaked out, hibernating, in dreamland, in repose, inactive, inert, napping, out, out cold, reposing, resting, sacked out, sawing logs, sleeping, slumbering, snoozing, snoring, somnolent.

- **Word:** Anaemic (Synonym denoting Meaning: pale)

  Other Synonyms: Bloodless, feeble, frail, infirm, pallid, sickly, wan, watery, weak.

  Antonyms: Ablaze, animated, aroused, blushing, burning, crimson, elated, embarrassed, enthused, exhilarated, feverish, florid, full-blooded, high, hot, inspired, intoxicated, pink, red, rosy, rubicund, ruddy, sanguine, thrilled.

- **Word:** Analyse (Synonym denoting Meaning: examine)

  Other Synonyms: Assay, chew over, confab, consider, estimate, evaluate, figure, figure out, hash, inspect, interpret, investigate, judge, kick around, rehash, resolve, scrutinize, sort out, spell out, study, talk game, test, think through.

  Antonyms: Avoid, blink, brush off, cold-shoulder, cut, cut dead, dial out, discount, disdain, evade, fail, forget, high hat, ice, live with, neglect, omit, overlook, overpass, pass over, play past, pooh-pooh, reject, scorn, slight, tune out, wink at.

- **Word:** Ancient (Synonym denoting Meaning: old)

  Other Synonyms: Age-old, aged, antediluvian, antiquated, antique, archaic, back number, been around, bygone, creak, early, elderly, fossil, hoary, moth-eaten, obsolete, old goat, old-fashioned, older, oldie, out-of-date, outmoded, primal, primeval, primordial, relic, remote, rusty, superannuated, timeworn, venerable.

  Antonyms: Abreast, au courant, current, existent, extant, fire new, in fashion, instant, just out, latest, mod, new, newfangled, now, present, present-day, recent, red-hot, topical, ultramodern, up, up-to-date, up-to-the-minute.

- **Word:** Angel (Synonym denoting Meaning: guardian)

  Other Synonyms: God's messenger, archangel, celestial being, cherub, divine messenger, guardian, heavenly being, holy being, seraph, spirit, spiritual being, sprite, supernatural being.

  Antonyms: Adversary, archfiend, beast, common enemy, dastard, enfant terrible, Evil One, fiend, hellion, imp, knave, Lucifer, Mephistopheles, monster, ogre, rogue, Satan, scamp, scoundrel, sin, the Dickens, villain.

B

- **Word:** Baby (Synonym denoting Meaning: infant)

  Other Synonyms: Angel face, babe, bambino, bundle, buttercup, button, cherub, chick, child, crawler, deduction, dividend, dumpling, kid, little angel, little darling, little doll, little one, lollypop, newborn, nipper, nursling, papoose, preemie, suckling, sugar, tad, tax write-off, toddler, tot, write-off, youngster.

  Antonyms: Boyish, girlish, growing, immature, juvenile, pubescent, puerile, teen, teenage, young, youthful.

- **Word:** Bachelor (Synonym denoting Meaning: single man)

  Other Synonyms: Available, bachelor girl, batch, celibate, eligible, misogamist, misogynist, single, single man, stag, unattached, unmarried man, virgin.

  Antonyms: Bedmate, bridegroom, buffalo, consort, cuckold, groom, head, helpmate, hubby, main man, man, mate, mister, monogamist, old man, other half, polygamist, spouse.

- **Word:** Back (Synonym denoting Meaning: end)

  Other Synonyms: Aback, abaft, aft, after, astern, back of, backward, behind, final, following, hind, hindmost, posterior, rear, rearmost, rearward, tail.

  Antonyms: Antecedent, foregoing, former, past, precedent, preceding, previous, prior.

- **Word:** Bad (Synonym denoting Meaning: poor)

  Other Synonyms: Abominable, amiss, atrocious, awful, bad news, beastly, blah, bottom out, bummer, careless, cheap, cheesy, crappy, cruddy, crummy, defective, deficient, dissatisfactory, downer, dreadful, erroneous, fallacious, faulty, garbage, god-awful, gross, grungy, icky, imperfect, inadequate, incorrect, inferior, junky, lousy, not good, off, poor, raunchy, rough, sad, sleazy, slipshod, stinking, substandard, synthetic, the pits, unacceptable, unsatisfactory.

  Antonyms: Adequate, admissible, all right, average, big, close, common, cool, decent, delightful, ducky, fair, far out, groovy, hip, hunky-dory, ice, kosher, large, okay, passable, peachy, peachy keen, pleasant, pleasing, respectable, right on, sharp, slick, standard, sufficient, swell, tolerable, trendy, unexceptional.

- **Word:** Bag (Synonym denoting Meaning: catch)

  Other Synonyms: Acquire, apprehend, capture, collar, gain, get, hook, kill, land, nail, net, seize, shoot, take, trap.

  Antonyms: Comp, complimentary, costless, for free, for love, for nothing, free lunch, free ride, freebie, gratis, gratuitous, handout, paper, unpaid, unrecompensed.

- **Word:** Banish (Synonym denoting Meaning: expel)

  Other Synonyms: Ban, cast out, deport, discard, discharge, dislodge, dismiss, dispel, drive away, eject, eliminate, eradicate, evict, exclude, excommunicate, exile, expatriate, expulse, extradite, isolate, ostracize, oust, outlaw, proscribe, relegate, remove, rusticate, sequester, shake off, shut out, transport.

  Antonyms: Accept, adapt, affiliate, affirm, appropriate, approve, assent, assume, borrow, embrace, endorse, espouse, follow, imitate, maintain, mimic, opt, ratify, seize, select, support, take on, take over, take up, tap, use, utilize.

- **Word:** Bank (Synonym denoting Meaning: collect)

  Other Synonyms: Amass, deposit, heap, hill, hoard, invest, lay aside, lay away, mass, mound, pile, put by, salt away, save, sock away, speculate, squirrel, stash.

  Antonyms: Acquit, ante up, come across, come through, contribute, cough up, deal, defray, dispense, disperse, distribute, divide, divvy, dole out, expend, fork out, give, lay out, lot out, measure out, outlay, partition, pay off, pay out, pony up, put out, shell out, use.

- **Word:** Barrier (Synonym denoting Meaning: obstruction)

  Other Synonyms: Bar, barricade, blank wall, blockade, bound, boundary, confines, curtain, ditch, enclosure, fence, fortification, gully, hurdle, impediment, limit, moat, obstacle, pale, palisade, railing, rampart, roadblock, stop, trench, wall.

  Antonyms: Aperture, breach, break, cavity, chink, cleft, crack, cranny, crevice, cut, discontinuity, door, fissure, gap, hatch, interstice, mouth, orifice, outlet, perforation, recess, rent, rift, rupture, scuttle, slit, slot, space, split, spout, tear, vent, window.

- **Word:** Base (Synonym denoting Meaning: vulgar)

  Other Synonyms: Abject, abominable, cheap, coarse, common, contemptible, corrupt, depraved, despicable, disgraceful, dishonourable, disreputable, foul, grovelling, humble, ignoble, immoral, indelicate, loathsome, lowly, mean, menial, offensive, paltry, pitiful, plebeian, poor, scandalous, servile, shameful, shoddy, sleazy, sordid, sorry, squalid, trashy, ugly, unworthy, vile, worthless, wretched.

Antonyms: Acceptable, ace, admirable, agreeable, bad, bully, capital, choice, commendable, congenial, crack, deluxe, excellent, exceptional, favourable, first-class, first-rate, gnarly, gratifying, great, honourable, nice, pleasing, positive, precious, prime, recherché, reputable, satisfactory, satisfying, select, shipshape, sound, spanking, splendid, sterling, stupendous, super, superb, superexcellent, superior, tip-top, valuable, wonderful, worthy.

- **Word:** Bashful (Synonym denoting Meaning: shy)

  Other Synonyms: Abashed, backward, blushful, blushing, chary, confused, constrained, coy, embarrassed, humble, modest, nervous, overmodest, recoiling, reserved, reticent, retiring, self-conscious, self-effacing, shamefaced, sheepish, shrinking, silent, timid, timorous, unassertive.

  Antonyms: Audacious, bold, brazen, brazenfaced, cheeky, cocksure, cocky, effervescent, flip, foolhardy, forward, hasty, headlong, heedless, hot-headed, ill-advised, impertinent, impetuous, impolitic, impudent, incautious, inconsiderate, indiscreet, insolent, madcap, nervy, precipitate, presuming, presumptuous, pushing, rash, reckless, rude, self-asserting, self-assertive, tactless, thoughtless, undiplomatic, untactful, uppity, vivacious.

- **Word:** Basic (Synonym denoting Meaning: elementary)

  Other Synonyms: Basal, capital, central, chief, elemental, essential, indispensable, inherent, intrinsic, key, main, necessary, primary, primitive, principal, radical, underlying, vital.

  Antonyms: Added, affixed, appended, further, increased, lagniappe, more, new, option, other, over-and-above, padding, perk, spare, supplementary, widow.

- **Word:** Beautiful (Synonym denoting Meaning: attractive)

  Other Synonyms: Admirable, alluring, angelic, appealing, beauteous, bewitching, charming, classy, comely, cute, dazzling, delicate, delightful, divine, elegant, enticing, excellent, exquisite, fair, fascinating, fine, foxy, good-looking, gorgeous, graceful, grand, handsome, ideal, lovely, nice, pleasing, pretty, radiant, ravishing, refined, resplendent, shapely, splendid, stunning, sublime, superb, symmetrical, taking, well-formed, wonderful.

Antonyms: Aberrant, abnormal, absurd, antic, bizarre, deformed, distorted, eerie, extravagant, extreme, fanciful, fantastic, flamboyant, freakish, gross, incongruous, ludicrous, malformed, misshapen, monstrous, odd, outlandish, perverted, preposterous, queer, ridiculous, strange, surrealistic, uncanny, unnatural, weird, weirdo, whimsical.

- **Word:** Behave (Synonym denoting Meaning: control)

  Other Synonyms: Be civil, be good, be nice, be orderly, comport oneself, control oneself, demean oneself, deport oneself, direct, discipline oneself, manage, manage oneself, play fair, shape up.

  Antonyms: Act up, be indecorous, blunder, cut up, misbehave.

- **Word:** Beloved (Synonym denoting Meaning: adored)

  Other Synonyms: Admired, cared for, cherished, darling, dear, dearest, doted on, endeared, esteemed, fair-haired, favourite, hallowed, highly regarded, highly valued, idolised, loved, pet, pleasing, popular, precious, prized, respected, revered, sweet, treasured, venerated, well-liked, worshiped.

  Antonyms: Abhorred, avoided, creepy, despised, detested, dippy, disesteemed, disfavoured, disliked, drip, dumpy, execrated, goon, gross, loathed, loser, lousy, nerd, obnoxious, ostracized, out, pain, ratty, rejected, scorned, shunned, sleazy, stinky, turkey, unaccepted, unattractive, uncared for, undesirable, unloved, unvalued, unwanted, unwelcome, weird, wimpy, zombie.

- **Word:** Below (Synonym denoting Meaning: lower)

  Other Synonyms: Beneath, down, down from, under, underneath.

Antonyms: Aloft, atop, beyond, high, on high, over, overhead, raised, superior, upon.

- **Word:** Bend (Synonym denoting Meaning: curve)

  Other Synonyms: Angle away, angle off, arch, bow, buckle, camber, careen, circle, contort, crimp, crinkle, crook, crouch, curl, deflect, deform, detour, double, droop, flex, genuflect, hook, incline, lean, loop, pervert, round, spiral, stoop, swerve, tilt, turn, twist, veer, verge, warp, waver, wilt, wind, yaw, zigzag.

  Antonyms: Adjust, alienate, coordinate, even, fix, line up, make parallel, order, range, regulate, straighten.

- **Word:** Beneficial (Synonym denoting Meaning: advantageous)

  Other Synonyms: Benign, constructive, favourable, favouring, gainful, good, healthful, helpful, profitable, propitious, salubrious, salutary, serviceable, toward, useful, valuable, wholesome, worthy.

  Antonyms:, Adverse, contrary, damaging, debit side, deleterious, depreciative, depreciatory, derogatory, detracting, disparaging, down side, dyslogistic, harmful, hurtful, ill-timed, inconvenient, inexpedient, injurious, inopportune, objectionable, pejorative, prejudicial, slighting, uncomplimentary, unfavourable, unprofitable.

- **Word:** Better (Synonym denoting Meaning: excellent)

  Other Synonyms: Bigger, choice, exceeding, exceptional, finer, fitter, greater, higher quality, improved, larger, more appropriate, more desirable, more fitting, more select, more suitable, more useful, more valuable, preferable, preferred, prominent, sharpened, sophisticated, superior, surpassing, worthier.

  Antonyms: Back seat, bottom man, bottom rung, entry level, flunky, junior, less, lesser, lower, menial, minor, minus, nether, peon, second banana, second fiddle, second-string, secondary, slave, smaller, subjacent, subordinate, subsidiary, under, underneath, yes man.

- **Word:** Bide (Synonym denoting Meaning: wait)

  Other Synonyms: Abide, attend, await, continue, dwell, hang around, hang in, hang out, linger, live, remain, reside, sit tight, stay, stick around, sweat it, tarry, watch for.

  Antonyms: Abscond, approach, beat it, bug out, cruise, decamp, depart, escape, exit, fare, flee, fly, get away, get going, get lost, get off, hightail, journey, lam, leave, light out, make for, mosey, move, move out, near, pass, proceed, progress, pull out, push off, push on, quit, repair, retire, run along, run away, set off, shove off, skip out, split, take flight, take leave, take off, tool, travel, vamoose, wend, withdraw.

- **Word:** Big (Synonym denoting Meaning: large)

  Other Synonyms: Ample, awash, barn door, brimming, bulky, bull, burly, capacious, chock-full, colossal, commodious, considerable, copious, crowded, enormous, extensive, fat, full, gigantic, heavy duty, heavyweight, hefty, huge, hulking, humungous, husky, immense, king sized, mammoth, massive, monster, oversize, packed, ponderous, prodigious, roomy, sizable, spacious, strapping, stuffed, substantial, super colossal, thundering, vast, voluminous, walloping, whopper, whopping.

  Antonyms: Babyish, bantam, brief, cramped, diminutive, dinky, dwarf, elfin, embryonic, fleeting, hardly any, hasty, immature, imperceptible, inappreciable, inconsiderable, infant, infinitesimal, insufficient, junior, light, Lilliputian, limited, meagre, microscopic, mini, miniature, minute, not big, not large, peanut, petite, pygmy, scant, short, short-lived, shrimp, shriveled, skimpy, slight, snub, sparse, stubby, stunted, teeny, tiny, toy, truncated, undersized, undeveloped, wee, wizened, young.

- **Word:** Blaze (Synonym denoting Meaning: burn)

  Other Synonyms: Beam, burst out, coruscate, explode, fire, flame, flare, flash, flicker, fulgurate, glare, gleam, glow, illuminate, illumine, incandesce, light, radiate, scintillate, shimmer, shine, sparkle.

Antonyms: Blot out, blow out, choke, douse, drown, out, quench, smother, snuff out, stamp out, stifle, suffocate, trample.

- **Word:** Bloody (Synonym denoting Meaning: bleeding)

  Other Synonyms: Blood-soaked, blood-spattered, bloodstained, crimson, ensanguined, gaping, gory, grisly, imbrued, open, raw, sanguinary, sanguine, wounded.

  Antonyms: Cold, cold-hearted, dull, impassible, indolent, insensible, insensitive, languid, lazy, lifeless, listless, passionless, sluggish, spiritless, torpid, unemotional, unkind.

- **Word:** Blossom (Synonym denoting Meaning: flower)

  Other Synonyms: Bloom, blow, burgeon, burst, effloresce, leaf, open, shoot, unfold.

  Antonyms: Blemish, contort, damage, deform, demolish, destroy, dilapidate, disfigure, distort, foul up, gum up, harm, hash up, impair, injure, louse up, mangle, mar, mess up, misshape, muck up, obliterate, ruin, scratch, screw up, spoil, sully, tarnish, trash, vandalize, wreck.

- **Word:** Blue (Synonym denoting Meaning: sad)

  Other Synonyms: Dejected, depressed, despondent, disconsolate, dismal, dispirited, down-hearted, downcast, fed up, gloomy, glum, low, melancholy, moody, unhappy, woebegone.

  Antonyms: Alert, animate, animated, blithe, blithesome, bouncy, brash, carefree, cheerful, cheery, chipper, chirpy, confident, convivial, devil-may-care, festive, forward, frivolous, frolicsome, fun-loving, gamesome, glad, gleeful, hilarious, insouciant, jocund, jolly, jovial, joyful, joyous, keen, light-hearted, lively, merry, mirthful, playful, pleasure-seeking, presuming, pushy, rollicking, self-assertive, sparkling, spirited, sportive, sprightly, sunny, vivacious, wild, zippy.

- **Word:** Blunder (Synonym denoting Meaning: botch)

  Other Synonyms: Blow, bobble, bollix, botch, bumble, bungle, confuse, err, flounder, flub, foul up, fumble, gum up, louse up, lurch, mess up, misjudge, mistake, muff up, screw up, slip up, stumble.

Antonyms: Achieve, arrive, attain, bring about, bring off, carry out, conclude, consummate, do, do justice, effect, finish, fulfil, gain, get someplace, get there, hit, make it, manage, nail it, perform, produce, pull off, rack up, reach, realise, score, sew up, unzip, win.

- **Word:** Boil (Synonym denoting Meaning: heat)

  Other Synonyms: Bubble, churn, coddle, cook, decoct, effervesce, evaporate, fizz, foam, froth, parboil, poach, seethe, simmer, smolder, steam, steep.

  Antonyms: Arctic, biting, bleak, brisk, chilly, cool, freezing, frigid, frosty, gelid, glacial, icy, nippy, raw, sharp, wintry.

- **Word:** Bold (Synonym denoting Meaning: brave)

  Other Synonyms: Adventurous, assuming, audacious, bantam, courageous, daring, dauntless, enterprising, fearless, forward, gallant, heroic, intrepid, resolute, unafraid, undaunted, valiant, valorous.

  Antonyms: Abashed, aghast, alarmed, anxious, apprehensive, aroused, blanched, cowardly, cowed, daunted, discouraged, disheartened, dismayed, distressed, disturbed, faint-hearted, frightened, frozen, horrified, in awe, intimidated, nervous, panic-stricken, perplexed, perturbed, petrified, rattled, run scared, scared, scared stiff, shocked, spooked, startled, stunned, suspicious, terrified, terror-stricken, timid, timorous, trembling, upset, worried.

- **Word:** Bear (Synonym denoting Meaning: bring)

  Other Synonyms: Buck, carry, convey, deliver, ferry, fetch, lug, move, pack, take, tote, transfer, transport.

  Antonyms: Beg off, brush off, corn, decline, demur, desist, ding, disaccord, disallow, disapprove, dispense with, dissent, dodge, evade, fluff off, hold back, hold off, hold out, ignore, make excuses, nix, not budge, not buy, pass up, protest, rebuff, regret, reject, repel, reprobate, repudiate, say no, send off, send regrets, set aside, shun, spurn, thumbs down, turn away, turn down, turn from, withdraw, withhold.

- **Word:** Beat (Synonym denoting Meaning: strike)

  Other Synonyms: Bang, bash, bat, batter, belt, box, break, bruise, buffet, cane, castigate, clout, club, collide, crush, cudgel, drub, flagellate, flail, flog, hammer, hit, knock, lambaste, lash, lick, maltreat, mash, maul, pelt, pommel, pound, punch, punish, ram, rap, slap, slug, smack, spank, strike, swat, thrash, thresh, thump, thwack, trounce, wallop, whale, whip.

  Antonyms: Abet, alleviate, assist, bail out, befriend, encourage, favour, go with, lighten, mitigate, promote, relieve, serve, straight out, subsidise, support, sustain.

- **Word:** Benefactor (Synonym denoting Meaning: donor)

  Other Synonyms: Aid, altruist, angel, assistant, backer, contributor, fairy godmother, fan, free ride, good Samaritan, helper, humanitarian, mark, meal ticket, patron, philanthropist, pigeon, promoter, protector, sponsor, subscriber, sugar daddy, supporter, well-wisher.

  Antonyms: Adversary, bad guy, bandit, competitor, contender, enemy, foe, match, meat, opponent, opposite number, rival.

- **Word:** Bilk (Synonym denoting Meaning: cheat)

  Other Synonyms: Bamboozle, beat, circumvent, con, deceive, defraud, disappoint, do, fleece, flimflam, foil, frustrate, gyp, overreach, rook, ruin, swindle, thwart, trick.

  Antonyms: Accord, administer, allow, ante up, award, bequeath, bestow, cede, come across, commit, confer, consign, convey, deed, deliver, dish out, dispense, dispose of, dole out, donate, endow, entrust, fork over, furnish, gift, grant, hand, hand over, heap upon, lavish upon, lay upon, lease, let have, make over, parcel out, part with, pass down, pass out, permit, pony up, present, provide, relinquish, remit, sell, shell out, subsidize, supply, throw in, tip, transfer, transmit, turn over, vouchsafe, will.

- **Word:** Blasé (Synonym denoting Meaning: nonchalant)

  Other Synonyms: Apathetic, bored, cloyed, cool, disenchanted, disentranced, fed up, glutted, indifferent, jaded, knowing, laid back, lukewarm, mellow, offhand, satiated, sick of, sophisticate, sophisticated, surfeited, unconcerned, unexcited, uninterested, unmoved, weary, world-weary.

  Antonyms: Acquisitive, agog, ambitious, antsy, appetent, ardent, athirst, avid, breathless, covetous, craving, desiring, desirous, dying to, earnest, enthusiastic, fervent, fervid, greedy, gung ho, hankering, heated, hot, hungry, impatient, intent, keen, longing, pining, raring, restive, restless, self-starting, solicitous, thirsty, vehement, voracious, warm-blooded, wild, wishful, yearning, zealous.

- **Word:** Block (Synonym denoting Meaning: obstruct)

  Other Synonyms: Arrest, bar, barricade, block out, blockade, brake, bung up, catch, charge, check, choke, clog, close, close off, close out, congest, cut off, dam, deter, fill, halt, hang up, hinder, hold up, impede, intercept, interfere, occlude, plug, prevent, shut off, shut out, stall, stonewall, stop, stop up, stopper, stymie, tackle, thwart.

  Antonyms: Bright, clarion, crystal, fair, fine, halcyon, light, luminous, pleasant, rainless, shining, shiny, sunny, sunshiny, unclouded.

- **Word:** Blow (Synonym denoting Meaning: leave)

  Other Synonyms: Depart, go, split.

  Antonyms: Access, alight, appear, attain, barge in, blow in, bob up, breeze in, bust in, buzz, check in, clock in, disembark, dismount, drop anchor, drop in, enter, fall by, fall in, get to, hit, hit town, land, make it, pop in, pop up, pull in, punch in, reach, report, roll in, show, show up, sign in, take place, turn up, visit.

- **Word:** Blissful (Synonym denoting Meaning: happy)

  Other Synonyms: Beatific, cool, crazy, delighted, delightful, dreamy, ecstatic, elated, enchanted, enraptured, euphoric, floating, flying, gone, heavenly, in ecstasy, joyful, joyous, mad, rapturous, sent, spaced out, turned on.

  Antonyms: Afflicted, depressed, disturbed, grieving, harmed, injured, oppressed, pained, peeved, persecuted, saddened, unhappy, woeful, worried.

C

- **Word:** Cabin (Synonym denoting Meaning: house)

  Other Synonyms: Berth, box, caboose, camp, chalet, compartment, cot, cottage, crib, deckhouse, home, hovel, hut, lodge, log house, quarters, room, shack, shanty, shed.

  Antonyms: chateau, citadel, donjon, fastness, fort, fortification, fortress, hold, keep, manor, mansion, palace, peel, seat, stronghold, tower, villa.

- **Word:** Cache (Synonym denoting Meaning: hide)

  Other Synonyms: Accumulate, bury, conceal, cover, ditch, duck, ensconce, lay away, maintain, park, plant, put away, save, screen, secrete, squirrel, squirrel away, stash, stash away, store.

  Antonyms: Advertise, arrange, bare, betray, boast, brandish, demonstrate, disclose, emblazon, evidence, evince, exhibit, expand, expose, extend, feature, flash, flaunt, flourish, glaze, grandstand, illustrate, impart, lay bare, lay out, make clear, make known, manifest, model, open, open out, parade, perform, present, promote, promulgate, publish, represent, reveal, set out, show off, showcase, sport, spread out, stretch out, trot out, uncover, unfold, unfurl, unmask, unroll, unveil.

- **Word:** Cad (Synonym denoting Meaning: lout)

  Other Synonyms: Bastard, boor, bounder, clown, creep, cur, curl, dog, heel, knave, louse, lout, maggot, rake, rascal, rat, rogue, rounder, scoundrel, stinker, worm.

Antonyms: Admirer, beloved, cavalier, escort, fiancé, flame, gentleman friend, inamorato, love, lover, paramour, squire, steady, suitor, swain, sweetheart, true love.

- **Word:** Cage (Synonym denoting Meaning: enclose)

  Other Synonyms: Close in, confine, coop up, enclose, envelop, fence in, hem, hold, imprison, incarcerate, jail, lock up, mew, pen, restrain, shut in, shut up.

  Antonyms: Comp, complimentary, costless, for free, for love, for nothing, free lunch, free ride, freebie, gratis, gratuitous, handout, paper, unpaid, unrecompensed.

- **Word:** Calamity (Synonym denoting Meaning: disaster)

  Other Synonyms: Adversity, affliction, blue ruin, cataclysm, catastrophe, collapse, cross, curtains, distress, downfall, hardship, holy mess, mess, misadventure, mischance, misfortune, mishap, reverse, ruin, scourge, trial, tribulation, visitation, Waterloo, woe, worst, wreck, wretchedness.

  Antonyms: Absolution, baptism, benediction, benison, commendation, consecration, dedication, grace, invocation, thanks, thanksgiving, unction.

- **Word:** Calculate (Synonym denoting Meaning: estimate)

  Other Synonyms: Account, add, adjust, appraise, assay, cast, cipher, compute, consider, count, determine, divide, dope out, enumerate, figure, forecast, foretell, gauge, guess, judge, keep tab, keep tabs, measure, multiply, number, rate, reckon, size up, subtract, sum, tally, tot, tote, value, weigh, work out.

  Antonyms: Assume, believe, conceive, conclude, deem, estimate, expect, fancy, feel, figure, gather, glean, guess, guesstimate, imagine, infer, judge, presume, pretend, suppose, surmise, suspect, theorise, think.

- **Word:** Calm (Synonym denoting Meaning: peaceful)

  Other Synonyms: At peace, bland, civil, cool, halcyon, harmonious, hushed, in order, inactive, inanimate, low-key, mild, motionless, pacific, pastoral, placid, quiescent, quiet, reposeful, reposing, restful, rural, serene, slow, smooth, soothing, standstill, still, tranquil, undisturbed, unruffled, windless.

Antonyms: Aflame, agitated, animated, annoyed, aroused, awakened, beside oneself, charged, delighted, discomposed, disconcerted, disturbed, eager, enthusiastic, feverish, fired up, frantic, high, hopped up, horny, hot, hyper, hysterical, inflamed, inspired, juiced up, jumpy, keyed up, moved, nervous, on edge, on fire, overwrought, passionate, piqued, provoked, roused, ruffled, steamed up, stimulated, stirred, thrilled, tumultuous, upset, weird, wild, worked up.

- **Word:** Cancel (Synonym denoting Meaning: call off)

  Other Synonyms: Abolish, abort, abrogate, annul, black out, blot out, break, break off, call off, countermand, cross out, cut, deface, delete, destroy, do in, efface, eliminate, eradicate, erase, expunge, finish off, kill, obliterate, off, omit, quash, remove, render invalid, repeal, repudiate, rescind, revoke, rub out, scratch out, scrub, sink, smash, squash, stamp across, strike out, torpedo, total, trash, trim, undo, wash out, wipe out, x out.

  Antonyms: Acquiesce, avow, concede, confess, grant, let on, own.

- **Word:** Canny (Synonym denoting Meaning: clever)

  Other Synonyms: Able, acute, adroit, artful, astute, cagey, careful, cautious, circumspect, cunning, dexterous, discreet, fancy footwork, foxy, frugal, ingenious, intelligent, judicious, knowing, nimble-witted, perspicacious, prudent, quick, quick-witted, sagacious, sharp, shrewd, skilful, slick, slippery, sly, smart, smooth, street smart, streetwise, subtle, wary, watchful, wise, worldly-wise.

  Antonyms: Absent-minded, abstracted, casual, cursory, disregardful, forgetful, hasty, heedless, improvident, imprudent, inaccurate, inadvertent, incautious, inconsiderate, indifferent, indiscreet, indolent, injudicious, irresponsible, lackadaisical, lax, loose, mindless, napping, negligent, nonchalant, oblivious, offhand, perfunctory, pococurante, reckless, regardless, remiss, slipshod, sloppy, thoughtless, unconcerned, unguarded, unheeding, unmindful, unobservant, unreflective, unthinking.

- **Word:** Canonical (Synonym denoting Meaning: accepted)

  Other Synonyms: Approved, authoritative, authorized, lawful, legal, official, orthodox, received, recognized, sanctioned, sound, statutory.

  Antonyms: Below par, crappy, damaged, disagreeable, displeasing, distasteful, exceptionable, half-assed, half-baked, ill-favoured, improper, inadmissible, insupportable, lemon, lousy, objectionable, obnoxious, offensive, reject, repugnant, seconds, sleazy, unappealing, undesirable, uninviting, unpleasant, unsatisfactory, unwanted, unwelcome, won't do.

- **Word:** Canyon (Synonym denoting Meaning: gulf)

  Other Synonyms: Coulee, glen, gorge, gulch, gully, ravine, valley.

  Antonyms: Alp, bank, bluff, butte, cliff, crag, dome, drift, elevation, eminence, glob, heap, height, hump, mass, mesa, mound, mount, palisade, peak, pike, pile, precipice, pyramid, range, ridge, shock, sierra, stack, ton, volcano.

- **Word:** Capable (Synonym denoting Meaning: able)

  Other Synonyms: Able, accomplished, adapted, adept, adequate, apt, au fait, clever, competent, dynamite, efficient, experienced, fireball, fitted, gifted, good, green thumb, intelligent, know-how, masterly, pro, proficient, proper, qualified, skilful, suited, talented, vet, veteran.

  Antonyms: Butterfingers, disqualified, feeble, impotent, inadequate, incompetent, ineffective, ineligible, inept, inexperienced, inexpert, insufficient, loser, lump, muff, naive, poor, powerless, turkey, unable, unequipped, unfit, unqualified, unskilled, unskilful, unsuited, weak, yo-yo.

- **Word:** Capacity (Synonym denoting Meaning: ability)

  Other Synonyms: Adequacy, aptitude, aptness, bent, brains, calibre, capability, cleverness, compass, competence, competency, efficiency, facility, faculty, forte, genius, gift, inclination, intelligence, knack, might, power, qualification, readiness, skill, stature, strength, talent.

Antonyms: Disability, disqualification, failure, frailty, impotence, inadequacy, inaptitude, incapability, incapacitation, incapacity, incompetence, ineffectiveness, ineffectualness, inefficacy, inefficiency, ineptitude, ineptness, insufficiency, in utility, lack, necessity, powerlessness, shortcoming, unfitness, weakness.

- **Word:** Capture (Synonym denoting Meaning: catch)

  Other Synonyms: Apprehend, arrest, bag, bust, catch, collar, conquer, gain control, get, grab, land, nab, nail, net, occupy, overwhelm, pick up, pinch, pull in, round up, run in, secure, seize, snare, snatch, take, take captive, take prisoner, trap.

  Antonyms: Comp, complimentary, costless, for free, for love, for nothing, free lunch, free ride, freebie, gratis, gratuitous, handout, paper, unpaid, unrecompensed.

- **Word:** Caravan (Synonym denoting Meaning: travellers)

  Other Synonyms: Band, camels, campers, cavalcade, expedition, procession, safari, train, troop.

  Antonyms: Alone, characteristic, definite, diacritic, diagnostic, different, discrete, distinct, especial, exclusive, express, identical, idiosyncratic, indivisible, lone, odd, only, original, own, particular, peculiar, personal, personalised, proper, reserved, respective, secluded, select, separate, several, single, singular, sole, solitary, special, specific, uncommon, unique, unitary, unusual.

- **Word:** Care (Synonym denoting Meaning: carefulness)

  Other Synonyms: Alertness, attending, attention, caution, circumspection, concentration, concern, conscientiousness, consideration, diligence, direction, discrimination, effort, enthusiasm, exactness, exertion, fastidiousness, forethought, heed, interest, management, meticulousness, nicety, pains, particularity, precaution, prudence, regard, scrupulousness, solicitude, thought, trouble, vigilance, wariness, watchfulness.

Antonyms: Carelessness, free-spiritedness, impulse, impulsiveness, intemperance, recklessness, spontaneity, thoughtlessness, unrestraint, wantonness, wildness.

- **Word:** Careful (Synonym denoting Meaning: cautious)

  Other Synonyms: Accurate, alert, apprehensive, assiduous, attentive, chary, choosy, circumspect, concerned, conscientious, conservative, cool, deliberate, discreet, exacting, fastidious, finicky, fussy, guarded, heedful, judicious, leery, meticulous, mindful, observant, particular, play safe, precise, prim, protective, provident, prudent, punctilious, regardful, religious, rigorous, scrupulous, self-disciplined, shy, sober, solicitous, thorough, thoughtful, vigilant, wary, watchful.

  Antonyms: Absent-minded, abstracted, casual, cursory, disregardful, forgetful, hasty, heedless, improvident, imprudent, inaccurate, inadvertent, incautious, inconsiderate, indifferent, indiscreet, indolent, injudicious, irresponsible, lackadaisical, lax, loose, mindless, napping, negligent, nonchalant, oblivious, offhand, perfunctory, pococurante, reckless, regardless, remiss, slipshod, sloppy, thoughtless, unconcerned, unguarded, unheeding, unmindful, unobservant, unreflective, unthinking.

- **Word:** Carry (Synonym denoting Meaning: accomplish)

  Other Synonyms: Affect, be victorious, capture, drive, effect, gain, get, impel, impress, influence, inspire, move, prevail, secure, spur, strike, sway, win.

  Antonyms: Abort, backslide, be defeated, be demoted, be ruined, blunder, break down, decline, deteriorate, fall, fall flat, fall short, fall through, fizzle, flop, flounder, fold, founder, go astray, go down, go downhill, go wrong, hit bottom, lose control, lose out, lose status, miscarry, miss, play into, run aground, slip.

- **Word:** Cash (Synonym denoting Meaning: money)

  Other Synonyms: Banknote, bread, buck, bullion, cabbage, chicken feed, coin, coinage, currency, dough, funds, investment, legal tender, lot, note, payment, pledge, principal, refund, remuneration, reserve, resources, riches, savings, scratch, security, skins, stock, supply, treasure, wampum, wherewithal.

  Antonyms: Ascribe, assign, charge, credit, input, lay, refer.

- **Word:** Castle (Synonym denoting Meaning: home)

  Other Synonyms: Citadel, donjon, fastness, fort, fortification, fortress, hold, keep, manor, mansion, palace, peel, seat, stronghold, tower, villa.

  Antonyms: Box, bungalow, cabana, cabin, caboose, camp, chalet, cot, home, house, hut, lodge, ranch, shack, shanty, small house.

- **Word:** Categorise (Synonym denoting Meaning: sort)

  Other Synonyms: Assort, class, classify, group, identify, peg, pigeonhole, rank out, tab, typecast.

  Antonyms: Ataxia, clutter, confusion, derangement, disarrangement, disarray, disorderliness, disorganisation, holy mess, huddle, irregularity, jumble, mess, muddle, rat's nest, shambles, snarl, untidiness.

- **Word:** Celebrity (Synonym denoting Meaning: dignitary)

  Other Synonyms: Ace, big cheese, big deal, big gun, big name, big shot, big stuff, bigwig, cynosure, famous person, figure, heavyweight, hero, hot dog, hotshot, immortal, lion, luminary, magnate, mahatma, major league, name, notable, personage, personality, somebody, someone, star, superstar, the cheese.

  Antonyms: Cipher, insignificancy, lightweight, little guy, menial, nix, nonentity, nothing, nullity, parvenu, small potato, squirt, upstart, wimp, zero, zilch, zip.

- **Word:** Cement (Synonym denoting Meaning: attach)

  Other Synonyms: Bind, blend, bond, cohere, combine,

connect, fasten, fuse, glue, gum, join, merge, mortar, paste, plaster, seal, solder, stick, unite, weld.

Antonyms: Bisect, branch, break, break down, carve, chop, cleave, cross, cut, cut up, demarcate, detach, disconnect, disengage, disentangle, disjoin, dislocate, dismember, dissect, dissever, dissociate, dissolve, disunite, divorce, fork, halve, intersect, isolate, loose, part, partition, pull away, quarter, rend, rupture, section, segment, segregate, sever, shear, split, subdivide, sunder, tear, unbind, undo, whack off.

- **Word:** Central (Synonym denoting Meaning: main)

  Other Synonyms: Axial, basic, cardinal, centre, centric, chief, dominant, equidistant, essential, focal, foremost, fundamental, important, inmost, inner, interior, intermediate, key, leading, master, mean, median, mid, middle, middlemost, midmost, midway, nuclear, outstanding, overriding, paramount, pivotal, predominant, primary, prime, principal, radical, ruling, salient, significant.

  Antonyms: Appearance, aspect, coating, cover, covering, exteriority, external, facade, face, finish, outside, polish, rind, shell, skin, superficies, surface, visible part.

- **Word:** Chain (Synonym denoting Meaning: manacle)

  Other Synonyms: Attach, bind, confine, connect, enslave, fetter, handcuff, hold, moor, restrain, shackle, tether, tie up, trammel.

  Antonyms: affranchise, deliver, discharge, disencumber, disenthrall, enfranchise, free, liberate, loose, loosen, manumit, release, unbind, unchain, unfetter, unshackle.

- **Word:** Challenge (Synonym denoting Meaning: question)

  Other Synonyms: Accost, arouse, ask for, assert, beard, brave, call for, call out, claim, confront, cross, dare, defy, demand, denounce, dispute, exact, face down, face off, hang in, impeach, impose, impugn, inquire, insist upon, investigate, invite competition, object to, provoke, query, question, reclaim, require, search out, stimulate, summon, tax, test, try, vindicate.

Antonyms: Acknowledgment, antiphon, back talk, band-aid, clause, comeback, comment, cooler, counterclaim, crack, disclosure, echo, elucidation, explanation, feedback, guff, interpretation, justification, key, lip, observation, parting shot, pay dirt, plea, quick fix, rebuttal, refutation, rejoinder, remark, repartee, report, resolution, response, result, retort, return, riposte, sign, solution, statement, thank-you note, topper, vindication, wisecrack.

- **Word:** Champion (Synonym denoting Meaning: defeater)

  Other Synonyms: Advocate, ally, backer, challenger, champ, conqueror, defender, endorser, exponent, expounder, guardian, hero, heroine, master, medalist, nonpareil, number one, numero uno, paladin, partisan, patron, proponent, protector, supporter, sympathiser, titleholder, top dog, upholder, vanquisher, victor, vindicator, warrior, white knight, winner.

  Antonyms: Also-ran, bankrupt, beat, bomb, born loser, bum, castaway, dead duck, deadbeat, defaulter, derelict, disappointment, dud, flop, flunky, good-for-nothing, has-been, incompetent, insolvent, loafer, loser, lumpy, might-have-been, moocher, ne'er-do-well, no-good, nobody, nonperformer, prodigal, stiff, turkey, underachiever, washout.

- **Word:** Channel (Synonym denoting Meaning: guide)

  Other Synonyms: Carry, conduct, convey, direct, funnel, pipe, route, send, siphon, transmit, transport.

  Antonyms: Adhere, arrest, bind, bottle up, carry, catch, check, cherish, clasp, cleave, clench, clinch, cling, clutch, confine, contain, cork up, cradle, detain, embrace, enclose, enjoy, fondle, freeze to, grasp, grip, handle, hang on, have, hug, imprison, keep, keep close, keep out, lock up, maintain, nourish, occupy, own, palm, possess, press, restrain, retain, secure, seize, squeeze, stay put, stick, take, trammel, vise, wield, withhold, wring.

- **Word:** Character (Synonym denoting Meaning: integrity)

  Other Synonyms: Courage, fame, honour, intelligence, mind, name, place, position, rank, rectitude, rep, report, reputation, repute, standing, station, status, strength, uprightness.

  Antonyms: Bribery, bribing, crime, crookedness, demoralization, dishonesty, exploitation, extortion, fiddling, fraud, fraudulency, graft, jobbery, malfeasance, misrepresentation, nepotism, payoff, payola, profiteering, racket, shadiness, shady deal, shuffle, skimming, squeeze, unscrupulousness, venality.

- **Word:** Charitable (Synonym denoting Meaning: generous)

  Other Synonyms: Accommodating, all heart, altruistic, beneficent, benevolent, benign, big, big-hearted, bountiful, eleemosynary, giving, good, helpful, humane, humanitarian, kind, kindly, lavish, liberal, obliging, philanthropic, sympathetic.

  Antonyms: Bargain, bargain-basement, bargain-counter, budget, buy, cheapo, competitive, cut-price, cut-rate, depreciated, economical, economy, economy-size, half-priced, irregular, low tariff, low-cost, low-priced, lowered, marked down, moderate, nominal, on sale, popularly-priced, real buy, reasonable, reduced, sale, slashed, standard, steal, stingy, thrifty, tight, utility.

- **Word:** Cheat (Synonym denoting Meaning: defraud)

  Other Synonyms: Bamboozle, beat, beguile, bilk, bleed, burn, caboodle, chisel, con, cozen, crib, cross, deceive, defraud, delude, diddle, do, double deal, double-cross, dupe, fast talk, finagle, fleece, flimflam, fudge, gouge, gyp, hoodwink, hose, jerk around, milk, mislead, ream, rip off, rook, rope in, sandbag, scam, screw, shaft, short, shuck, skin, stiff, sucker, swindle, take, take in, take out, trick, trim, two-time, victimize.

  Antonyms: Accord, add, afford, ante up, assign, bequeath, bequest, bestow, chip in, come through, commit, confer, devote, dispense, dole out, dower, endow, enrich, furnish, give, give away, go Dutch, grant, hand out, kick in, pitch in, pony up, present, proffer, provide, sacrifice, share, subscribe, subsidize, supply, tender, will.

- **Word:** Check (Synonym denoting Meaning: inspect)

  Other Synonyms: Analyse, ascertain, audit, balance account, Candle, case, compare, confirm, correct, count, enquire about, find out, frisk, go through, investigate, keep account, look at, look over, look see, make sure, monitor, note, overlook, probe, prove, quiz, read, review, scout out, scrutinise, study, tell, test, try, verify.

  Antonyms: Blink at, brush aside, brush away, brush off, cold-shoulder, contemn, despise, discount, disdain, disobey, disparage, fail, forget, laugh off, let go, let pass, live with, miss, neglect, omit, overlook, overpass, pass over, pooh pooh, scorn, slight, snub, tune out, vilipend, wink at.

D

- **Word:** Daft (Synonym denoting Meaning: stupid)

  Other Synonyms: Absurd, asinine, baked, bedlamite, bonkers, cracked, crackers, crazy, daffy, demented, deranged, dopey, flaky, foolish, fried, giddy, idiotic, inane, insane, lunatic, mad, mental, nuts, nutty, ridiculous, screwy, silly, simple, totally baked, touched, unbalanced, unhinged, unsound, wacky, whacko, witless.

  Antonyms: All there, analytical, balanced, calm, cerebral, circumspect, cognitive, collected, cool, deductive, deliberate, discerning, discriminating, enlightened, far-sighted, impartial, intellectual, intelligent, judicious, knowing, level-headed, logical, lucid, normal, objective, perspicacious, philosophic, prudent, ratiocinative, reasonable, reasoning, reflective, sagacious, sane, sensible, sober, sound, stable, synthetic, thinking, thoughtful, together, well-advised, wise.

- **Word:** Daily (Synonym denoting Meaning: every day)

  Other Synonyms: Circadian, common, commonplace,

constantly, cyclic, day-to-day, diurnal, everyday, often, once daily, ordinary, per idem, periodic, quotidian, regular, regularly, routine.

Antonyms: Alternate, arrested, broken, checked, cyclic, cyclical, discontinuing, discontinuous, epochal, every other, fitful, herky-jerky, infrequent, interrupted, isochronal, isochronous, iterant, iterative, metrical, occasional, periodic, periodical, punctuated, recurrent, recurring, rhythmic, rhythmical, seasonal, serial, shifting, spasmodic, sporadic, stop-and-go, touch-and-go, willy-nilly.

- **Word:** Dam (Synonym denoting Meaning: block)

  Other Synonyms: Bar, barricade, brake, check, choke, clog, close, confine, hinder, hold, hold back, impede, obstruct, repress, restrain, restrict, retard, slow, stop up, suppress.

  Antonyms: Comp, complimentary, costless, for free, for love, for nothing, free lunch, free ride, freebie, gratis, gratuitous, handout, paper, unpaid, unrecompensed.

- **Word:** Damage (Synonym denoting Meaning: injury)

  Other Synonyms: Accident, adulteration, adversity, affliction, bane, blemish, blow, breakage, bruise, casualty, catastrophe, contamination, corruption, debasement, depreciation, deprivation, destruction, deterioration, detriment, devastation, disservice, disturbance, evil, hardship, harm, hurt, illness, impairment, infliction, knockout, marring, mischief, mishap, mutilation, outrage, pollution, ravage, reverse, ruin, ruining, spoilage, stroke, suffering, waste, wound, wreckage, wrecking.

  Antonyms: Advance, advancement, amelioration, amendment, augmentation, betterment, change, civilization, correction, cultivation, development, elevation, enhancement, enrichment, furtherance, gain, growth, increase, preferment, progress, progression, promotion, rally, reclamation, recovery, rectification, reformation, regeneration, renovation, revision, rise, upbeat, upgrade, upswing.

- **Word:** Damp (Synonym denoting Meaning: humid)

  Other Synonyms: Clammy, cloudy, dank, dewy, drenched, dripping, drippy, drizzly, misty, moist, muggy, oozy, saturated, soaked, soaking, sodden, soggy, sopping, steamy, sticky, vaporous, waterlogged, wet,.

  Antonyms: Barren, bone-dry, desert, dusty, parched, thirsty, waterless.

- **Word:** Dangerous (Synonym denoting Meaning: hazardous)

  Other Synonyms: Alarming, bad, breakneck, chancy, critical, deadly, delicate, dynamite, exposed, fatal, formidable, hairy, heavy, hot, impending, impregnable, insecure, jeopardous, loaded, malignant, menacing, mortal, nasty, parlous, perilous, portentous, precarious, pressing, queasy, risky, serious, serpentine, shaky, speculative, terrible, thorny, threatening, ticklish, touch-and-go, touchy, treacherous, ugly, unhealthy, unsafe, unstable, urgent, viperous, vulnerable.

  Antonyms: Adequate, agreeable, ample, appropriate, at rest, cared for, cheerful, commodious, complacent, contented, convenient, cozy, cushy, delightful, easy, enjoyable, enjoying, gratified, hale, happy, healthy, hearty, loose, loose-fitting, luxurious, made well, palatial, pleasant, pleased, protected, relaxed, relaxing, relieved, rested, restful, restored, rich, roomy, satisfactory, satisfying, serene, sheltered, snug, soft, soothed, spacious, strengthened, untroubled, useful, warm, well-off.

- **Word:** Dapper (Synonym denoting Meaning: well-groomed)

  Other Synonyms: Active, bandbox, brisk, chic, chichi, classy, clean, dainty, dashing, doggy, jaunty, natty, neat, nice, nifty, nimble, posh, prim, rakish, ritzy, sassy, sharp, showy, smart, snazzy, snug, spiff, spiffy, spruce, spry, stylish, swank, swanky, swell, trim, turned out.

  Antonyms: Beat up, bedraggled, blowzy, dirty, disarranged, disarrayed, disordered, frowzy, grubby, ill-kempt, messed up, messy, mussed up, raunchy, ruffled, rumpled, sleazy, slipshod, sloppy, slovenly, tousled, uncombed, unkempt, untidy.

- **Word:** Dare (Synonym denoting Meaning: challenge)

  Other Synonyms: Beard, brave, bully, confront, cope, defy, denounce, disregard, face, face off, front, goad, insult, laugh at, meet, mock, muster courage, oppose, provoke, resist, scorn, spurn, square off, taunt, threaten.

  Antonyms: Abstain, avert, bypass, circumlocute, circumvent, deflect, desist, ditch, divert, dodge, duck, elude, escape, eschew, evade, fake out, fend off, flee, hide, hold off, jump, keep clear, lay low, obviate, recoil, shake, shake off, shirk, shrink from, shuffle off, shun, shy, sidestep, skip, skip town, skirt, stay away, stay out, stutter step, turn aside, ward off, weave, withdraw.

- **Word:** Dark (Synonym denoting Meaning: not light)

  Other Synonyms: Black, blackish, caliginous, clouded, cloudy, crepuscular, darkened, dim, dingy, drab, dull, dun, dusk, duskish, dusky, faint, foggy, gloomy, grimy, ill-lighted, indistinct, inky, lightless, lurid, misty, murky, nebulous, obscure, opaque, overcast, pitch-black, pitch-dark, pitchy, shaded, shadowy, shady, sombre, sooty, stygian, sunless, tenebrous, unlighted, unlit, vague.

  Antonyms: Ablaze, aglow, alight, argent, beaming, blazing, brilliant, burning, burnished, coruscating, dazzling, effulgent, flashing, fulgent, glaring, gleaming, glistening, glittering, glossy, glowing, golden, illuminated, illumined, incandescent, intense, irradiated, lambent, light, lighted, luminous, lustrous, limpid, moonlit, phosphorescent, polished, radiant, resplendent, scintillating, shimmering, shiny, silvery, sparkling, sunny, twinkling, vivid.

- **Word:** Dash (Synonym denoting Meaning: run)

  Other Synonyms: Boil, bolt, bound, career, charge, chase, course, dart, fly, gallop, haste, hasten, hurry, lash, race, rush, rush act, rush period, scamper, scoot, scurry, shoot, speed, spring, sprint, tear.

  Antonyms: Boondoggle, dawdle, diddle, dilly-dally, drag, fool around, fool with, fritter away, hang about, horse around, idle, jerk off, lag, linger, loiter, lollygag, mess around, monkey, monkey around, play around, poke, procrastinate, put off, putter, screw around, tarry, trail, trifle with, waste time, while away.

- **Word:** Dawn (Synonym denoting Meaning: daybreak)

  Other Synonyms: Aurora, bright, cockcrow, dawning, day peep, daybreak, daylight, early bright, first blush, first light, light, morn, morning, sunrise, sunup, wee hours.

  Antonyms: Dark, duskish, evening, eventide, gloaming, gloom, night, nightfall, sundown, sunset, twilight.

- **Word:** Day (Synonym denoting Meaning: light)

  Other Synonyms: Astronomical day, bright, dawn-to-dark, daylight, daytime, diurnal course, early bright, light, nautical day, sidereal day, sunlight, sunrise-to-sunset, sunshine, twenty-four hours, working day.

  Antonyms: Black, blackish, caliginous, clouded, cloudy, crepuscular, darkened, dim, dingy, drab, dull, dun, dusk, duskish, dusky, faint, foggy, gloomy, grimy, ill-lighted, indistinct, inky, lightless, lurid, misty, murky, nebulous, obscure, opaque, overcast, pitch-black, pitch-dark, pitchy, shaded, shadowy, shady, sombre, sooty, stygian, sunless, tenebrous, unlighted, unlit, vague.

- **Word:** Dead (Synonym denoting Meaning: not alive)

  Other Synonyms: Asleep, belly up, bloodless, breathless, buried, cadaverous, checked out, cold, cut off, deceased, defunct, departed, done for, erased, expired, extinct, gone, inanimate, inert, late, lifeless, liquidated, mortified, no more, not existing, passed away, perished, reposing, rubbed out, snuffed out, spiritless, stiff, unanimated, washed up, wasted.

  Antonyms: Animate, around, awake, breathing, cognizant, conscious, dynamic, existing, extant, functioning, growing, knowing, live, living, mortal, operative, running, subsisting, viable, vital, working.

- **Word:** Deaf (Synonym denoting Meaning: unhearing)

  Other Synonyms: Deafened, earless, stone deaf.

  Antonyms: Audition, auditory, auditory range, detecting, distinguishing, ear, earshot, effect, extent, faculty, hearing distance, listening, perception, range, reach, recording.

- **Word:** Deal (Synonym denoting Meaning: manage)

  Other Synonyms: Act, approach, attend to, behave, behave toward, clear, concern, conduct oneself, consider, control, cope with, deal with, direct, discuss, hack, hack it, handle, live with, make it, oversee, play, review, rid, see to, serve, take, treat, unburden, use.

  Antonyms: Blink at, brush aside, brush away, brush off, cold-shoulder, contemn, despise, discount, disdain, disobey, disparage, fail, forget, laugh off, let go, let pass, live with, miss, neglect, omit, overlook, overpass, pass over, pooh pooh, scorn, slight, snub, tune out, vilipend, wink at.

- **Word:** Death (Synonym denoting Meaning: end)

  Other Synonyms: Afterlife, annihilation, bereavement, casualty, cessation, curtains, darkness, decease, demise, departure, destruction, dissolution, downfall, dying, end, ending, eradication, eternal rest, euthanasia, exit, expiration, extermination, extinction, fatality, finis, finish, future home, grave, grim reaper, heaven, loss, mortality, necrosis, obliteration, oblivion, paradise, parting, passing, passing over, quietus, release, repose, ruin, ruination, silence, sleep, termination, tomb, un.

  Antonyms: Actuality, animation, big game, journey, life, living, presence, rat race, reality, subsistence, vitality, world.

- **Word:** Decent (Synonym denoting Meaning: respectable)

  Other Synonyms: Appropriate, approved, becoming, befitting, chaste, clean, comely, conforming, continent, correct, decorous, delicate, ethical, fit, fitting, good, honest, honourable, immaculate, mannerly, modest, moral, nice, noble, polite, presentable, proper, prudent, pure, reserved, right, seemly, spotless, stainless, standard, straight, straight arrow, straight shooter, suitable, trustworthy, unblemished, undefiled, untarnished, upright, virtuous, worthy.

Antonyms: Abnormal, at odds, awkward, bad form, discordant, discrepant, erroneous, false, ill-advised, ill-timed, imprudent, inaccurate, inadmissible, inadvisable, inapplicable, inapposite, inappropriate, inapt, incongruous, incorrect, inexpedient, infelicitous, inharmonious, inopportune, irregular, ludicrous, malapropos, odd, off base, preposterous, unapt, unbefitting, uncalled-for, uncomely, undue, unfit, unfitting, unseasonable, unsuitable, unsuited, untimely, unwarranted, wrong.

- **Word:** Deceptive (Synonym denoting Meaning: dishonest)

  Other Synonyms: Ambiguous, beguiling, bum, catchy, crafty, cunning, deceitful, deceiving, deluding, delusive, delusory, designing, disingenuous, fake, fallacious, false, fishy, foxy, fraudulent, illusory, imposturous, indirect, insidious, knavish, lying, misleading, mock, oblique, off, phony, plausible, rascal, roguish, scheming, seeming, serpentine, shifty, slick, slippery, sly, sneaky, snide, specious, spurious, subtle, treacherous, tricky, two faced, underhanded, unreliable, wily.

  Antonyms: Aboveboard, apparent, artless, bare-faced, blunt, bold, brazen, candid, direct, downright, easy, familiar, flat-out, forthright, free, guileless, heart-to-heart, ingenuous, matter-of-fact, naive, natural, open, outright, outspoken, plain, plain-spoken, real, scrupulous, sincere, straight, straight-forward, transparent, truthful, unconcealed, undisguised, uninhibited, unreserved, unrestricted, up front, upright.

- **Word:** Defensive (Synonym denoting Meaning: protective)

  Other Synonyms: Arresting, averting, balking, checking, conservative, coping with, defending, foiling, forestalling, frustrating, guarding, in opposition, interrupting, opposing, preservative, preventive, protecting, resistive, safeguarding, thwarting, uptight, watchful, withstanding.

Antonyms: Abhorrent, abusive, annoying, biting, blue, crumb, cutting, detestable, disagreeable, discourteous, displeasing, disrespectful, distasteful, dreadful, embarrassing, evil, foul, ghastly, grisly, gross, hideous, horrible, horrid, insolent, invidious, irritating, nauseating, objectionable, obnoxious, odious, off-colour, offending, opprobrious, outrageous, repellent, reprehensible, repugnant, repulsive, revolting, rotten, rude, shocking, stinking, terrible, uncivil, unmannerly.

- **Word:** Desire (Synonym denoting Meaning: want)

  Other Synonyms: Admiration, ambition, appetite, ardour, aspiration, attraction, avidity, concupiscence, covetousness, craving, craze, cupidity, devotion, doting, eagerness, fancy, fascination, fervour, fondness, frenzy, greed, hankering, hunger, inclination, infatuation, itch, lasciviousness, lechery, libido, liking, longing, love, lust, mania, motive, need, passion, predilection, proclivity, propensity, rapaciousness, rapture, ravenousness, relish, salacity, solicitude, thirst, urge, voracity, will, wish, yearning.

  Antonyms: Abhorrence, abomination, allergy, animosity, antagonism, antipathy, detestation, disfavour, disgust, disinclination, disliking, displeasure, dissatisfaction, distaste, dread, hate, hatred, horror, hostility, indisposition, loathing, odium, opposition, reluctance, repugnance, repulsion, revulsion, unwillingness.

- **Word:** Destiny (Synonym denoting Meaning: fate)

  Other Synonyms: Afterlife, break, breaks, certainty, circumstance, conclusion, condition, constellation, cup, design, divine decree, doom, expectation, finality, foreordination, fortune, future, happenstance, hereafter, horoscope, inevitability, intent, intention, karma, kismet, lot, luck, objective, ordinance, portion, predestination, predetermination, prospect, serendipity, the beads, the stars, weird.

  Antonyms: Blow, calamity, casualty, collision, crack-up, disaster, event, fender-bender, fluke, hazard, misadventure, misfortune, mishap, pileup, rack-up, setback, shunt, slip-up, smash, smash-up, stack-up, total, wrack-up.

- **Word:** Dignity (Synonym denoting Meaning: excellence)

  Other Synonyms: Address, cachet, character, consequence, courtliness, culture, decency, decorum, distinction, elevation, eminence, ethics, etiquette, glory, grace, grandeur, gravity, greatness, hauteur, honour, importance, loftiness, majesty, merit, morality, nobleness, perfection, poise, prestige, propriety, quality, rank, regard, renown, respectability, seemliness, self-respect, significance, solemnity, splendour, standing, state, stateliness, station, stature, status, sublimity, virtue, worth.

  Antonyms: Barbarism, blooper, blunder, boner, boo-boo, break, faux pas, gaffe, gaucherie, goof, immodesty, impudence, incongruity, incorrectness, indecency, indecorum, inelegance, mistake, rudeness, slip, solecism, unseemliness, unsuitability, vulgarism, vulgarity.

- **Word:** Discuss (Synonym denoting Meaning: talk)

  Other Synonyms: Altercate, argue, bounce off, canvass, compare notes, confabulate, confer, consider, consult with, contend, contest, converse, debate, deliberate, descant, discourse about, dispute, dissert, dissertate, examine, explain, figure, get together, go into, groupthink, hash over, hold forth, jaw, kick about, knock around, moot, rap, reason about, review, sift, take up, talk about, thrash out, toss around, ventilate, weigh.

  Antonyms: Be morose, be silent, brood, frown, gloom, glower, gripe, grouse, grump, look sullen, lower, moon, mump, nope, scowl, take on.

- **Word:** Disguise (Synonym denoting Meaning: mask)

  Other Synonyms: Affect, age, alter, antique, assume, beard, belie, camouflage, change, cloak, colour, conceal, counterfeit, cover, cover up, deacon, deceive, dissemble, dissimulate, doctor up, dress up, fake, falsify, feign, front, fudge, garble, gloss over, hide, make like, make up, masquerade, muffle, obfuscate, obscure, pretend, redo, screen, secrete, sham, shroud, simulate, touch up, varnish, veil, wear cheaters, whitewash.

Antonyms: Advertise, arrange, bare, betray, boast, brandish, demonstrate, disclose, emblazon, evidence, evince, exhibit, expand, expose, extend, feature, flash, flaunt, flourish, glaze, grandstand, illustrate, impart, lay bare, lay out, make clear, make known, manifest, model, open, open out, parade, perform, present, promote, promulgate, publish, represent, reveal, set out, show off, showcase, sport, spread out, stretch out, trot out, uncover, unfold, unfurl, unmask, unroll, unveil.

- **Word:** Divinity (Synonym denoting Meaning: god)

  Other Synonyms: Celestial, Dad, deity, divine nature, genius, goddess, godhead, godhood, godliness, guardian spirit, higher power, holiness, Lord, Man Upstairs, sanctity, spirit.

  Antonyms: Adversary, archfiend, beast, common enemy, dastard, enfant terrible, Evil One, fiend, hellion, imp, knave, Lucifer, Mephistopheles, monster, ogre, rogue, Satan, scamp, scoundrel, sin, the Dickens, villain.

- **Word:** Dumb (Synonym denoting Meaning: unintelligent)

  Other Synonyms: Dense, dim-witted, dodo, doltish, dull, dumb bunny, dumb head, dumb ox, dumbbell, dumdum, dummy, feebleminded, foolish, moronic, simple-minded, stupid, thick.

  Antonyms: Ablaze, aglow, alight, argent, beaming, blazing, brilliant, burning, burnished, coruscating, dazzling, effulgent, flashing, fulgent, glaring, gleaming, glistening, glittering, glossy, glowing, golden, illuminated, illumined, incandescent, intense, irradiated, lambent, light, lighted, luminous, lustrous, limpid, moonlit, phosphorescent, polished, radiant, resplendent, scintillating, shimmering, shiny, silvery, sparkling, sunny, twinkling, vivid.

- **Word:** Disarm (Synonym denoting Meaning: cripple)

  Other Synonyms: Conciliate, cripple, deactivate, debilitate, deescalate, demilitarise, demobilise, disable, disband, disqualify, incapacitate, invalidate, occupy, pacify, paralyse, prostrate, strip, subdue, subjugate, unarm, weaken.

Antonyms: Bender, bough, bow, branch, fin, flapper, flipper, handle, hook, member, offshoot, projection, prong, rod, stump, wing.

- **Word:** Diaphanous (Synonym denoting Meaning: fine)

  Other Synonyms: Chiffon, clear, delicate, filmy, flimsy, gauzy, gossamer, light, pellucid, pure, see-through, sheer, thin, tiffany, translucent, transparent.

  Antonyms: Blurred, cloudy, dark, darkened, dim, dirty, dull, dusky, filmy, foggy, frosty, fuliginous, gloomy, hazy, impenetrable, misty, muddied, muddy, murky, non-translucent, non-transparent, obfuscated, shady, smoky, sooty, thick, turbid.

- **Word:** Die-hard (Synonym denoting Meaning: uncompromising)

  Other Synonyms: Conservative, convinced, dyed-in-the-wool, extreme, extremist, firm, fogyish, immovable, inflexible, intransigent, old-line, orthodox, Philistine, reactionary, right, standpat, Tory, traditionalistic, ultraconservative.

  Antonyms: Compromising, delicate, difficult, embarrassed, inconvenient, inopportune, painful, perplexing, sticky, thorny, ticklish, troublesome, trying, uncomfortable, unpleasant, untimely.

- **Word:** Decay (Synonym denoting Meaning: collapse)

  Other Synonyms: Adulteration, atrophy, blight, caries, consumption, corrosion, crumbling, decadence, decline, decomposition, decrease, decrepitude, degeneracy, degeneration, depreciation, deterioration, dilapidation, disintegration, disrepair, dissolution, downfall, dying, extinction, fading, failing, gangrene, impairment, mortification, perishing, putrefaction, putrescence, putridity, rot, rotting, ruin, ruination, rust, senescence, spoilage, spoliation, wasting, withering.

  Antonyms: Advance, advancement, augmentation, beefing up, boost, build-up, crop, cultivation, enlargement, evolution, evolvement, expansion, extension, fleshing out, flowering, gain, germination, growing, heightening, hike, improvement, increase, maturation, maturing, multiplication, produce, production, progress, proliferation, prosperity, rise, sprouting, stretching, success, surge, swell, thickening, unfolding, up, upping, vegetation, widening.

- **Word:** Deliberation (Synonym denoting Meaning: discussion)

  Other Synonyms: Application, attention, brainwork, calculation, care, carefulness, caution, cerebration, cogitation, confabulation, conference, consideration, consultation, debate, forethought, heed, meditation, prudence, purpose, reflection, speculation, study, ventilation, wariness.

  Antonyms: Carelessness, free-spiritedness, impulse, impulsiveness, intemperance, recklessness, spontaneity, thoughtlessness, unrestraint, wantonness, wildness.

- **Word:** Dear (Synonym denoting Meaning: beloved)

  Other Synonyms: Baby, blue-eyed, cherished, close, darling, doll face, endeared, esteemed, fair-haired, familiar, favourite, intimate, loved, pet, precious, prized, respected, sugar, sweet face, sweetie, toots, tootsie, tootsie, treasured.

  Antonyms: Abominable, annoying, bothersome, defective, disagreeable, disliked, displeasing, distasteful, dreaded, icky, inadmissible, incommodious, inconvenient, inexpedient, insufferable, loathed, loathsome, objectionable, obnoxious, offensive, outcast, rejected, repellent, repugnant, scorned, shunned, troublesome, unacceptable, unattractive, unlikable, unpleasing, unpopular, unsatisfactory, unsavoury, unsought, unsuitable, unwanted, unwelcome, unwished for, useless.

E

- **Word:** Early (Synonym denoting Meaning: beginning)

  Other Synonyms: Aboriginal, ancient, antecedent,

antediluvian, antiquated, brand-new, budding, early bird, fresh, initial, maiden, new, original, preceding, premier, previous, primal, prime, primeval, primitive, primordial, prior, pristine, raw.

Antonyms: Absolute, all out, clear, clinching, cogent, compelling, convincing, deciding, decisive, demonstrative, determinant, determinative, final, flat out, incontrovertible, indisputable, irrefutable, irrevocable, litmus test, precise, resolving, revealing, settling, straight out, telling, ultimate, unambiguous, unanswerable, unarguable, unconditional, undeniable, unmistakable, unquestionable.

- **Word:** Earnest (Synonym denoting Meaning: enthusiastic)

  Other Synonyms: Ardent, busy, devoted, diligent, eager, fervent, fervid, heartfelt, impassioned, industrious, keen, passionate, perseverant, purposeful, sedulous, sincere, urgent, vehement, warm, wholehearted, zealous.

  Antonyms: Blah, callous, cold, cool, draggy, drippy, emotionless, flat, impassive, indifferent, insensible, laid back, languid, moony, passive, stoic, stolid, uncaring, unconcerned, unemotional, unfeeling, uninterested, unmoved, unresponsive, untouched, wimpy.

- **Word:** Easy (Synonym denoting Meaning: not difficult)

  Other Synonyms: Accessible, apparent, basic, child's play, cinch, clear, easily done, effortless, elementary, evident, facile, inconsiderable, light, little, manageable, manifest, mere, no bother, no problem, no sweat, no trouble, not burdensome, obvious, painless, paltry, picnic, plain, plain sailing, pushover, royal, simple, slight, smooth, snap, straightforward, uncomplicated, undemanding, uninvolved, wieldy, yielding.

  Antonyms: Ambitious, arduous, backbreaking, ball-buster, bothersome, burdensome, challenging, crucial, demanding, effortful, exacting, formidable, galling, Gargantuan, hard, hard-won, heavy, herculean, immense, intricate, irritating, laboured, labourious, man-sized, no picnic, not easy, onerous, painful, problem, problematic, prohibitive, rigid, severe, stiff, strenuous, titanic, toilsome, tough, troublesome, trying, unyielding, uphill, upstream, wearisome

- **Word:** Eat (Synonym denoting Meaning: erode)

  Other Synonyms: Bite, condense, corrode, crumble, decay, decompose, disappear, disintegrate, dissipate, dissolve, drain, exhaust, gnaw, liquefy, melt, nibble, rot, run through, rust, spill, squander, use, vanish, waste away, wear.

  Antonyms: Assemble, bring about, carpenter, cast, compile, compose, contrive, engineer, erect, evolve, fabricate, fashion, fit together, forge, form, frame, jerry-build, knock out, make, manufacture, model, prefab, produce, put together, put up, raise, rear, reconstruct, sculpture, set up, synthesise, throw together, throw up.

- **Word:** Economical (Synonym denoting Meaning: saving)

  Other Synonyms: Avaricious, canny, careful, chary, circumspect, close, closefisted, cost-effective, curmudgeonly, economizing, efficient, frugal, meagre, mean, methodical, miserly, money-saving, niggardly, parsimonious, penny-pinching, penny-wise, penurious, practical, provident, prudent, prudential, saving, Scotch, scrimping, skimping, spare, sparing, stingy, thrifty, tight, time-saving, watchful, work-saving.

  Antonyms: Big-ticket, costly, dear, excessive, executive, exorbitant, extravagant, fancy, high, highway robbery, holdup, immoderate, inordinate, invaluable, lavish, overpriced, plush, posh, pretty penny, pricey, rich, ritzy, sky-high, steep, stiff, swank, too high, uneconomical, unreasonable, upscale, valuable.

- **Word:** Ecstasy (Synonym denoting Meaning: bliss)

  Other Synonyms: Beatitude, blessedness, cool, delectation, delight, delirium, ebullience, elation, enchantment, enthusiasm, euphoria, exaltation, far out, felicity, fervour, frenzy, gladness, gone, happiness, heaven, inspiration, intoxication, joy, joyfulness, paradise, rapture, ravishment, rhapsody, seventh heaven, trance, transport, twilight zone.

Antonyms: Abasement, abjection, abjectness, blahs, bleakness, blow-out, blue funk, blues, bummer, cheerlessness, dejection, desolation, desperation, despondency, disconsolation, discouragement, dispiritedness, distress, dole, dolefulness, downheartedness, dreariness, dullness, dumps, ennui, gloom, gloominess, heavy-heartedness, hopelessness, lowness, melancholia, melancholy, misery, mortification, qualm, sadness, sorrow, trouble, unhappiness, woefulness, worry.

- **Word:** Edge (Synonym denoting Meaning: border)

  Other Synonyms: Bend, bound, boundary, brim, brink, butt, circumference, contour, corner, crook, crust, curb, end, extremity, frame, fringe, frontier, hem, hook, ledge, limb, limit, line, lip, margin, moulding, mouth, outline, outskirt, peak, perimeter, periphery, point, portal, rim, ring, shore, side, skirt, split, strand, term, threshold, tip, trimming, turn, verge.

  Antonyms: Axis, bull's-eye, centrality, core, cynosure, equidistance, essence, focal point, focus, gist, heart, hotbed, hub, inside, interior, intermediacy, kernel, kernel, mainstream, marrow, midpoint, midst, nave, navel, nucleus, pith, pivot, place, polestar, quick, radiant, root, seat.

- **Word:** Edible (Synonym denoting Meaning: eatable)

  Other Synonyms: Comestible, digestible, esculent, fit, good, harmless, nourishing, nutritious, nutritive, palatable, savoury, succulent, tasty, toothsome, wholesome.

  Antonyms: Abominable, awful, beastly, cloying, creepy, detestable, distasteful, foul, frightful, ghastly, gross, gruesome, hateful, hideous, horrid, horrific, icky, loathsome, lousy, macabre, monstrous, nasty, nauseating, nerdy, noisome, objectionable, obnoxious, odious, offensive, outrageous, repellent, repugnant, repulsive, revolting, rotten, satiating, scandalous, shameless, shocking, sleazy, stinking, surfeiting, vile, vulgar, yucky.

- **Word:** Efficient (Synonym denoting Meaning: effective)

  Other Synonyms: Able, accomplished, active, adapted, adept, adequate, apt, businesslike, capable, clever, competent, conducive, decisive, deft, dynamic, economic, economical, effectual, efficacious, energetic, equal to, experienced, expert, familiar with, fitted, good at, good for, handy, masterly, organized, potent, powerful, practiced, productive, proficient, profitable, qualified, ready, saving, shrewd, skilled, skilful, systematic, talented, tough, useful, valuable, virtuous, well-organized, workmanlike.

Antonyms: Amateur, amateurish, awkward, bungling, bush, bush league, clumsy, disqualified, floundering, helpless, inadequate, incapable, incapacitated, ineffectual, inefficient, ineligible, inept, inexperienced, inexpert, insufficient, maladroit, raw, skill less, unable, unequipped, unfit, unfitted, unhandy, uninitiated, unqualified, unskilled, untrained, useless.

- **Word:** Effort (Synonym denoting Meaning: work)

  Other Synonyms: Accomplishment, achievement, act, aim, application, aspiration, attempt, battle, crack, creation, deed, discipline, drill, elbow grease, endeavour, energy, enterprise, essay, exercise, exertion, feat, fling, force, go, industry, intention, job, labour, pains, power, product, production, pull, purpose, push, resolution, shot, spurt, stab, strain, stress, stretch, strife, striving, struggle, sweat, tension, toil, training, travail, trial, trouble, try, tug, undertaking, venture, whack.

  Antonyms: Apathy, dilatoriness, do-nothingness, dormancy, dreaminess, drowsiness, dullness, faineance, heaviness, idleness, inactivity, indolence, inertia, inertness, lackadaisicalness, languidness, languorousness, laxness, leadenness, leisureliness, lethargy, listlessness, neglectfulness, negligence, passivity, remissness, slackness, sleepiness, sloth, slothfulness, slowness, sluggishness, stolidity, tardiness, weariness.

- **Word:** Elaborate (Synonym denoting Meaning: intricate)

  Other Synonyms: Busy, careful, complex, complicated, decorated, detailed, elegant, embellished, exact, extensive, extravagant, fancy, fussy, garnished, hi tech, highly-wrought, imposing, involved, knotty, laboured, labyrinthine, luxurious, many-faceted, minute, ornamented, ornate, ostentatious, overdone, overworked, painstaking, perfected, plush, posh, precise, prodigious, refined, showy, skilful, sophisticated, studied, thorough.

Antonyms: Accepted, average, banal, bourgeois, casual, characteristic, colloquial, commonplace, conventional, current, customary, daily, everyday, familiar, frequent, general, habitual, hackneyed, homely, humdrum, informal, mediocre, monotonous, natural, obscure, passable, plain, prevailing, prevalent, probably, prosaic, regular, routine, run-of-the-mill, simple, stale, standard, stereotyped, stock, trite, trivial, typical, undistinguished, universal, unvaried, usual, wearisome, workaday.

- **Word:** Elective (Synonym denoting Meaning: optional)

  Other Synonyms: Constituent, discretionary, electoral, facultative, nonobligatory, not compulsory, selective, voluntary, voting.

  Antonyms: De rigueur, forced, imperative, imperious, mandatory, necessary, obligatory, required, requisite.

- **Word:** Elegant (Synonym denoting Meaning: beautiful)

  Other Synonyms: Affected, appropriate, apt, aristocratic, artistic, august, chic, choice, classic, clever, comely, courtly, cultivated, cultured, dainty, delicate, dignified, effective, exquisite, fancy, fashionable, fine, genteel, graceful, grand, handsome, ingenious, luxurious, majestic, modish, neat, nice, noble, opulent, ornamented, ornate, ostentatious, overdone, polished, rare, recherché, refined, rich, select, simple, stately, stuffy, stylish, sumptuous, superior, turgid, well-bred.

  Antonyms: Base, bawdy, blue, boorish, brutish, cheap, common, crass, crude, dirty, earthy, filthy, foul, foul-mouthed, gross, gruff, immodest, impolite, improper, impure, indelicate, inelegant, loutish, low, lowbred, mean, nasty, obscene, off-colour, offensive, raffish, raunchy, raw, ribald, rough, roughneck, rude, scatological, smutty, tacky, uncivil, uncouth, uncultivated, uncultured, unrefined, vulgar.

- **Word:** Element (Synonym denoting Meaning: feature)

  Other Synonyms: Aspect, basic, basis, bit, component, constituent, detail, drop, essential, facet, factor, feature, fundamental, hint, ingredient, item, material, matter, member, part, particle, particular, piece, portion, principle, root, section, stem, subdivision, trace, unit, view.

  Antonyms: Blended, complex, compound, conglomerate, mixed, synthesised.

- **Word:** Elevate (Synonym denoting Meaning: lift up)

  Other Synonyms: Drag, dredge, erect, fetch up, heighten, hike up, hoist, jack up, levitate, lift, poise, pump, put up, pyramid, raise, ramp, rear, shoot up, stilt, take up, tilt, uphold, uplift, upraise.

  Antonyms: Abate, calm down, check, contract, crumble, curb, curtail, cut down, decay, decline, degenerate, depreciate, deteriorate, devaluate, die down, diminish, droop, drop, drop off, dry up, dwindle, ease, ebb, evaporate, fade, fall off, lessen, let up, lighten, lose edge, lower, modify, narrow down, peter out, quell, quiet, reduce, restrain, run low, settle, shrink, shrivel, sink, slack off, slacken, slash, slow down, slump, soften, subside, tail off, wane, waste, weaken, wear, wither.

- **Word:** Emigrant (Synonym denoting Meaning: foreigner)

  Other Synonyms: Alien, colonist, displaced person, evacuee, exile, expatriate, fugitive, immigrant, migrant, outcast, pilgrim, refugee, traveller, wanderer, wayfarer, émigré.

  Antonyms: Aborigine, anthropophagus, brute, bushman, cruel person, islander, man-eater, native, ogre, ogress, primitive, ruffian, savage, tribesman.

- **Word:** Emotion (Synonym denoting Meaning: mental state)

  Other Synonyms: Affect, affection, affectivity, agitation, anger, ardour, commotion, concern, desire, despair, despondency, disturbance, drive, ecstasy, elation, empathy, excitability, excitement, feeling, fervour, grief, gut reaction, happiness, inspiration, joy, love, melancholy, passion, perturbation, pride, rage, remorse, responsiveness, sadness, satisfaction, sensation, sensibility, sensitiveness, sentiment, shame, sorrow, sympathy, thrill, tremor, vehemence, vibes, warmth, zeal.

Antonyms: Aloofness, coldness, coolness, detachment, disinterest, dispassion, disregard, dullness, half-heartedness, heedlessness, indifference, insensibility, insensitivity, insouciance, lassitude, lethargy, listlessness, passiveness, passivity, stoicism, unconcern, unresponsiveness.

- **Word:** Empower (Synonym denoting Meaning: authorise)

  Other Synonyms: Accredit, allow, capacitate, charge, commission, delegate, enable, entitle, entrust, grant, invest, license, OK, okay, permit, privilege, qualify, sanction, vest, warrant.

  Antonyms: Abjure, cancel, censor, debar, deny, ding, disavow, disclaim, dismiss, disown, embargo, exclude, forbid, keep back, kill, nix, pass on, prohibit, proscribe, put down, rebuff, refuse, repudiate, shut out, veto, withhold, zing.

- **Word:** Empty (Synonym denoting Meaning: void)

  Other Synonyms: Abandoned, bare, barren, blank, clear, dead, deflated, depleted, desert, deserted, desolate, despoiled, destitute, devoid, dry, evacuated, exhausted, forsaken, godforsaken, hollow, lacking, stark, unfilled, unfurnished, uninhabited, unoccupied, vacant, vacated, vacuous, void, wanting, waste.

  Antonyms: All, entire, exhaustive, faultless, full, full-dress, gross, imperforate, intact, integral, integrated, organic, outright, plenary, replete, the works, thorough, thoroughgoing, unabbreviated, unabridged, unbroken, uncondensed, uncut, undiminished, undivided, undocked, unexpurgated, unimpaired, unitary, unreduced, whole, whole enchilada, whole-hog, whole-length.

- **Word:** Enclose (Synonym denoting Meaning: surround)

  Other Synonyms: Block of, blockade, bound, box up, cage, circle, circumscribe, close in, confine, coop, corral, cover, encase, encircle, encompass, enfold, enshroud, environ, fence, fence off, hedge, hem in, imbue, imimplant, impound, imprison, include, induct, insert, intern, jail, limit, lock in, lock up, mew, pen, restrict, set apart, shut in, veil, wall in, wrap.

  Antonyms: Comp, complimentary, costless, for free, for love, for nothing, free lunch, free ride, freebie, gratis, gratuitous, handout, paper, unpaid, unrecompensed.

- **Word:** Endear (Synonym denoting Meaning: attract)

  Other Synonyms: Attach, bind, captivate, charm, cherish, engage, prize, treasure, value, win.

  Antonyms: Come between, disaffect, disunite, divide, divorce, estrange, make indifferent, part, separate, set against, turn away, turn off, wean.

- **Word:** Energise (Synonym denoting Meaning: activate)

  Other Synonyms: Animate, arm, build-up, electrify, empower, enable, enliven, excite, fortify, goose, innervate, inspirit, invigorate, jazz up, juice up, liven up, motivate, pep up, prime, pump up, quicken, reinforce, start up, stimulate, strengthen, sustain, switch on, trigger, turn on, vitalise, work up, zap.

  Antonyms: Bankrupt, burn out, conk out, cripple, debilitate, disable, do in, drain, draw, enervate, enfeeble, fag, fatigue, frazzle, impoverish, knock out, overdo, overexert, overextend, overwork, peter out, poop, poop out, prostrate, run ragged, sap, suck dry, tire, tire out, tucker, use up, weaken, wear down.

- **Word:** Enervate (Synonym denoting Meaning: tire)

  Other Synonyms: Bush, castrate, debilitate, devitalize, disable, emasculate, enfeeble, exhaust, fatigue, incapacitate, jade, paralyse, prostrate, sap, unman, unnerve, unstring, wash out, weaken, wear, wear out, weary.

  Antonyms: Actuate, arouse, call up, energize, impel, mobilize, motivate, move, prompt, propel, rouse, start, stimulate, stir, switch on, trigger, turn on

- **Word:** Enfold (Synonym denoting Meaning: embrace)

  Other Synonyms: Bear hug, cinch, clasp, clinch, clutch, cover, drape, encase, enclose, encompass, enshroud, envelop, envelope, enwrap, fold, girdle, grab, hold, hug, invest, press, shroud, squeeze, surround, swathe, veil, wrap, wrap up.

  Antonyms: Bare, breach, break in, break out, broach, burst, bust in, come apart, crack, disclose, display, disrupt, expand, expose, fissure, free, gap, gape, hole, jimmy, kick in, lacerate, lance, penetrate, perforate, pierce, pop, puncture, release, reveal, rupture, separate, sever, slit, slot, split, spread, tap, unblock, unbolt, unclose, unclothe, uncork, uncover, undo, unfasten, unfold, unfurl, unlatch, unlock, unroll, unseal, unshut, unstop, untie, unwrap, vent, ventilate, yawn, yawp.

- **Word:** Enforce (Synonym denoting Meaning: administer)

  Other Synonyms: Accomplish, administrate, apply, carry out, coerce, commandeer, compel, constrain, crack down, demand, dictate, discharge, dragoon, drive, effect, egg on, emphasize, exact, execute, exert, expect, extort, force upon, fortify, fulfil, goad, hound, impel, implement, impose, incite, insist on, invoke, lash, lean on, make, necessitate, oblige, perform, press, prosecute, reinforce, require, sanction, spur, strain, stress, strong-arm, support, urge, whip, wrest.

  Antonyms: Carelessness, free-spiritedness, impulse, impulsiveness, intemperance, recklessness, spontaneity, thoughtlessness, unrestraint, wantonness, wildness.

- **Word:** Engagement (Synonym denoting Meaning: pledge)

  Other Synonyms: Assurance, betrothal, betrothing, bond, commitment, compact, contract, espousal, match, oath, obligation, pact, plight, promise, troth, undertaking, vow, word, zero hour.

  Antonyms: Disengagement, disjoining, dissolution, disunion, division, divorce, divorcement, partition, rupture, separation, severing, split-up.

- **Word:** Enjoy (Synonym denoting Meaning: like)

  Other Synonyms: Adore, appreciate, be entertained, be pleased, cotton to, delight in, dig, dote on, drink in, eat up, fancy, flip for, flip over, funk, go, groove on, have fun, like, love, luxuriate in, mind, pleasure in, rejoice in, relish, revel in, savour, savvy, step out, take to.

  Antonyms: Abhor, abominate, allergic to, chill, contemn, deride, detest, disdain, disregard, eschew, execrate, flout, hate, loathe, neglect, put down, reject, renounce, repudiate, revile, run down, scorn, shun, slight, snub, spurn, trash, undervalue, wipe out.

- **Word:** Enlarge (Synonym denoting Meaning: increase)

  Other Synonyms: Add to, amplify, augment, beef up, blow up, boost, broaden, build, bulk, develop, diffuse, dilate, distend, elaborate, elongate, embroider, exaggerate, expand, expatiate, extend, grow, grow larger, heighten, inflate, jack up, jazz up, lengthen, magnify, make larger, mount, multiply, pad, rise, slap on, snowball, spread, stretch, swell, upsurge, wax, widen.

  Antonyms: Abbreviate, abstract, blue pencil, chop, clip, compress, concentrate, condense, contract, curtail, cut, decrease, digest, diminish, lessen, limit, narrow, nutshell, reduce, restrict, slash, snip, summarise, trim, truncate.

- **Word:** Enough (Synonym denoting Meaning: plenty)

  Other Synonyms: Abundant, acceptable, adequate, ample, bellyful, bounteous, bountiful, comfortable, competent, complete, copious, decent, enough already, fed up, full, had it, last straw, lavish, plenteous, plentiful, replete, satisfying, sufficient, sufficient, sufficing, suitable, that's it, unlimited.

  Antonyms: Absent, away, bankrupt, bereft, burned out, cooked, cut off, defective, deficient, deprived, destitute, devoid, disappointing, empty, failing, faulty, gone, half-assed, half-baked, imperfect, in default, inadequate, incomplete, inferior, less, minus, missing, needed, omitted, patchy, poor, scant, scanty, scarce, short, shy, sketchy, substandard, unfulfilled, unsound.

- **Word:** Enter (Synonym denoting Meaning: come in)

  Other Synonyms: Access, arrive, barge in, blow in, break in, breeze in, burst in, bust in, butt in, come, come in, crack, crawl, creep, crowd in, drive in, drop in, fall into, gain entree, get in, go in, horn in, immigrate, infiltrate, ingress, insert, insinuate, introduce, intrude, invade, jump in, make way, move in, pass into, penetrate, pierce, pile in, pop in, probe, rush in, slip, sneak, work in, worm in, wriggle.

  Antonyms: Abandon, abdicate, absent, beat it, blast off, blow, cut out, decamp, desert, disappear, emigrate, escape, evacuate, exit, get away, go, go away, go forth, make feet, march out, migrate, move on, move out, part, perish, pull out, quit, remove, retire, sally forth, say goodbye, scram, secede, set forth, shove off, slip away, split, start, start out, take leave, tergiversate.

- **Word:** Enterprise (Synonym denoting Meaning: resourcefulness)

  Other Synonyms: Activity, adventurousness, alertness, ambition, audacity, boldness, courage, daring, dash, drive, eagerness, energy, enthusiasm, force, foresight, get-up-and-go, gumption, hustle, industry, initiative, inventiveness, pluck, push, readiness, resource, self-reliance, spirit, vigour, zeal.

  Antonyms: Aloofness, coldness, coolness, detachment, disinterest, dispassion, disregard, dullness, half-heartedness, heedlessness, indifference, insensibility, insensitivity, insouciance, lassitude, lethargy, listlessness, passiveness, passivity, stoicism, unconcern, unresponsiveness.

F

- **Word:** Fabulous (Synonym denoting Meaning: wonderful)

  Other Synonyms: Aces, amazing, astonishing, astounding,

bang-up, best, breathtaking, cool, crack, dilly, extravagant, fantastic, fictitious, first class, gone, greatest, groovy, immense, in spades, inconceivable, incredible, legendary, mind-blowing, out-of-this-world, outrageous, peachy, phenomenal, primo, prodigious, remarkable, spectacular, striking, stupendous, super, superb, terrific, top drawer, tops, turn-on, unbelievable, unreal, wicked, wondrous.

Antonyms: Accepted, average, banal, bourgeois, casual, characteristic, colloquial, commonplace, conventional, current, customary, daily, everyday, familiar, frequent, general, habitual, hackneyed, homely, humdrum, informal, mediocre, monotonous, natural, obscure, passable, plain, prevailing, prevalent, probably, prosaic, regular, routine, run-of-the-mill, simple, stale, standard, stereotyped, stock, trite, trivial, typical, undistinguished, universal, unvaried, usual, wearisome, work-a-day.

- **Word:** Fact (Synonym denoting Meaning: detail)

  Other Synonyms: Accomplishment, act, action, actuality, adventure, affair, being, case, circumstance, conception, consideration, construction, creation, data, datum, deed, entity, episode, event, evidence, experience, factor, fait accompli, feature, happening, incident, information, item, manifestation, occurrence, organism, particular, performance, phenomenon, point, proceeding, specific, statistic, transaction, truism.

  Antonyms: Accident, break, chance, chance happening, crisis, crossroads, emergency, event, eventuality, exigency, fortuity, happening, incident, juncture, likelihood, occasion, odds, opportunity, pass, pinch, predicament, probability, strait, turning point, uncertainty, zero hour.

- **Word:** Faculty (Synonym denoting Meaning: ability)

  Other Synonyms: Adroitness, aptitude, aptness, bent, capability, capacity, cleverness, dexterity, facility, flair, forte, genius, gift, instinct, intelligence, knack, leaning, nose, peculiarity, penchant, pistol, power, predilection, proclivity, propensity, property, quality, readiness, reason, right stuff, sense, skill, strength, talent, turn, wits.

Antonyms: Disability, disqualification, failure, frailty, impotence, inadequacy, inaptitude, incapability, incapacitation, incapacity, incompetence, ineffectiveness, ineffectualness, inefficacy, inefficiency, ineptitude, ineptness, insufficiency, inutility, lack, necessity, powerlessness, shortcoming, unfitness, weakness.

- **Word:** Fail (Synonym denoting Meaning: be unsuccessful)

  Other Synonyms: Abort, backslide, be defeated, be demoted, be ruined, blunder, break down, decline, deteriorate, fall, fall flat, fall short, fall through, fizzle, flop, flounder, fold, founder, go astray, go down, go downhill, go wrong, hit bottom, lose control, lose out, lose status, miscarry, miss, play into, run aground, slip.

  Antonyms: Achieve, arrive, attain, bring about, bring off, carry out, conclude, consummate, do, do justice, effect, finish, fulfil, gain, get someplace, get there, hit, make it, manage, nail it, perform, produce, pull off, rack up, reach, realise, score, sew up, unzip, win.

- **Word:** Fair (Synonym denoting Meaning: impartial)

  Other Synonyms: Above board, benevolent, blameless, candid, civil, clean, courteous, decent, disinterested, dispassionate, equal, equitable, even-handed, frank, generous, good, honest, honourable, just, lawful, legitimate, moderate, non-partisan, objective, on up-and-up, open, pious, praiseworthy, principled, proper, reasonable, respectable, righteous, scrupulous, sincere, square, straight, straightforward, temperate, trustworthy, unbiased, uncoloured, uncorrupted, unprejudiced, upright, virtuous.

  Antonyms: Biased, dogmatic, narrow, narrow-minded, obstinate, opinionated, partial, partisan, sectarian, slanted, small-minded, twisted, unfair, warped.

- **Word:** Faith (Synonym denoting Meaning: belief)

  Other Synonyms: Canon, church, communion, confession, connection, conviction, credo, creed, cult, denomination, doctrine, dogma, doxy, gospel, orthodoxy, persuasion, piety, piousness, principle, profession, religion, revelation, sect, teaching, tenet, theism, theology, worship.

  Antonyms: Atheism, distrust, dubiety, incredulity, mistrust, nihilism, rejection, repudiation, skepticism, spurning, unbelief, unfaith.

- **Word:** Fallow (Synonym denoting Meaning: inactive)

  Other Synonyms: Dormant, idle, inert, neglected, quiescent, resting, slack, uncultivated, undeveloped, unplanted, unproductive, unseeded, untilled, unused, vacant, virgin.

  Antonyms: Alive, at work, bustling, effective, efficacious, exertive, flowing, functioning, going, hasty, impelling, in force, in play, in process, mobile, movable, moving, operating, operative, progressive, pushing, rapid, restless, rolling, running, rushing, rustling, shifting, simmering, speeding, speedy, streaming, swarming, travelling, turning, walking, working.

- **Word:** Falsehood (Synonym denoting Meaning: lie)

  Other Synonyms: Canard, cover-up, deceit, deception, dishonesty, dissimulation, distortion, equivocation, erroneousness, error, fable, fabrication, fakery, fallaciousness, fallacy, falseness, falsity, feigning, fib, fiction, figment, fraud, half truth, hogwash, line, mendacity, misstatement, perjury, pretence, prevarication, sham, story, tale, untruth, untruthfulness, whopper, yarn.

  Antonyms: Actual, actually, existing, genuinely, in effect, in fact, real, really, tangible, truly, veritably.

- **Word:** Famine (Synonym denoting Meaning: hunger)

  Other Synonyms: Dearth, destitution, drought, misery, paucity, poverty, scarcity, starvation, want.

  Antonyms: Affluence, ampleness, bounty, copiousness, fortune, opulence, plentitude, plenty, profusion, prosperity, prosperousness, riches, wealth.

- **Word:** Famous (Synonym denoting Meaning: notable)

  Other Synonyms: Acclaimed, applauded, august, brilliant, celebrated, conspicuous, distinguished, elevated, eminent, exalted, excellent, extraordinary, foremost, glorious, grand, great, honoured, illustrious, important, imposing, in limelight, in spotlight, influential, leading, lionised, memorable, mighty, much-publicised, noble, noted, noteworthy, notorious, of note, outstanding, peerless, powerful, pre-eminent, prominent, recognized, remarkable, renowned, reputable, signal, splendid, talked of, well-known.

  Antonyms: Bearding, incognito, nameless, pseudo, pseudonymous, secret, unacknowledged, unattested, unclaimed, undesignated, undisclosed, unidentified, unnamed, unsigned, unspecified.

- **Word:** Fare (Synonym denoting Meaning: get along)

  Other Synonyms: Advance, do, get by, get on, go, handle, happen, journey, make headway, make out, manage, muddle through, pass, proceed, progress, prosper, prove, shift, stagger, turn out.

  Antonyms: Aid, anchor, backbone, brace, bulwark, buttress, crutch, linchpin, main man, maintainer, old standby, pillar, prop, right-hand man, sinew, staff, standby, stay, strength, supporter, sustainer, upholder.

- **Word:** Fatal (Synonym denoting Meaning: deadly)

  Other Synonyms: Baleful, baneful, calamitous, cataclysmic, catastrophic, deathly, destructive, disastrous, fateful, final, ill-fated, ill-starred, incurable, inevitable, killing, lethal, malefic, malignant, mortal, pernicious, pestilent, pestilential, ruinous, terminal, virulent.

  Antonyms: Amiable, benevolent, benignant, complaisant, favourable, friendly, generous, genial, gentle, good, good-hearted, gracious, kind, liberal, merciful, mild, obliging, sympathetic.

- **Word:** Fatty (Synonym denoting Meaning: chubby)

  Other Synonyms: Blubbery, cholesterol-filled, fat, fatlike, greasy, lardaceous, lardy, oily, oleaginous, rich, unctuous.

  Antonyms: Angle, be off, be slanted, bear on, beetle, bow, cant, careen, cock, curve, decline, deflect, dip, divert, drift, droop, fasten on, hang on, heel, incline, jut, list, nod, overhang, pitch, place, prop, recline, repose, rest, rest on, roll, sag, sheer, sink, slant, slope, tilt, tip, turn, twist, veer.

- **Word:** Fear (Synonym denoting Meaning: alarm)

  Other Synonyms: Abhorrence, agitation, angst, anxiety, apprehensiveness, aversion, awe, bugbear, chicken heartedness, cold feet, cold sweat, concern, consternation, cowardice, creeps, despair, discomposure, dismay, disquietude, distress, doubt, dread, faintheartedness, foreboding, fright, funk, horror, jitters, misgiving, nightmare, panic, phobia, presentiment, qualm, recreancy, reverence, revulsion, scare, suspicion, terror, timidity, trembling, tremor, trepidation, unease, uneasiness, worry.

  Antonyms: Aggressiveness, aplomb, arrogance, assuredness, audacity, boldness, bravery, certainty, certitude, conviction, coolness, courage, effrontery, faith, firmness, impudence, nerve, poise, presumption, security, self-confidence, self-reliance, sureness, surety, temerity, trust.

- **Word:** Feast (Synonym denoting Meaning: eat)

  Other Synonyms: Banquet, eat sumptuously, entertain, gorge, indulge, overindulge, regale, stuff, treat.

  Antonyms: Abjure, abnegate, avoid, cease, constrain, curb, decline, deny oneself, do without, eschew, evade, fast, forbear, forgo, give up, keep from, pass, pass up, quit, refrain, refuse, renounce, shun, sit out, spurn, starve, stop, withhold.

- **Word:** Feature (Synonym denoting Meaning: stress)

  Other Synonyms: Accentuate, advertise, blaze, emphasize, give prominence, headline, italicise, make conspicuous, mark, play up, point up, present, promote, set off, spotlight, star, underline, underscore.

Antonyms: Blink at, brush aside, brush away, brush off, cold-shoulder, contemn, despise, discount, disdain, disobey, disparage, fail, forget, laugh off, let go, let pass, live with, miss, neglect, omit, overlook, overpass, pass over, pooh pooh, scorn, slight, snub, tune out, vilipend, wink at.

- **Word:** Female (Synonym denoting Meaning: womanly)

  Other Synonyms: Changeable, child-bearing, delicate, effeminate, effete, fair, feminine, fertile, gentle, girlish, girly, graceful, ladylike, maidenly, matronly, modest, oviparous, petticoat, pistil-bearing, pure, refined, reproductive, sensitive, she-stuff, shy, soft, tender, twisty, virgin, weak, womanish.

  Antonyms: Macho, manful, manlike, manly, potent, virile.

- **Word:** Festive (Synonym denoting Meaning: celebratory)

  Other Synonyms: Blithe, bouncy, carnival, cheery, chipper, chirpy, convivial, decorated, festal, gala, gay, gleeful, grooving, happy, hearty, holiday, jocund, jolly, jovial, joyful, joyous, jubilant, juiced up, jumping, light-hearted, merry, mirthful, peppy, perky, rocking, snappy, swinging, upbeat, zippy.

  Antonyms: Bad, bleeding, blue, blue funk, bummed out, cast down, crestfallen, crummy, dejected, despondent, destroyed, disconsolate, dispirited, down, downcast, downhearted, dragged, fed up, glum, grim, hurting, in pain, let down, low, low down, low-spirited, lugubrious, melancholy, moody, morose, pessimistic, ripped, sad, sob story, spiritless, taken down, torn up, unhappy, weeper, woebegone.

- **Word:** Fetter (Synonym denoting Meaning: hold)

  Other Synonyms: Bind, chain, check, clog, confine, cuff, curb, drag feet, encumber, hamper, hamstring, handcuff, hang up, hinder, hobble, hog-tie, hold captive, leash, manacle, repress, restrain, restrict, shackle, tie, tie up, trammel.

Antonyms: Comp, complimentary, costless, for free, for love, for nothing, free lunch, free ride, freebie, gratis, gratuitous, handout, paper, unpaid, unrecompensed.

- **Word:** Fence (Synonym denoting Meaning: enclose)

  Other Synonyms: Bound, cage, circumscribe, confine, coop, corral, defend, encircle, fortify, girdle, guard, hedge, hem, immew, pen, protect, rail, restrict, secure, separate, surround, wall.

  Antonyms: Absolve, acquit, bail out, cast loose, clear, commute, deliver, discharge, disengage, dispense, drop, emancipate, exculpate, excuse, exempt, exonerate, extricate, free, give off, give out, issue, leak, let off, liberate, lifeboat, loose, loosen, manumit, open up, set free, set loose, spring, surrender, take out, turn loose, turn out, unbind, unchain, undo, unfasten, unfetter, unleash, unloose, unshackle, untie, vent, yield.

- **Word:** Fervent (Synonym denoting Meaning: enthusiastic)

  Other Synonyms: Animated, ardent, blazing, burning, devout, dying to, eager, earnest, ecstatic, emotional, enthused, excited, fervid, fiery, glowing, gotta have, gung ho, heartfelt, hearty, hopped up, hot, hot for, hot-blooded, impassioned, intense, passionate, perfervid, pious, religious, responsive, serious, sincere, tender, unfeigned, vehement, warm, warm-hearted, wholehearted, zealous.

  Antonyms: Blah, callous, cold, cool, drippy, emotionless, flat, impassive, indifferent, insensible, laid back, languid, moony, passive, stoic, stolid, uncaring, unconcerned, unemotional, unfeeling, uninterested, unmoved, unresponsive, untouched, wimpy.

- **Word:** Farewell (Synonym denoting Meaning: departure)

  Other Synonyms: Adieu, adieus, adieux, bye-bye, cheerio, goodbye, leave-taking, parting, salutation, send-off, so long, ta-ta, valediction.

  Antonyms: Accosting, acknowledgement, address, aloha,

attention, best wishes, blow, card, compliments, good wishes, hail, hello, heralding, hi, high five, highball, how-do-you-do, howdy, kindness, letter, nod, note, notice, ovation, reception, regards, respects, rub, rumble, salaam, salutation, salute, speaking to, testimonial, tumble, ushering in, what's happening.

- **Word:** Fascism (Synonym denoting Meaning: dictatorship)

  Other Synonyms: Absolutism, autocracy, bureaucracy, demagogy, despotism, nazism, one-party system, party government, racism, regimentation, totalitarianism.

  Antonyms: Capitalism, commonwealth, egalitarianism, emancipation, equalitarianism, equality, free enterprise, freedom, justice, laissez faire, liberal government, private ownership, representative government, republic, suffrage.

- **Word:** Fasten (Synonym denoting Meaning: join)

  Other Synonyms: Adhere, affix, anchor, attach, band, bar, batten, belt, bind, bolt, bond, brace, button, catch, cement, chain, cleave, close, cohere, connect, couple, embed, establish, fix, freeze to, girth, glue, grip, hitch, hitch on, hold, hook, hook up, implant, infix, jam, knot, lace, leash, link, lock, lodge, make firm, moor, mortise, nail, rivet, rope, screw, seal, secure, set, settle, solder, stay put, stick, strengthen, string, tack on, tag, tie, tighten, truss, unite, wedge, weld.

  Antonyms: Abstract, cut off, disaffiliate, disassemble, disassociate, disengage, disentangle, disjoin, dismount, dissociate, disunite, divide, divorce, free, isolate, loose, loosen, part, remove, segregate, separate, sever, sunder, take apart, tear off, uncouple, unfasten, unfix, unhitch, withdraw.

- **Word:** Fathom (Synonym denoting Meaning: understand)

  Other Synonyms: Appreciate, apprehend, catch, cognize, comprehend, dig, discern, divine, estimate, figure out, follow, gauge, grasp, have, interpret, know, measure, penetrate, perceive, pierce, pinpoint, plumb, probe, recognise, savvy, sound, unravel.

Antonyms: Abash, amaze, astonish, astound, baffle, ball up, befog, bewilder, blend, bug, commingle, confute, discombobulate, discomfit, discountenance, dumbfound, embarrass, faze, fiddle, flabbergast, jumble, misidentify, mix, mix up, mystify, nonplus, perplex, pose, puzzle, rattle, screw up, startle, surprise, throw.

- **Word:** Fearful (Synonym denoting Meaning: alarmed)

  Other Synonyms: Aflutter, afraid, aghast, agitated, anxious, apprehensive, diffident, discomposed, disquieted, disturbed, faint-hearted, frightened, goose bumpy, hesitant, intimidated, jittery, jumpy, lily-livered, mousy, nerveless, nervous, nervy, panicky, perturbed, phobic, pusillanimous, quivery, run scared, scared, shaky, sheepish, shrinking, shy, skittish, solicitous, spineless, tense, timid, timorous, tremulous, uneasy, unmanly, weak-kneed, worried, yellow.

  Antonyms: Adventurous, assuming, audacious, bantam, courageous, daring, dauntless, enterprising, fearless, forward, gallant, heroic, resolute, unafraid, undaunted, valiant, valorous.

- **Word:** Feeling (Synonym denoting Meaning: touch)

  Other Synonyms: Activity, awareness, consciousness, enjoyment, excitability, excitation, excitement, feel, motility, motor response, pain, perceiving, perception, pleasure, reaction, receptivity, reflex, responsiveness, sensation, sense, sensibility, sensitivity, sensuality, tactility, tangibility, titillation, touch.

  Antonyms: Alienation, aloofness, apathy, callousness, carelessness, cold shoulder, cold-bloodedness, coldness, coolness, detachment, disdain, disinterest, disinterestedness, dispassion, disregard, equity, heedlessness, immunity, impartiality, impassiveness, impassivity, inattention, inertia, insensitivity, insouciance, isolationism, lack, lethargy, listlessness, negligence, neutrality, nonchalance, non-interference, objectivity, stoicism, torpor, unconcern, unmindfulness.

- **Word:** Fade (Synonym denoting Meaning: lose colour)

  Other Synonyms: Become colourless, blanch, bleach, blench, clear, decolourise, dim, disappear, discolour, dissolve, dull, etiolate, evanish, evaporate, grow dim, lose brightness, lose lustre, muddy, pale, tarnish, tone down, vanish, wash out.

Antonyms: Buff up, burnish, clear up, enliven, gleam, glow, grow sunny, illuminate, illumine, intensify, kindle, light up, lighten, polish, punch up.

- **Word:** Fairy (Synonym denoting Meaning: pixie)

  Other Synonyms: Bogie, brownie, dwarf, elf, enchantress, genie, gnome, goblin, gremlin, hob, imp, leprechaun, mermaid, nymph, puck, siren, sprite, sylph.

  Antonyms: Bogey, bogeyman, demon, devil, fiend, giant, monster, monstrosity.

- **Word:** Faithful (Synonym denoting Meaning: loyal)

  Other Synonyms: Affectionate, allegiant, ardent, attached, behind one, circumspect, confiding, conscientious, constant, dependable, devoted, dutiful, dyed-in-the-wool, enduring, fast, firm, genuine, hard-core, honest, honourable, incorruptible, loving, obedient, patriotic, reliable, resolute, scrupulous, sincere, staunch, steadfast, steady, straight, sure, tried, true, true-blue, trustworthy, trusty, truthful, unchanging, unswerving, unwavering, upright, veracious.

  Antonyms: Abuse, aspersion, backstabbing, belittlement, bitchiness, calumniation, calumny, cattiness, defamation, denigration, depreciation, detraction, disparagement, gossip, invective, lie, malice, obloquy, scandal, slander, spite, spitefulness, tale, vilification, vituperation.

- **Word:** Fallacy (Synonym denoting Meaning: misconception)

  Other Synonyms: Aberration, ambiguity, artifice, bias, casuistry, cavil, deceit, deception, deceptiveness, delusion, deviation, elusion, equivocation, erratum, erroneousness, error, evasion, falsehood, faultiness, flaw, heresy, illogicality, illusion, inconsistency, inexactness, invalidity, misapprehension, miscalculation, misinterpretation, mistake, non sequitur, notion, paradox, perversion, preconception, prejudice, quibbling, quirk, solecism, sophism, sophistry, speciousness, subterfuge, u, untruth.

Antonyms: Accuracy, actuality, authenticity, axiom, case, certainty, correctness, dope, exactitude, exactness, fact, facts, factualism, factuality, factualness, genuineness, gospel, gospel truth, honest truth, infallibility, inside track, law, legitimacy, maxim, naked truth, nitty-gritty, perfection, picture, plain talk, precision, principle, rectitude, rightness, scoop, score, straight dope, trueness, truism, truthfulness, validity, veracity, verisimilitude, verity, whole story.

G

- **Word:** Gamble (Synonym denoting Meaning: chance)

  Other Synonyms: Back, bet, brave, cast lots, challenge, chance, dare, defy, endanger, face, game, get down, hazard, imperil, jeopardise, lot, play, plunge, put, risk, set, speculate, stake, tempt fortune, venture, wager.

  Antonyms: Accurate, alert, apprehensive, assiduous, attentive, chary, choosy, circumspect, concerned, conscientious, conservative, cool, deliberate, discreet, exacting, fastidious, finicky, fussy, guarded, heedful, judicious, leery, meticulous, mindful, observant, particular, play safe, precise, prim, protective, provident, prudent, punctilious, regardful, religious, rigorous, scrupulous, self-disciplined, shy, sober, solicitous, thorough, thoughtful, vigilant, wary, watchful.

- **Word:** Gas (Synonym denoting Meaning: something not liquid or solid)

  Other Synonyms: Anesthetic, effluvium, fumes, miasma, smoke, stream, vapour, volatile substance.

  Antonyms: Aqueous, au jus, damp, dissolved, dulcet, flowing, fluent, fluidic, fusible, juicy, liquefied, luscious, mellifluent, mellifluous, mellow, melted, melting, moist, molten, moving, pulpy, running, runny, sappy, serous, smooth, soft, solvent, splashing, succulent, thawed, thin, uncongealed, viscous, watery, wet.

- **Word:** Generally (Synonym denoting Meaning: mainly)

  Other Synonyms: About, almost always, altogether, approximately, broadly, chiefly, commonly, conventionally, customarily, en masse, extensively, habitually, largely, mostly, normally, on average, ordinarily, overall, popularly, practically, predominantly, primarily, principally, publicly, regularly, roughly, roundly, thereabouts, typically, universally, usually, widely.

  Antonyms: Almost never, barely, exceptionally, extra, extraordinarily, extremely, finely, hardly, hardly ever, infrequently, little, notably, remarkably, scarcely ever, seldom, singularly, uncommon, uncommonly, infrequently, unusually.

- **Word:** General (Synonym denoting Meaning: common)

  Other Synonyms: Familiar, ordinary, universal, commonplace, frequent, popular, usual customary, habitual, prevalent, everyday, normal, public.

  Antonyms: Exceptional, infrequent, rare, singular, uncommon, unknown, unusual.

- **Word:** Generous (Synonym denoting Meaning: kind)

  Other Synonyms: Bountiful, free, liberal, noble, chivalrous, free-handed, magnanimous, open-handed, disinterested, free-hearted, munificent, open-hearted.

  Antonyms: Avaricious, greedy, mean, niggardly, penurious, rapacious, close, ignoble, miserly, petty, illiberal.

- **Word:** Genius (Synonym denoting Meaning: intelligent)

  Other Synonyms: Talent, talents.

  Antonyms: Folly, imbecility, obtuseness, senselessness, stupidity.

- **Word:** Gift (Synonym denoting Meaning: present)

  Other Synonyms: Benefaction, boon, bribe, grant, largess, bequest, bounty, donation, gratuity.

Antonyms: Compensation, earnings, guerdon, penalty, remuneration, wages.

- **Word:** Govern (Synonym denoting Meaning: command)

  Other Synonyms: Curb, influence, mold, reign over, rule control, direct, manage, reign, restrain, sway.

  Antonyms: Be in subjection, be subject, comply, obey, submit, yield.

- **Word:** Grief (Synonym denoting Meaning: sadness)

  Other Synonyms: Affliction, melancholy, regret, sorrow, trouble, distress, mourning, sadness, tribulation.

  Antonyms: Blessedness, delight, gladness, pleasure, bliss, ecstasy, gratification, rapture, cheer, enjoyment, joy, rejoicing, comfort, felicity, merriment, satisfaction, contentment, gaiety, mirth, triumph.

- **Word:** Grant (Synonym denoting Meaning: admit)

  Other Synonyms: Yield, concede, allow, give, bestow, confer, deign, vouchsafe, convey, transfer, allot, accord, cede, impart.

  Antonyms: Withhold, withdraw, reserve, resume, deny, refuse.

- **Word:** Graphic (Synonym denoting Meaning: lively)

  Other Synonyms: Vivid, picturesque, well-drawn, striking, telling, illustrative, pictorial, descriptive, forcible, feeling, described.

  Antonyms: Hazy, obscure, indefinite.

- **Word:** Grasp (Synonym denoting Meaning: clasp)

  Other Synonyms: Gripe, seize, grip, grapple, catch, clutch, clinch, lay hold of, hold, retain, comprehend.

  Antonyms: Loose, lose, abandon, relinquish, surrender, release, miss, misunderstand.

- **Word:** Grateful (Synonym denoting Meaning: thankful)

  Other Synonyms: Obliged, indebted, beholden, agreeable, acceptable, pleasing, pleasant, delightful, gratifying, welcome, charming, satisfying, delicious, savory, nice, cordial, luscious, refreshing, invigorating, comforting, soothing, alleviating.

Antonyms: Unpleasant, unacceptable, disobliged, ungrateful, disagreeable.

- **Word:** Gratification (Synonym denoting Meaning: happiness)

  Other Synonyms: Satisfaction, indulgence, enjoyment, delight, pleasure, fruition, reward, recompense.

  Antonyms: Pain, dislike, disappointment, abstinence, stinting, discipline, abnegation.

- **Word:** Gratify (Synonym denoting Meaning: happy)

  Other Synonyms: Please, delight, gladden, indulge, satisfy, humor, fulfill.

  Antonyms: Displease, dissatisfy, stint, deprive, deny, discipline.

- **Word:** Gratitude (Synonym denoting Meaning: thank)

  Other Synonyms: Thankfulness, obligation, gratefulness.

  Antonyms: Thanklessness, ingratitude, ungratefulness, resentment, oblivion, indignation.

- **Word:** Gratuitous (Synonym denoting Meaning: voluntary)

  Other Synonyms: Free, uncompensated, groundless, unwarranted, unsought, unnecessary, spontaneous, baseless, unrecompensed.

  Antonyms: Compulsory, involuntary, obligatory, necessitated, warranted, well-founded, unwilling, enforced, enjoined.

- **Word:** Grave (Synonym denoting Meaning: weighty)

  Other Synonyms: Important, serious, cogent, momentous, sober, sedate, thoughtful, staid, solemn, plain, subdued, quiet, silent, sad, pressing, deBomber, aggravated, heavy.

  Antonyms: Joyous, merry, unimportant, facetious, ridiculous, trivial, light, frivolous, futile, trifling, petty, slight.

- **Word:** Great (Synonym denoting Meaning: big)

  Other Synonyms: Large, vast, huge, bulky, ample, immense, gigantic, enormous, much, excessive, high, numerous, countless, considerable, important, weighty, distinguished, eminent, exalted, prominent, excellent, elevated, celebrated, noted, famed, illustrious, famous, renowned, august, grand, dignified, noble, sublime, majestic, lofty, generous, magnanimous, chivalrous, high-minded, sumptuous, rich, magnificent, difficult, onerous, hard, burdensome, grievous, chief, principal, main, leading, grand, superior, preeminent, protracted, noticeable.

Antonyms: Little, narrow, scanty, puny, few, short, mean, ignoble, weak, unimportant.

- **Word:** Greediness (Synonym denoting Meaning: hunger)

  Other Synonyms: Avidity, voracity, ravenousness, gluttony, eagerness, longing, greed, intense desire, grasping, avarice, rapacity, selfishness.

  Antonyms: Generosity, prodigality, benevolence.

- **Word:** Greedy (Synonym denoting Meaning: hungry)

  Other Synonyms: Voracious, ravenous, insatiable, gluttonous, insatiate, rapacious, eager, desirous, selfish, grasping, avaricious.

  Antonyms: Abstemious, abstinent, contented, apathetic, indifferent, generous, unselfish.

- **Word:** Grievance (Synonym denoting Meaning: hardship)

  Other Synonyms: Wrong, injury, burden, oppression, affliction, trial, sorrow, grief, distress, woe, complaint, trouble, injustice.

  Antonyms: Congratulation, boon, benefit, rejoicing, privilege, alleviation, riddance, disburdenment.

- **Word:** Grieve (Synonym denoting Meaning: pain)

  Other Synonyms: Afflict,, hurt, distress, sadden, agonize, sorrow, mourn, lament, suffer, bewail, burden, annoy, wound, complain, deplore.

  Antonyms: Ease, soothe, console, please, rejoice, exult, alleviate, gratify, content, satisfy.

- **Word:** Grievous (Synonym denoting Meaning: painful)

  Other Synonyms: Sad, heavy, distressing, afflictive, deplorable, lamentable, hurtful, injurious, noxious, mischievous, detrimental, calamitous, atrocious, heinous, outrageous, intolerable, dreadful, flagrant, aggravated, sorrowful, baleful, burdensome, unhappy, disastrous.

  Antonyms: Pleasant, joyous, delightful, glad, consolatory, acceptable, welcome, grateful, light, trivial, trifling.

- **Word:** Grim (Synonym denoting Meaning: cruel)

  Other Synonyms: Fierce, ruthless, savage, ferocious, frightful, horrible, hideous, dire, horrid, appalling, terrific, dreadful, ugly, ghastly, sullen, stern.

  Antonyms: Mild, attractive, benign, placid, docile.

- **Word:** Gross (Synonym denoting Meaning: aggregate)

  Other Synonyms: Great, large, big, bulky: dense, thick, coarse, rough, rude, unrefined, unseemly, unbecoming, indelicate, sensual, impure, vulgar, low, broad, enormous, flagrant, shameful, outrageous, grievous, palpable, manifest, glaring, whole, total, entire, vicious, animal, bloated.

  Antonyms: Partial, component, net, refined, pure, elegant, delicate, subtle.

- **Word:** Grotesque (Synonym denoting Meaning: droll)

  Other Synonyms: Fantastic, whimsical, fanciful, odd, unnatural, strong, wild, bizarre, extravagant, ludicrous, absurd, ridiculous, antic, burlesque, quaint, old, archaic, distorted.

  Antonyms: Classic, chaste, graceful, fine, severe, regular, fashionable, symmetrical, typical, formal, normal.

- **Word:** Ground (Synonym denoting Meaning: support)

  Other Synonyms: Basis, base, groundwork, foundation, sod, soil, clod, earth, loam, turf, region, territory, country, land, domain, estate, acres, field, motive, consideration, reason, cause, account, inducement, premise, plea.

Antonyms: Superstructure, statement, argument, inference, deduction, product, development, result, effect, ocean, sea, deep main, waters.

- **Word:** Grounded (Synonym denoting Meaning: rooted)

  Other Synonyms: Established, initiated, inaugurated, trained, prepared, fixed, set, indoctrinated.

  Antonyms: Ungrounded, unprepared, uninitiated, baseless, unfounded, groundless, unauthorised.

- **Word:** Groundless (Synonym denoting Meaning: vain)

  Other Synonyms: Supposititious, unfounded, false, baseless, fanciful, chimerical, gratuitous.

  Antonyms: Well-founded, authoritative, substantial, actual.

- **Word:** Group (Synonym denoting Meaning: clump)

  Other Synonyms: Cluster, collection, assemblage, order, bunch, knot, class, assembly, collocation.

  Antonyms: Individual, crowd, isolation, medley, confusion, dispersion, distribution, scattering.

- **Word:** Grovel (Synonym denoting Meaning: creep)

  Other Synonyms: Creep, crawl, fawn, cringe, lie, grub, wallow.

  Antonyms: Soar, aspire, mount, rise, domineer, intimidate, dictate.

- **Word:** Grow (Synonym denoting Meaning: increase)

  Other Synonyms: Enlarge, swell, expand, extend, augment, vegetate, shout, sprout, advance, wax, progress, improve, adhere, raise, produce, cultivate, accrue, become, amplify.

  Antonyms: Diminish, recede, contract, fail, stop, die, wane, decline, subside, ebb, decay, depreciate, crumble, weak.

- **Word:** Grandiloquence (Synonym denoting Meaning: bombast)

  Other Synonyms: Turgidity, verbosity, pomposity, grandiosity, stiltedness, euphuism.

Antonyms: Simplicity, unaffectedness, vernacular.

- **Word:** Grudge (Synonym denoting Meaning: hatred)

  Other Synonyms: Pique, rancor, spite, malice, malevolence, grievance, aversion, dissatisfaction, discontent, refusal.

  Antonyms: Welcome, satisfaction, approval, contentment, benefaction, complacency, bestowal.

- **Word:** Guardian (Synonym denoting Meaning: warden)

  Other Synonyms: Keeper, protector, defender, preserver, custodian, conservator.

  Antonyms: Pupil, ward, traitor, betrayer, charge, minor.

- **Word:** Guess (Synonym denoting Meaning: divine)

  Other Synonyms: Conjecture, surmise, mistrust, suspect, find out, solve, penetrate, fathom, suppose, think, believe, fancy, imagine, hazard, risk.

  Antonyms: Examine, prove, investigate, establish, demonstrate, deduce, elaborate, illustrate.

- **Word:** Guide (Synonym denoting Meaning: instructor)

  Other Synonyms: Director, conductor, pilot, mentor, monitor, adviser, instructor, counsellor, clue, key, itinerary.

  Antonyms: Follower, disciple, imitator, pupil.

- **Word:** Guile (Synonym denoting Meaning: cleverness)

  Other Synonyms: Cunning, craft, subtlety, artifice, artfulness, deceit, duplicity, deception, fraud, wiles, trickery, treachery, insidiousness, hypocrisy.

  Antonyms: Frankness, simplicity, honesty, candor, generosity, sincerity, truth, veracity.

- **Word:** Guilt (Synonym denoting Meaning: feeling of sin)

  Other Synonyms: Guiltiness, culpability, criminality, wrong, offensiveness, wickedness, ill desert, iniquity, sin, offense.

  Antonyms: Innocence, purity, godliness, righteousness.

- **Word:** Gush (Synonym denoting Meaning: bürst)

  Other Synonyms: Stream, flow, rush, spout, pour out, flow out, sentimentalize, be overeffusive.

  Antonyms: Drip, drop, filter, ooze, percolate, dribble, drain, strain, trickle.

- **Word:** Gust (Synonym denoting Meaning: taste)

  Other Synonyms: Relish, zest, liking, pleasure, enjoyment, delight, delectation, gratification, turn, fancy, favour, blast, squall, fit, outburst, burst, paroxysm, puff, breeze, gale.

  Antonyms: Calm, tranquility, subsidence, composure, restraint, zephyr, insipidity, tastelessness.

H

- **Word:** Honest (Synonym denoting Meaning: true)

  Other Synonyms: Candid, frank, ingenuous, equitable, genuine, just, trustworthy, fair, good, sincere, trusty, faithful, honourable, straightforward, upright.

  Antonyms: Deceitful, faithless, hypocritical, perfidious, unfaithful, dishonest, false, lying, traitorous, unscrupulous, disingenuous, fraudulent, mendacious, treacherous, untrue.

- **Word:** Horizontal (Synonym denoting Meaning: regular)

  Other Synonyms: Even, flat, level, plain, plane.

  Antonyms: Broken, inclined, rolling, rugged, sloping, hilly, irregular, rough, slanting, uneven.

- **Word:** Habitual (Synonym denoting Meaning: usual)

  Other Synonyms: Accepted, accustomed, addicted, addicting, automatic, chronic, common, confirmed, constant, continual, conventional, customary, cyclic, disciplined, established, familiar, fixed, frequent, hardened, ingrained, inveterate, iterated, iterative, mechanical.

  Antonyms: Abnormal, amazing, astonishing, atypical, awe-inspiring, awesome, bizarre, conspicuous, curious, different, distinguished, eminent, exceptional, extraordinary, far out, important, inconceivable, incredible, memorable, noteworthy, odd, outstanding.

- **Word:** Heaven (Synonym denoting Meaning: utopia)

  Other Synonyms: Afterworld, arcadia, atmosphere, azure, beyond, bliss, Canaan, dreamland, ecstasy, Elysium, empyrean, enchantment, eternal home, eternal rest, eternity, fairyland, felicity, firmament, glory, great unknown, happiness, harmony, heights, hereafter.

  Antonyms: Abandon, abyss, affliction, agony, anguish, blue blazes, bottomless pit, difficulty, emergency, everlasting fire, grave, Hades, hell-fire, hot place, infernal regions, inferno, limbo, lower world, martyrdom, misery, nether world, nightmare, ordeal.

- **Word:** Heavy (Synonym denoting Meaning: weighty)

  Other Synonyms: Abundant, ample, awkward, beefy, big, built, bulky, burdensome, chunky, considerable, copious, corpulent, cumbersome, cumbrous, elephantine, enceinte, excessive, expectant, expecting, fat, fatso, fatty, fleshy, gravid, gross, hefty, huge, laden.

  Antonyms: Agile, airy, atmospheric, buoyant, crumbly, dainty, delicate, downy, easy, effervescent, ethereal, featherweight, feathery, filmy, flimsy, floatable, floating, fluffy, friable, frothy, graceful, inconsequential, insubstantial, light-footed.

- **Word:** Height (Synonym denoting Meaning: altitude)

  Other Synonyms: Acme, apex, apogee, brow, ceiling, crest, crown, cusp, elevation, extent, highness, hill, loftiness, mountain, peak, pinnacle, pitch, prominence, rise, solstice, stature, summit, tallness, tip, tiptop, top, vertex, zenith.

  Antonyms: Basement, basis, bed, bedrock, bottom, foot, footing, ground, groundwork, infrastructure, lowest point, pedestal, rest, root, seat, seating, stand, substratum, substructure, support, underpinning.

- **Word:** Hide (Synonym denoting Meaning: conceal)

  Other Synonyms: Adumbrate, blot out, bury, cache, camouflage, cloak, cover, curtain, disguise, dissemble, ditch, duck, eclipse, ensconce, go underground, harbour, hold back, hole up, hush up, keep from, keep secret, lie low, lock up, mask, not tell, obscure, plant, protect.

  Antonyms: Advertise, arrange, bare, betray, boast, brandish, demonstrate, disclose, emblazon, evidence, evince, exhibit, expand, expose, extend, feature, flash, flaunt, flourish, glaze, grandstand, illustrate, impart, lay bare, lay out, make clear, make known.

- **Word:** Hill (Synonym denoting Meaning: uprising)

  Other Synonyms: Acclivity, Acropolis, ascent, bluff, bread-and-cheese, butte, cliff, climb, cradle hill, down, drift, dune, elevation, eminence, esker, fell, foothill, gradient, headland, heap, height, highland, hillock, hilltop, hummock, inclination, incline, knoll, mesa, mound.

  Antonyms: Basin, bottom, canyon, channel, coulee, dale, dell, depression, dingle, glen, gorge, lowland, notch, plain, swale, trough, vale.

- **Word:** Hint (Synonym denoting Meaning: indication)

  Other Synonyms: Adumbration, advice, allusion, announcement, clue, communication, connotation, denotation, evidence, glimmering, help, idea, implication, impression, inference, information, inkling, innuendo, insinuation, intimation, iota, lead, mention.

  Antonyms: Audible, bold, categorical, clean-cut, clear, clear-cut, clearly defined, complete, crisp, definitive, determined, distinct, distinguishable, downright, explicit, express, fixed, forthright, full, graphic, incisive, marked, minute, not vague, obvious.

- **Word:** Honest (Synonym denoting Meaning: truthful)

  Other Synonyms: Above board, authentic, bona fide, candid, conscientious, decent, direct, equitable, ethical, fair, forthright, frank, genuine, high-minded, honourable, impartial, ingenuous, just, lawabiding, no lie, open, outright, plain, proper, real, reliable, reputable.

Antonyms: Backbiting, bent, bluffing, cheating, corrupt, crafty, crooked, cunning, deceitful, deceiving, deceptive, designing, disreputable, double-crossing, double-dealing, elusive, false, fraudulent, guileful, hoodwinking, knavish, mendacious, misleading, perfidious, roguish, shady, shifty, sinister, slippery, sneaking, sneaky, swindling.

- **Word:** Hopeful (Synonym denoting Meaning: optimistic)

  Other Synonyms: Anticipating, anticipative, assured, at ease, blithe, buoyant, calm, cheerful, comfortable, confident, content, eager, elated, emboldened; enthusiastic, expectant, expecting, faithful, forward-looking, high, hoping, inspirited, light-hearted, pollyannaish, reassured, rose-coloured, rosy, sanguine, satisfied, serene, trustful, trusting, unflagging, upbeat.

  Antonyms: Bleak, cynical, dark, dejected, depressed, despairing, discouraged, distrustful, downhearted, foreboding, gloomy, glum, hopeless, melancholy, misanthropic, morbid, morose, realistic, resigned, sad, sullen, troubled, worried.

- **Word:** House (Synonym denoting Meaning: habitat)

  Other Synonyms: Abode, apartment, box, building, bullpen, castle, cave, co-op, condo, condominium, crash pad, crib, cubby-hole, den, diggings, digs, domicile, dump, dwelling, edifice, flat, flophouse, habitation, home, home plate, homestead, joint, kennel, layout.

  Antonyms: Box, bungalow, cabana, cabin, camp, chalet, cot, cottage, crib, den, dugout, dump, hovel, hutch, lean-to, lodge, log house, pigeonhole, refuge, shack, shanty, shed, shelter, summer house, tepee, wigwam.

- **Word:** Housing (Synonym denoting Meaning: accommodation)

  Other Synonyms: Apartment, condominium, construction,

digs, dwelling, habitation, home, house, quarter, residence, roof, shelter, sheltering, stopping place.

Antonyms: Boom town, borough, burg, capital, centre, conurbation, downtown, dumb, hamlet, megalopolis, metropolis, metropolitan area, municipality, place, port, suburb.

- **Word:** Huge (Synonym denoting Meaning: large)

  Other Synonyms: Big mother, bulky, colossal, cyclopean, elephantine, enormous, extensive, gargantuan, giant, gigantic, great, gross, humongous, immeasurable, immense, jumbo, king-size, leviathan, lusty, magnificent, mammoth, massive, mighty, monster.

  Antonyms: Baby, bantam, bitty, cramped, diminutive, dwarf, humble, immature, inadequate, inconsequential, inconsiderable, insufficient, limited, little, meagre, microscopic, mini, miniature, minuscule, minute, modest, monkey, narrow, paltry, petite.

- **Word:** Humble (Synonym denoting Meaning: meek)

  Other Synonyms: Apprehensive, backward, bashful, biddable, blushing, content, courteous, deferential, docile, fearful, gentle, hesitant, lowly, manageable, mild, modest, obliging, obsequious, ordinary, polite, quiet, reserved, respectful, retiring, reverential, sedate, self-conscious, self-effacing, servile, sheepish, shy, simple, soft.

  Antonyms: Aloof, assuming, audacious, autocratic, bossy, bragging, cavalier, cheeky, cocky, cold shoulder, conceited, contemptuous, cool, disdainful, domineering, ego trip, egoistic, haughty, high-handed, imperious, insolent, know-it-all, lordly.

- **Word:** Humid (Synonym denoting Meaning: damp)

  Other Synonyms: Boiling, clammy, close, dank, moist, mucky, muggy, oozy, oppressive, sodden, soggy, steamy, sticky, stifling, stuffy, sultry, sweaty, sweltering, watery, wet.

  Antonyms: Anhydrous, arid, athirst, baked, bald, bare, barren, dehydrated, depleted, desert, desiccant, desiccated, drained, dried up, droughty, dusty, evaporated, exhausted, hard, impoverished, juiceless, not irrigated, parched, rainless, sapless, sapped, sear, shriveled, stale, thirsty, torrid, waterless.

- **Word:** Humidity (Synonym denoting Meaning: dampness)

  Other Synonyms: Clamminess, damp, dampness, dankness, dew, dewiness, evaporation, heaviness, humidness, liquidity, moistness, moisture, mugginess, oppressiveness, sogginess, steam, steaminess, stickiness, sultriness, sweatiness, swelter, thickness, vaporization, wet, wetness.

  Antonyms: Boredom, colourlessness, continuance, continuity, dreariness, dryness, dullness, ennui, equability, evenness, flatness, humdrum, identicalness, invariability, levelness, likeness, monotone, monotonousness, oneness, repetitiousness, repetitiveness, routine, similarity, tediousness, tedium, tiresomeness, unchangeableness, uniformity.

- **Word:** Hungry (Synonym denoting Meaning: starving)

  Other Synonyms: Athirst, avid, carnivorous, covetous, craving, desirous, eager, edacious, empty, esurient, famished, famishing, fly light, greedy, hankering, hoggish, hollow, hungered, insatiate, keen, munchies, omnivorous, piggish, rapacious, ravenous, starved, starving, unfilled, unsatisfied, voracious, yearning.

  Antonyms: Abounding, abundant, adequate, awash, big, bounteous, brimming, burdened, bursting, chock-full, chock block, competent, complete, crammed, crowded, entire, extravagant, glutted, gorged, imbued, impregnated, intact, jam full, jam-packed, jammed, laden, lavish, loaded, overflowing, packed, padded, plenteous, plentiful, plethoric.

- **Word:** Hysteria (Synonym denoting Meaning: upset)

  Other Synonyms: Agitation, delirium, excitement, feverishness, frenzy, hysterics, madness, mirth, nervousness, panic, unreason.

  Antonyms: Calmness, dispassion, doldrums, hush, impassivity, imperturbation, lull, patience, peace, peacefulness, placidity, quiet, quietness, repose, rest, restraint, serenity, silence, stillness, stoicism, tranquility.

- **Word:** Heavy (Synonym denoting Meaning: weighty)

  Other Synonyms: Ponderous, oppressive, grievous, severe, cumbersome, afflictive, dull, sluggish, inert, inactive, stupid, torpid, indolent, slow, lifeless, inanimate, dejected, depressed, sorrowful, sad, gloomy, despondent, melancholy, disconsolate, weary, tiresome, wearisome, loaded, encumbered, burdened.

  Antonyms: Light, trifling, trivial, agile, active, joyous, brisk, alleviative, quick, consolatory, buoyant, inspiriting, animating.

- **Word:** Heterogeneous (Synonym denoting Meaning: confused)

  Other Synonyms: Unlike, variant, various,, conglomerate, mingled, mixed, miscellaneous, dissimilar, non-homogeneous, alien, strange, different, opposed, contrary, contrasted.

  Antonyms: Homogeneous, identical, like, same, pure, uniform, similar, alike, accordant, congruous.

- **Word:** High (Synonym denoting Meaning: prominent)

  Other Synonyms: Superior, distinguished, preeminent, dignified, great, admirable, recondite, abstruse, occult, profound, dark, obscure, transcendental, proud, haughty, arrogant, supercilious, lordly, boastful, ostentatious, bragging, vain-glorious, despotic, domineering, overbearing, tyrannical, turbulent, violent, strong.

  Antonyms: Low, base, degraded, inferior, mean, short, stunted, depressed, dwarfed, ignoble.

- **Word:** Hinder (Synonym denoting Meaning: delay)

  Other Synonyms: Embarrass, oppose, prevent, stay, stop, retard, hamper, impede, baffle, en-cumber, check, bar, clog, counteract, frustrate, foil, interrupt, obstruct, resist, thwart, block, balk, debar.

  Antonyms: Quicken, hasten, speed, accelerate, expedite, enable, facilitate, promote.

- **Word:** Hold (Synonym denoting Meaning: possess)

  Other Synonyms: Retain, have, occupy, clasp, grasp, clutch, clinch, restrain, confine, im-prison, detain, bind, fasten, unite, connect, stop, stay, arrest, suspend, withhold, sup-port, maintain, sustain, continue, prosecute, embrace, entertain, cherish, heed, regard.

Antonyms: Drop, surrender, fail, abandon, desert, release, forego, vacate, concede, break, cease, speed, accelerate, give, dispense, disperse.

- **Word:** Hollow (Synonym denoting Meaning: empty)

  Other Synonyms: Void, vacant, vacuous, cavernous, insincere, false, faithless, hypocritical, treacherous, deceitful, false-hearted, pharisaical, artificial, concave, insubstantial, flimsy, transparent, senseless, unsound, deep, low, rumbling.

  Antonyms: Full, solid, firm, sincere, well-stored, strong, true, sound, genuine, substantial.

- **Word:** Honest (Synonym denoting Meaning: honourable)

  Other Synonyms: Fair, open, straightforward, equitable, upright, virtuous, conscientious, just, true, faithful, trusty, reliable, trustworthy, genuine, thorough, decent, reputable, respectable, creditable, suitable, proper, chaste, truthful, ingenuous, sincere, frank, unreserved, candid, good.

  Antonyms: Lying, unscrupulous, mendacious, untrue, deceitful, dishonest, false, hypocritical, fraudulent, disingenuous, perfidious, faithless, treacherous, unfaithful, traitorous, dishonourable, improper, wrong, insincere, vicious.

- **Word:** Honour (Synonym denoting Meaning: veneration)

  Other Synonyms: Reverence, respect, homage, deference, civility, dignity, elevation, distinction, majesty, reputation, repute, fame, esteem, credit, glory, consideration, integrity, probity, rectitude, pride, nobility, eminence, high-mindedness, spirit, self-respect.

  Antonyms: Contempt, irreverence, disrespect, slight, obscurity, demoralization, degradation, debasement, disgrace, cowardice, infamy, dishonour.

- **Word:** Horrible (Synonym denoting Meaning: horrid)

  Other Synonyms: Frightful, terrible, terrific, alarming, appalling, horrific, horrifying, formidable, awful, harrowing, fearful, abominable, ghastly, detestable, hateful, direful.

  Antonyms: Lovely, desirable, enjoyable, attractive, beautiful, fair, pleasant, amiable.

- **Word:** Hot (Synonym denoting Meaning: burning)

  Other Synonyms: Fiery, scalding, heated, very warm, irascible, impetuous, excitable, passion-ate, hasty, furious, violent, ardent, fervent, vehement, eager, glowing, animated, fervid, biting, pungent, sharp, acrid, peppery, stinging, piquant, high-flavoured, choleric.

  Antonyms: Cold, frigid, cool, arctic, chilled, chilly, boreal, bleak, wintry, frosty, icy, apathetic, unresponsive, unfeeling, stoical, passionless, uninspiring, dull, dead, indifferent, unconcerned.

- **Word:** Hypocrisy (Synonym denoting Meaning: formalism)

  Other Synonyms: Cant, pietism, sanctimoniousness, assumed piety, deceit, deception, dissimulation, false profession, imposture, sanctimony, pretense, sham, affectation.

  Antonyms: Sincerity, transparency, truth, honesty, genuineness, candor, frankness, open-ness, ingenuousness, truthfulness.

I

- **Word:** Idiocy (Synonym denoting Meaning: stupidity)

  Other Synonyms: Asininity, cretinism, derangement, fatuity, fatuousness, foolishness, imbecility, inanity, insanity, insipidity, lunacy, madness, senselessness.

  Antonyms: Accurate, actual, corporeal, definite, detailed, explicit, material, objective, particular, precise, real, sensible, solid, specific, substantial, tangible.

- **Word:** Idiot (Synonym denoting Meaning: stupid)

  Other Synonyms: Ass, blockhead, boob, booby, cretin,

dimwit, donkey, dork, dumb ox, dumbbell, dunce, dunderhead, fool, halfwit, ignoramus, imbecile, jackass, jerk, kook, meathead, mental defective, moron, nincompoop, ninny, nitwit, pinhead, pointy head.

Antonyms: Adding machine, analogue, brain, calculator, clone, compatible, data processor, digital, electronic brain, laptop, mainframe, micro, microcomputer, mini, minicomputer, number cruncher, personal computer, thinking machine.

- **Word:** Idle (Synonym denoting Meaning: unused)

  Other Synonyms: Abandoned, asleep, barren, closed down, dead, deserted, down, dusty, empty, gathering dust, inactive, inert, jobless, laid-off, leisured, mothballed, motionless, passive, quiet, redundant, resting, rusty, sleepy, stationary, still, uncultivated, unemployed, unoccupied, untouched, unused, vacant, void, waste, workless.

  Antonyms: Aid, associate with, be into, be participant, chip in, come in, compete, concur, cooperate, engage, engage in, enter into, go into, join in, perform, play, share, sit in, strive, tune in.

- **Word:** Ignite (Synonym denoting Meaning: fire)

  Other Synonyms: Burn, catch fire, enkindle, fire, flare up, inflame, kindle, light, set alight, start up, take fire, touch off.

  Antonyms: Become dark, burn out, cease, darken, die, die out, expire, fade out, flicker, stop shining.

- **Word:** Ignoble (Synonym denoting Meaning: lowly)

  Other Synonyms: Abject, base, baseborn, coarse, common, contemptible, corrupt, craven, dastardly, degenerate, degraded, despicable, disgraceful, dishonourable, heinous, humble, infamous, inferior, lewd, low, mean, menial, modest, ordinary, peasant, petty, plain.

  Antonyms: Archduchess, aristocrat, blue blood, bluestocking, count, countess, empress, gentleman, gentlewoman, lace curtain, lady, lord, nobleman, noblewoman, patrician, peer, prince, princess, royalty, silk stocking.

- **Word:** Illegitimate (Synonym denoting Meaning: illegal)

  Other Synonyms: Adulterine, baseborn, bastard, by blow, contraband, fatherless, illegal, illicit, improper, invalid, love child, misbegotten, natural, spurious, supposititious, unauthorised, unconstitutional, unlawful, unsanctioned, wicked, wrong.

  Antonyms: Accepted, accredited, acknowledged, admissible, appropriate, authorised, canonical, certain, cogent, consistent, correct, customary, fair, front door, genuine, innocent, just, justifiable, kosher, lawful, legit, licit, logical, natural, normal, official, orthodox, probable, proper, real, reasonable, received, recognized, regular, reliable.

- **Word:** Illuminate (Synonym denoting Meaning: light)

  Other Synonyms: Brighten, fire, floodlight, highlight, ignite, illume, illumine, irradiate, kindle, light, light up, lighten, limelight, spot, spotlight.

  Antonyms: Becloud, bedim, blacken, cloud over, cloud up, deepen, dim, eclipse, fog, grey, haze, make dim, murk, obfuscate, obscure, overcast, overshadow, shade, shadow.

- **Word:** Idea (Synonym denoting Meaning: concept)

  Other Synonyms: Conception, impression, judgement, plan, opinion, purpose, conceit, design, fancy, pattern, thought, theory, belief, image, imagination, notion, supposition, ideal, apprehension, fantasy, model, sentiment, archetype, doctrine, understanding, fiction.

  Antonyms: Object, form, subject, substance, fact, actuality, reality.

- **Word:** Ignorant (Synonym denoting Meaning: illiterate)

  Other Synonyms: Unlearned, unlettered, unskilled, untaught, untutored, uneducated, ill-in-formed, uninstructed, uninformed.

  Antonyms: Educated, learned, instructed, sage, wise, skilled, cultured, trained, well-informed.

- **Word:** Illustrate (Synonym denoting Meaning: elucidate)

  Other Synonyms: Explain, exemplify, make clear, interpret, demonstrate, represent, embody,paint, image, adorn with pictures.

  Antonyms: Obscure, misinterpret, confuse, mystify, darken, misrepresent.

- **Word:** Illustrious (Synonym denoting Meaning: glorious)

  Other Synonyms: Splendid, brilliant, bright, radiant, famous, famed, noted, renowned, distinguished, celebrated, eminent, signal, remarkable, conspicuous, deathless, noble.

  Antonyms: Ignominious, disgraceful, infamous, inglorious, disreputable.

- **Word:** Image (Synonym denoting Meaning: statue)

  Other Synonyms: Idol, object of worship, likeness, efigure, resemblance, similitude, representation, picture, trope, metaphor, idea, copy, conception, fiction, shadow, vision.

  Antonyms: Person, original, sub- stance, subject, object, reality, truth, verity.

- **Word:** Imagine (Synonym denoting Meaning: conceive)

  Other Synonyms: Think, image, fancy, picture, devise, contrive, frame, project, invent, create, mold, suppose, assume, deem, apprehend, believe, surmise, understand, fabricate, presume.

  Antonyms: Represent, exhibit, depict, prove, demonstrate, verify, substantiate.

- **Word:** Imbecility (Synonym denoting Meaning: weakness)

  Other Synonyms: Debility, feebleness, infirmity, helplessness, foolishness, childishness, idiocy, fatuity, dotage, senility.

  Antonyms: Strength, energy, virility, vigor, power.

- **Word:** Immaculate (Synonym denoting Meaning: spotless)

  Other Synonyms: Unspotted, stainless, unsullied, unsoiled, untainted, untarnished, clean, pure, undefiled, innocent, guiltless, sinless, faultless, fair, holy, saintly, virgin, unpolluted.

Antonyms: Impure, corrupt, contaminated, defiled, polluted, tainted, spotted.

- **Word:** Immanent (Synonym denoting Meaning: intrinsic)

  Other Synonyms: Inherent, internal, indwelling, empirical, innate, subjective, congenital, ingrained, natural, implicit.

  Antonyms: Emanant, transitive, developed, projectile, phenomenal, explicit, accidental, transcendental, transeunt.

- **Word:** Immature (Synonym denoting Meaning: unripe)

  Other Synonyms: Crude, raw, green, unformed, unprepared, imperfect, rudimentary, unfinished, premature, hasty, unseasonable, untimely, undeveloped.

  Antonyms: Ripe, complete, developed, mature, finished.

- **Word:** Immediately (Synonym denoting Meaning: presently)

  Other Synonyms: Instant, straightway, directly, forthwith, at once, now, right off, instantly, without delay.

  Antonyms: Hereafter, by and by, after a while, sometime.

- **Word:** Impatience (Synonym denoting Meaning: uneasiness)

  Other Synonyms: Disquietude, restlessness, haste, vehemence, eagerness, precipitation, impetuosity, heat, violence of temper, irritability, irritableness.

  Antonyms: Patience, calmness, endurance, composure, leniency, submission, forbearance, long-suffering.

- **Word:** Imperative (Synonym denoting Meaning: commanding)

  Other Synonyms: Authoritative, peremptory, binding, obligatory, urgent, irresistible, dictatorial, inexorable, compulsory.

  Antonyms: Indulgent, lenient, mild, optional, entreative.

- **Word:** Imperious (Synonym denoting Meaning: magisterial)

  Other Synonyms: Dictatorial, despotic, domineering,

tyrannical, overbearing, lordly, haughty, arrogant, authoritative, exacting.

Antonyms: Yielding, compliant, submissive, gentle, mild, docile, ductile.

- **Word:** Implication (Synonym denoting Meaning: entanglement)

  Other Synonyms: Involution, inference, conclusion, intricacy, complication, concealment, latency, allusion, insinuation, innuendo, adumbration.

  Antonyms: Arrangement, system, orderliness, manifestation, expression, exposition, demonstration, production.

- **Word:** Important (Synonym denoting Meaning: grave)

  Other Synonyms: Weighty, momentous, serious, material, significant, influential, prominent, pompous, self-important, consequential, expressive, leading, main, relevant, considerable, essential, great, dignified.

  Antonyms: Insignificant, trivial, inconsiderable, irrelevant, secondary, petty, mean, minor, unimportant.

- **Word:** Imposition (Synonym denoting Meaning: imposing)

  Other Synonyms: Putting, placing, laying, burden, levy, tax, constraint, oppression, injunction, deception, fraud, artifice, trickery, cheating, presumption, exaction, encroachment.

  Antonyms: Sanction, warrant, truth, verity, fact, certainty, verification, genuine, authenticity, honesty.

- **Word:** Improve (Synonym denoting Meaning: mend)

  Other Synonyms: Gain, become better, get on, gain ground, increase, rise, be enhanced, better, amend, ameliorate, rectify, progress, use, make productive, correct, reform.

  Antonyms: Debase, deteriorate, vitiate, spoil, mar, impair, injure, depress.

- **Word:** Impudence (Synonym denoting Meaning: assurance)

  Other Synonyms: Boldness, impertinence, pertness, rudeness, sauciness, effrontery, forwardness, incivility, insolence, presumption, officiousness, intrusiveness.

Antonyms: Bashfulness, humility, diffidence, meekness, lowliness, modesty, submissiveness, coyness, obsequiousness, abasement.

- **Word:** Impulse (Synonym denoting Meaning: thrust)

  Other Synonyms: Push, impetus, passion, instinct, proclivity, inclination, appetite, motive, influence, incitement, instigation, incentive, force, sudden thought.

  Antonyms: Deliberation, premeditation, rebuff, repulse.

- **Word:** Inauguration (Synonym denoting Meaning: investiture)

  Other Synonyms: Installation, induction, consecration, institution, initiation, commencement, formal opening, beginning, origination.

  Antonyms: Dismissal, discharge, valediction, valedictory, close, conclusion, end, termination.

- **Word:** Incentive (Synonym denoting Meaning: inducement)

  Other Synonyms: Incitement, spur, impulse, stimulant, goad, motive, cause, encouragement, rousing, excitation.

  Antonyms: Deterrent, prohibition, learning, discouragement, dissuasion.

- **Word:** Incident (Synonym denoting Meaning: happening)

  Other Synonyms: Liable, belonging, pertaining, appertaining, natural, relating, falling, impinging, casual, occasional, pertinent, fortuitous, concurrent, concomitant, accidental.

  Antonyms: Regular, systematic, disconnected, independent, irrelative, inherent, essential, immanent, invariable, uniform.

- **Word:** Inclination (Synonym denoting Meaning: inclining)

  Other Synonyms: Slope, leaning, slant, trend, verging, obliquity, disposition, predilection, bent, bias, proclivity, proneness, tendency, leaning, aptitude, propensity, desire, wish, fondness, liking, partiality, aptness, attachment, affection.

Antonyms: Tangency, disinclination, divergence, ineptitude, inaptness, dislike.

- **Word:** Incline (Synonym denoting Meaning: slant)

  Other Synonyms: Lean, slope, trend, verge, tend, be disposed, have a desire or propensity, dispose, predispose, turn, bias, bend, bow, bear, dip, induce, prompt.

  Antonyms: Deter, restrain, check, ascend, rise, indispose, disincline.

- **Word:** Incongruous (Synonym denoting Meaning: inconsistent)

  Other Synonyms: Unsuitable, absurd, conflicting, discordant, discrepant, repugnant, incompatible, inapposite, contrary, contradictory, inappropriate, inharmonious, ill-matched, irreconcilable, mismatched.

  Antonyms: Consistent, harmonious, suitable, accordant, compatible.

- **Word:** Increase (Synonym denoting Meaning: accession)

  Other Synonyms: Growth, extension, augmentation, addition, enlargement, expansion, increment, product, produce, gain, profit, offspring, issue, progeny, descendants.

  Antonyms: Deduction, detraction, diminution, contraction, loss, waste, detriment, curtailment, reduction, expenditure, impoverishment.

- **Word:** Indication (Synonym denoting Meaning: indicating sign)

  Other Synonyms: Mark, note, index, symptom, token, hint, suggestion, manifestation, evidence, demonstration, proof.

  Antonyms: Silence, surmise, misdirection, misguidance.

- **Word:** Indifference (Synonym denoting Meaning: neutrality)

  Other Synonyms: Impartiality, disinterestedness, unconcern, apathy, coolness, negligence, carelessness, inattention, heedlessness, triviality, insignificance, unimportance, inferiority, insensibility, composure.

Antonyms: Importance, interest, significance, weight, gravity, affection, ardor, eagerness.

- **Word:** Indifferent (Synonym denoting Meaning: neutral

  Other Synonyms: Unbiased, impartial, disinterested, cool, unconcerned, unmoved, cold, inattentive, apathetic, dead, regardless, heedless, unmindful, equal, all the same, all one, just the same, passable, tolerable, ordinary, middling, mediocre, rather poor, lukewarm, careless.

  Antonyms: Anxious, careful, susceptible, sympathetic, sensitive.

- **Word:** Individual (Synonym denoting Meaning: particular)

  Other Synonyms: Special, separate, single, unique, one, peculiar, personal, positive, decided, unconventional, independent, specific, indivisible, singular, identical, idiosyncratic.

  Antonyms: General, common, collective, plural, universal.

- **Word:** Indulge (Synonym denoting Meaning: gratify)

  Other Synonyms: Yield, satisfy, humour, pamper, favour, allow, permit, suffer, cherish, foster, harbour, spoil, revel, grovel.

  Antonyms: Thwart, deny, disappoint, discard, contradict, renounce, counteract, mortify, abjure, discipline.

- **Word:** Industry (Synonym denoting Meaning: diligence)

  Other Synonyms: Labour, application, assiduity, attention, constancy, exertion, intentness, patience, perseverance, persistence, sedulousness, pains, effort, activity, toil.

  Antonyms: Idleness, inattention, neglect, negligence, sloth, remissness, changeableness, indolence, inconstancy, inactivity, fickleness, ease.

- **Word:** Inferiority (Synonym denoting Meaning: subordination)

  Other Synonyms: Deficiency, imperfection, minority, poverty, subjection, servitude, depression mediocrity.

Antonyms: Superiority, eminence, excellence, majority, elevation, independence, mastery, exaltation.

- **Word:** Infinite (Synonym denoting Meaning: absolute)

  Other Synonyms: Illimitable, limitless, boundless, interminable, eternal, unlimited, un-measured, measureless, unfathomable, unconditioned, numberless, unbounded, immeasurable, innumerable, countless.

  Antonyms: Brief, bounded, relative, short, limited, finite, restricted, transient, transitory, small, little, evanescent, circumscribed, measurable, moderate, narrow, shallow, infinitesimal.

- **Word:** Infirm (Synonym denoting Meaning: weak)

  Other Synonyms: Feeble, frail, debilitated, enfeebled, weakened, faltering, wavering, irresolute, vacillating, unsound, unstable, insecure, decrepit, lame, failing, impotent.

  Antonyms: Sound, forcible, firm, strong, sure, cogent, healthy, healthful.

- **Word:** Inflame (Synonym denoting Meaning: excite)

  Other Synonyms: Stimulate, incite, enkindle, rouse, animate, inspirit, work up, fire, irritate, exasperate, anger, nettle, provoke, enrage, incense, madden, infuriate, fan, embitter.

  Antonyms: Quench, extinguish, allay, cool, pacify, quiet.

- **Word:** Inflated (Synonym denoting Meaning: distended)

  Other Synonyms: Swollen, bloated, tumid, turgid, bombastic, stilted, declamatory, rhetorical, high- flown, pompous.

  Antonyms: Simple, plain, unaffected, concise, laconic, explicit, brief.

- **Word:** Influence (Synonym denoting Meaning: authority)

  Other Synonyms: Ascendency, control, predominance, sway, reputation, weight of character, credit, influx, inflow, effect, causation, impulse, affection, power, weight, prestige.

Antonyms: Inefficiency, ineffectiveness, inefficacy, nullity, inoperativeness, neutrality.

- **Word:** Inform (Synonym denoting Meaning: quicken)

  Other Synonyms: Animate, inspire, acquaint, apprise, mention to, notify, advise, tell, educate, enlighten, instruct, impart, communicate.

  Antonyms: Misjudge, deceive, hoodwink, misinform, mystify.

- **Word:** Ingenuous (Synonym denoting Meaning: artless)

  Other Synonyms: Open, candid, frank, sincere, straight-forward, honest, transparent, guileless, truthful, childlike, naive, noble, generous, honourable.

  Antonyms: Mean, reserved, sly, insincere, disingenuous.

- **Word:** Inherent (Synonym denoting Meaning: sticking fast)

  Other Synonyms: Adhering, essential, immanent, inborn, inbred, native, natural, subjective, innate, intrinsic, inhering, congenital, indispensable, indwelling, infixed, internal, ingrained, inseparable, inwrought.

  Antonyms: Extrinsic, superficial, fortuitous, casual, accidental, external, outward, superfluous, transient, unconnected, supplemental, incidental, subsidiary, superadded, foreign, extraneous, separable, temporary.

- **Word:** Injurious (Synonym denoting Meaning: wrong)

  Other Synonyms: Unjust, iniquitous, hurtful, detrimental, pernicious, deleterious, noxious, deadly, mischievous, baneful, fatal, destructive, damaging, ruinous, disadvantageous, libelous, slanderous, prejudicial.

  Antonyms: Helpful, advantageous, beneficial, salutary, profitable.

- **Word:** Innocent (Synonym denoting Meaning: pure)

  Other Synonyms: Sinless, virtuous, upright, stainless, right, faultless, guileless, clear, clean, blameless, guiltless, harmless, inoffensive, righteous, spotless, immaculate, innocuous.

Antonyms: Criminal, culpable, immoral, guilty, blameworthy.

- **Word:** Instance (Synonym denoting Meaning: request)

  Other Synonyms: Impulse, instigation, incitement, solicitation, importunity, pressure, urgency, illustration, example, citation, case, exemplification, specification, entreaty, point, prompting, persuasion, occurrence.

  Antonyms: Dissuasion, warning, deprecation, reluctance, rule, principle, statement.

- **Word:** Intact (Synonym denoting Meaning: untouched)

  Other Synonyms: Unhurt, unharmed, uninjured, whole, entire, unbroken, un-diminished, safe, inviolate, sacred, undefiled, uncorrupted, uncontaminated.

  Antonyms: Defiled, hurt, touched, injured, corrupt, affected, contaminated.

- **Word:** Integrity (Synonym denoting Meaning: completeness)

  Other Synonyms: Entirety, wholeness, honesty, rectitude, virtue, goodness, principle, uprightness, honour, probity, candor, truthfulness, conscientiousness.

  Antonyms: Fraud, meanness, rascality, duplicity, unfairness, underhandedness.

J

- **Word:** Jest (Synonym denoting Meaning: joke)

  Other Synonyms: Banter, bon mot, crack, fun, funny, gag, game, hoax, jape, jive, jolly, laugh, one-liner, play, pleasantry, prank, quip, rib, rib-tickler, ridicule, sally, spoof, sport, wisecrack, witticism.

  Antonyms: Chant, drag out, drone, extend, intone, lengthen, prolong, pronounce slowly, protract, utter.

- **Word:** Joke (Synonym denoting Meaning: fun)

  Other Synonyms: Antic, bon mot, buffoonery, burlesque, caper, caprice, chestnut, clowning, dido, drollery, epigram, escapade, farce, frolic, gag, gambol, game, ha-ha, hoodwinking, horseplay, humour, jape, jest, lark, laugh, mischief, mummery, one-liner, parody, payoff, play, pleasantry, prank, pun, put-on, quip, quirk, raillery, repartee, revel, rib, sally, saw.

Antonyms: Allay, alleviate, assuage, be enough, blunt, calm, compose, conciliate, content, diminish, do, ease, gratify, lessen, lull, meet halfway, mitigate, placate, propitiate, quell, quench, quiet, serve, soften, soothe, subdue, sweeten, tranquillize.

- **Word:** Jolly (Synonym denoting Meaning: joyful)

  Other Synonyms: Bithe, blithesome, bouncy, carefree, cheerful, chipper, chirpy, convivial, daffy, delightful, enjoyable, entertaining, festive, for grins, frolicsome, funny, gay, gladsome, gleeful, happy, hilarious, jocund, jokey, joshing, joviall, joyous, jubilant.

  Antonyms: Bereaved, bitter, blue, cheerless, dejected, depressed, despairing, despondent, disconsolate, dismal, distressed, doleful, down, downcast, forlorn, gloomy, glum, grief-stricken, grieved, heartbroken, heartsick, heavy-hearted, hurting, in doldrums, in grief, languishing, low, low-spirited, lugubrious, melancholy, morbid, morose, mournful.

- **Word:** Joy (Synonym denoting Meaning: happiness)

  Other Synonyms: Alleviation, amusement, animation, bliss, charm, cheer, comfort, delectation, delight, diversion, ecstasy, elation, exaltation, exultation, exulting, felicity, festivity, frolic, fruition, gaiety, gem, gladness, glee, good humour, gratification, hilarity, humour, indulgence, jewel, jubilance, liveliness, luxury, merriment, mirth, pleasure, pride, prize.

  Antonyms: Abhorrence, anathema, aversion, bother, curse, detestation, disgust, evil, hate, hatred, horror, loathing, nuisance, plague, revulsion, shame, torment, wickedness.

- **Word:** Junior (Synonym denoting Meaning: younger)

  Other Synonyms: Inferior, lesser, lower, minor, second-string, secondary, subordinate.

Antonyms: Ancient, back number, dean, doyen, elder, elderly person, first born, golden-ager, gramps, granny, head, master, old folks, old fossil, old geezer, old-timer, oldster, patriarch, pensioner, pops, relic, retired person, senior citizen, superior.

- **Word:** Justice (Synonym denoting Meaning: lawfulness)

  Other Synonyms: Amends, appeal, authority, authorization, charter, code, compensation, consideration, constitutionality, correction, credo, creed, decree, due process, equity, evenness, fair play, fair treatment, fairness, hearing, honesty, impartiality, integrity, judicatory, judicature, justness, law, legal process, legality, legalization, legitimacy.

  Antonyms: Abuse, breach, crime, crying shame, damage, dirty deal, discrimination, encroachment, favouritism, grievance, inequality, inequity, infraction, infringement, iniquity, malfeasance, malpractice, maltreatment, miscarriage, mischief, negligence, offence, one-sidedness, oppression, outrage, partiality, partisanship, prejudice, railroad.

- **Word:** Juvenile (Synonym denoting Meaning: childish)

  Other Synonyms: Adolescent, babyish, beardless, blooming, boyish, budding, callow, childlike, developing, formative, fresh, girlish, green, growing, immature, inexperienced, infant, infantile, jejune, junior, kid stuff, milk-fed, naive, pubescent, puerile, teenage.

  Antonyms: Complete, cultivated, cultured, developed, fit, full-blown, full-fledged, full-grown, fully grown, grown, grown-up, manly, matured, mellow, mellowed, of age, perfected, prepared, prime, ready, ripe, ripened, seasoned, settled, sophisticated, womanly.

- **Word:** Jade (Synonym denoting Meaning: tire)

  Other Synonyms: Weary, fatigue, exhaust, fag, worry, harass, oppress.

  Antonyms: Refresh, recruit, invigorate, inspirit.

- **Word:** Jaunty (Synonym denoting Meaning: airy)

  Other Synonyms: Showy, finical, fluttering, gay, fine, bedizened, flighty, fantastic, flaunting.

  Antonyms: Staid, sober, sedate, dignified, demure.

- **Word:** Jealous (Synonym denoting Meaning: envious)

  Other Synonyms: Suspicious, resentful, covetous, invidious, anxious, apprehensive, solicitous, zealous, watchful.

  Antonyms: Indifferent, genial, tm envious, liberal, self-denying.

- **Word:** Jeer (Synonym denoting Meaning: scoff)

  Other Synonyms: Taunt, jibe, sneer, flout, mock, jest, deride, banter.

  Antonyms: Flatter, compliment, praise, adulate, cringe.

- **Word:** Jejune (Synonym denoting Meaning: empty)

  Other Synonyms: Barren, meager, dry, sterile, bare, lean, uninteresting, thin, scant, poverty-stricken, poor, void.

  Antonyms: Full, rich, exuberant, racy, interesting, overwrought, redundant, abundant.

- **Word:** Jocose (Synonym denoting Meaning: humorous)

  Other Synonyms: Facetious, witty, droll, funny, comical, jocular, sportive, merry, waggish.

  Antonyms: Melancholy, serious, earnest, grave, lugubrious.

- **Word:** Jocund (Synonym denoting Meaning: joyous)

  Other Synonyms: Joyful, merry, frolicsome, blithe, jolly, sportive, lively, playful, airy, gay.

  Antonyms: Melancholy, dull, sorrowful, grave, mournful, cheerless, rueful, doleful, careworn.

- **Word:** Join (Synonym denoting Meaning: add)

  Other Synonyms: Attach, annex, connect, couple, link, unite, conjoin, cement, adjoin, be adjacent to, connect with, associate with, confederate, league.

Antonyms: Separate, disconnect, disjoin, subtract, sever.

- **Word:** Jollification (Synonym denoting Meaning: revelry)

  Other Synonyms: Conviviality, festivity, revel, carousal, wassail, carouse, fun, carnival.

  Antonyms: Weariness, tediousness, soberness, monotony.

- **Word:** Jolly (Synonym denoting Meaning: merry)

  Other Synonyms: Joyous, gay, joviall, mirthful, jocund, sportive, jocular, funny, sprightly, facetious, waggish, blithe, blithesome, cheery, cheerful, portly, bouncing, stout, plump.

  Antonyms: Sad, mournful, cheerless, mirthless, joyless, lugubrious, gloomy, morose.

- **Word:** Jostle (Synonym denoting Meaning: push)

  Other Synonyms: Crowd, hustle, collide, strike against, shake, in- commode, joggle, jog, jolt.

  Antonyms: Cear, lead, convoy, pilot, precede, extricate, attend.

- **Word:** Jot (Synonym denoting Meaning: iota)

  Other Synonyms: Whit, particle, atom, grain, bit, mite, scrap, scintilla, cipher, trifle, idea, thought, morsel, fraction.

  Antonyms: World, mass, volume, heap, bulk.

- **Word:** Jovial (Synonym denoting Meaning: merry)

  Other Synonyms: Joyous, gay, festive, mirthful, jolly, gleeful, hilarious, genial, convivial.

  Antonyms: Gloomy, lugubrious, melancholy, saturnine.

- **Word:** Joyful (Synonym denoting Meaning: glad)

  Other Synonyms: Joyous, merry, jubilant, jocund, happy, jolly, joviall, elate, elated, delighted, buoyant.

  Antonyms: Grave, solemn, mournful, sad, melancholy.

- **Word:** Jubilant (Synonym denoting Meaning: rejoicing)

  Other Synonyms: Exultant, triumphant, joyous, festive, exulting, congratulatory.

Antonyms: Doleful, sorrowful, remorseful, wailing, penitent, lugubrious.

- **Word:** Judge (Synonym denoting Meaning: justice)

  Other Synonyms: Referee, arbiter, arbitrator, magistrate, authority, critic, connoisseur.

  Antonyms: Criminal, novice, tyro, ignoramus.

- **Word:** Judgement (Synonym denoting Meaning: discernment)

  Other Synonyms: Estimate, award, criticism, understanding, discrimination, intelligence, taste, sagacity, penetration, wisdom, brains, prudence, sense, determination, decision, opinion, notion, conclusion, judiciousness, intellect, verdict, sentence, reward, condemnation.

  Antonyms: Argument, speculation, inquiry, proposition, investigation, consideration, evidence, pleading, pronouncement, fickleness, impulsiveness.

- **Word:** Judicious (Synonym denoting Meaning: discreet)

  Other Synonyms: Wise, prudent, sagacious, sensible, reasonable, rational, sober, sound, staid, politic, enlightened, well-considered, well-chosen, discerning, thoughtful.

  Antonyms: Silly, imprudent, indiscreet, illjudged, inexpedient, rash, impolitic, blind, foolish.

- **Word:** Juggle (Synonym denoting Meaning: cheat)

  Other Synonyms: Conjure, impose, trick, practice jugglery, deceive, defraud, beguile, swindle, mystify, mislead, overreach.

  Antonyms: Expose, enlighten, undeceive, detect, reveal, correct.

- **Word:** Jump (Synonym denoting Meaning: leap)

  Other Synonyms: Skip, bound, hop, spring, vault, caper, bounce, jolt, overleap, coincide, agree, accord.

  Antonyms: Walk, pace, promenade, dance.

- **Word:** Junction (Synonym denoting Meaning: joining)

  Other Synonyms: Union, combination, coalition, connection, linking, coupling, joint, juncture, angle, fastening, attachment, alliance, confederacy.

Antonyms: Division, separation, disconnection, hiatus, chasm, uncoupling, disunion, continuity.

- **Word:** Jurisdiction (Synonym denoting Meaning: right)

  Other Synonyms: Authority, sphere, judicature, legal power, government, control, sway, administration, magistracy.

  Antonyms: Immunity, exemption, freedom, independence.

- **Word:** Just (Synonym denoting Meaning: upright)

  Other Synonyms: Righteous, honest, true, conforming to justice, exact, normal, reasonable, due, equitable, fair, impartial, right, rightful, lawful, fair-minded, blameless, honourable, straight- forward, virtuous, uncorrupt, accurate, correct, deserved, fit, merited, appropriate, suitable, happy, proper, harmonious.

  Antonyms: Evil, untrue, unjust, dishonest, prejudiced, unfair, unreasonable, partial, unlawful, blameworthy, corrupt, dishonourable, inaccurate, incorrect, undeserved, unfit, inappropriate, inharmonious.

- **Word:** Juvenile (Synonym denoting Meaning: young)

  Other Synonyms: Youthful, puerile, childish, boyish, girlish, infantine, immature, adolescent.

  Antonyms: Mature, elderly, aged, senile, adult, manly, womanly, superannuated.

K

- **Word:** Keep (Synonym denoting Meaning: commemorate)

  Other Synonyms: Adhere to, bless, celebrate, comply with, consecrate, fulfil, hold, honour, laud, obey, observe, perform, praise, regard, respect, ritualize, sanctify, solemnize.

  Antonyms: Abandon, abdicate, absent, beat it, blast off, blow, cut out, decamp, desert, disappear, emigrate, escape, evacuate, exit, get away, go, go away, go forth, make feet, march out, migrate, move on, part, pull out, quit, remove, retire, sally.

- **Word:** Kidnap (Synonym denoting Meaning: abduct)

  Other Synonyms: Body snatch, bundle off, capture, carry away, carry off, coax, decoy, entice, grab, hijack, hold, impress, inveigh, lure, pirate, ravish, remove, seduce, seize, shanghai, skyjack, snatch, spirit away, steal, waylay.

  Antonyms: Absolve, acquit, bail out, cast loose, clear, commute, deliver, discharge, disengage, dispense, drop, emancipate, exculpate, excuse, exempt, exonerate, extricate, free, give off, give out, issue, leak, let off, liberate, lifeboat, loose, loosen, manumit, open up, set free, set loose, spring, surrender, take out, turn loose, turn out, unbind, unchain.

- **Word:** Kill (Synonym denoting Meaning: destroy)

  Other Synonyms: Annihilate, asphyxiate, assassinate, blow away, bump off, butcher, chill, cream, croak, crucify, dispatch, do in, drown, dump, electrocute, eradicate, erase, execute, exterminate, extirpate, finish off, get, guillotine, hang, hit, ice, immolate, knock off, liquidate, lynch, massacre, murder, obliterate, off.

  Antonyms: Accept, adapt, affiliate, affirm, appropriate, approve, assent, assume, borrow, embrace, endorse, espouse, follow, imitate, maintain, mimic, opt, ratify, seize, select, support, take on, take over, take up, tap, use, utilize.

- **Word:** Knight (Synonym denoting Meaning: charlatan)

  Other Synonyms: Daredevil, entrepreneur, explorer, fortune-hunter, gambler, globethero, heroine, knight, madcap, mercenary, opportunist, pioneer, pirate, rogue, romantic, soldier, speculator, stunt man, swashbuckler, traveller, voyager.

  Antonyms: Acquaintance, bystander, friend, homebody, home-grown, nearby resident, next-door neighbour.

- **Word:** Knowing (Synonym denoting Meaning: experienced)

  Other Synonyms: Alive, apprehensive, astute, awake, aware, brainy, bright, brilliant, canny, clever, cognizant, competent, conscious, conversant, cool, crack, deliberate, discerning, expert, insightful, intelligent, intended, intentional, into, judicious, knowledgeable, observant, perceptive, percipient, qualified, quick, quick-witted, sagacious, sage.

Antonyms: Artless, childlike, credulous, frank, fresh, green, guileless, gullible, ignorant, inexperienced, ingenuous, innocuous, inoffensive, lily white, low tech, open, raw, safe, simple, soft, square, inartificial, unfamiliar, unobjectionable.

- **Word:** Keen (Synonym denoting Meaning: sharp)

  Other Synonyms: Acute, bitter, severe, piercing, stinging, eager, vehement, fierce, prompt, ardent, cutting, biting, sarcastic, penetrating, satirical, shrewd, poignant, acrimonious, caustic, discerning, quick, astute.

  Antonyms: Blunt, dull, languid, blind, indifferent, obtuse, undiscerning, slow, simple.

- **Word:** Keeping (Synonym denoting Meaning: charge)

  Other Synonyms: Guardianship, custody, care, holding, preservation, restraint, maintenance, support, feed, provision, harmony, consistency, congruity, conformity, agreement.

  Antonyms: Neglect, abuse, disregard, abandonment, destruction, nonsupport, betrayal, disagreement, incongruity.

- **Word:** Ken (Synonym denoting Meaning: sight)

  Other Synonyms: View, cognizance, knowledge, survey, range.

  Antonyms: Ignorance, oversight, inexperience, inobservance.

- **Word:** Key (Synonym denoting Meaning: lock opener)

  Other Synonyms: Clue, guide, solution, explanation, keynote, tonic, wedge, clamp, lever.

  Antonyms: Mystification, confusion, mystery, secret, problem.

- **Word:** Kick (Synonym denoting Meaning: strike)

  Other Synonyms: Recoil, resist, rebel, spurn.

  Antonyms: Caress, soothe, flatter, obey.

- **Word:** Kill (Synonym denoting Meaning: murder)

  Other Synonyms: Massacre, assassinate, butcher, execute, dispatch, slay, slaughter, put to death.

  Antonyms: Resuscitate, vivify, reanimate, revivify, quicken, enliven.

- **Word:** Kin (Synonym denoting Meaning: family)

  Other Synonyms: Blood, consanguinity, descent, race, relationship, kind, kindred, affinity, alliance.

  Antonyms: Strangership, inaffinity, alienage, foreignership.

- **Word:** Kind (Synonym denoting Meaning: benign)

  Other Synonyms: Indulgent, humane, compassionate, gentle, tender, beneficent, propitious, generous, forbearing, lenient, bounteous, clement, mild, good, obliging, bland, friendly, amicable, philanthropic, charitable, sympathetic, affectionate, tender-hearted.

  Antonyms: Harsh, severe, hard, cruel, unkind, rough, stern, forbidding, austere, crabbed, illiberal.

- **Word:** Kindle (Synonym denoting Meaning: light)

  Other Synonyms: Ignite, inflame, enkindle, set on fire, excite, arouse, awaken, stir up, stimulate, incite, animate, foment, exasperate, provoke, enrage.

  Antonyms: Quench, suppress, extinguish, allay.

- **Word:** Kindness (Synonym denoting Meaning: kindliness)

  Other Synonyms: Benevolence, humanity, charity, sympathy, amiability, good nature, mildness, gentleness, softness.

  Antonyms: Harshness, cruelty, severity, sternness, roughness, austerity.

- **Word:** Kindred (Synonym denoting Meaning: relationship)

  Other Synonyms: Consanguinity, affinity, relations, kin, kith and kin, relatives, kinsmen, kinsfolk.

  Antonyms: Disconnection, strangers, foreigners.

- **Word:** Kingly (Synonym denoting Meaning: regal)

  Other Synonyms: Royal, monarchical, imperial, august, sovereign, noble, splendid, magnificent, imposing, grand, majestic.

  Antonyms: Plebeian, humble, popular, commonplace, simple, vulgar.

- **Word:** Knack (Synonym denoting Meaning: toy)

  Other Synonyms: Plaything, gimcrack, dexterity, skill, facility, aptness, aptitude, expertness, quickness.

  Antonyms: Clumsiness, awkwardness, ineptitude.

- **Word:** Knave (Synonym denoting Meaning: villain)

  Other Synonyms: Rascal, rogue, scoundrel, cheat, scamp, miscreant, swindler, scapegrace.

  Antonyms: Gentleman, hero, gull, dupe, simpleton.

- **Word:** Knavish (Synonym denoting Meaning: cheating)

  Other Synonyms: Mischievous, roguish, waggish, fraudulent, villainous.

  Antonyms: Honest, upright, honourable.

- **Word:** Knot (Synonym denoting Meaning: tie)

  Other Synonyms: Bond, intricacy, connection, entanglement, complication, joint, group, band, clique, gang, crew.

  Antonyms: Loosening, unfastening, unraveling, dispersion, solution, simplification, evenness, smoothness, individual.

- **Word:** Knotty (Synonym denoting Meaning: knotted)

  Other Synonyms: Difficult, intricate, perplexed, tough, hard, complicated.

  Antonyms: Plain, simple, obvious, easy, smooth, uninvolved.

- **Word:** Know (Synonym denoting Meaning: perceive)

  Other Synonyms: Apprehend, understand, be convinced or assured, acquaint, recognize, distinguish, comprehend.

Antonyms: Be ignorant or illiterate, overlook, misunderstand, misconstrue.

- **Word:** Knowledge (Synonym denoting Meaning: learning)

  Other Synonyms: Wisdom, scholarship, science, comprehension, cognition, erudition, intelligence, light, lore, perception, recognition, acquaintance, intuition, experience, information, apprehension, notice, understanding, conversance, cognizance, familiarity, instruction, enlightenment, acquirements, attainments.

  Antonyms: Ignorance, illiteracy, unfamiliarity, rudeness, inexperience, misapprehension, conception, misunderstanding.

L

- **Word:** Lack (Synonym denoting Meaning: deficiency)

  Other Synonyms: Abridgement, absence, curtailment, dearth, decrease, default, defect, deficit, depletion, deprivation, destitution, distress, exigency, exiguity, inadequacy, inferiority, insufficiency, loss, meagreness, miss, necessity, need, paucity, poverty.

  Antonyms: Accept, acquire, admit, annex, bear, carry, chalk up, compass, corner, enjoy, gain, get, hog, hold, include, keep, land, lock up, obtain, occupy, own, pick up, possess, procure, receive, retain, secure, sit on, take, take in, teem with.

- **Word:** Lady (Synonym denoting Meaning: woman)

  Other Synonyms: Adult, babe, bag, baroness, bitch, broad, butterfly, countess, dame, doll, duchess, empress, female, gal, gentlewoman, girl, little woman, mama, mare, matron, missus, mistress, noblewoman, old bag, old lady, old woman, petticoat.

  Antonyms: Ape, beau, beefcake, blade, bloke, boy, boyfriend, buster, butch, cat, chap, daddy, dude, fellow, gent, gentleman, guy, he, hunk, husband, jock, lord, lover, macho, master, mister, old man, papa, partner, pops, sir, spouse, stud, swain, wolf.

- **Word:** Land (Synonym denoting Meaning: earth)

  Other Synonyms: Acreage, acres, area, barren, beach, continent, country, countryside, dirt, district, earth, estate, expanse, extent, farming, farmland, fatherland, field, ground, grounds, holding, home, homeland, loam, mainland, manor, motherland, nation, old sod.

  Antonyms: Abig drink, big pond, blue, bounding main, brine, briny, briny deep, deep, drink, expanse, main, multitude, number, ocean, plethora, pond, profusion, sheet, sink, splash, surf, swell, waves.

- **Word:** Landlord (Synonym denoting Meaning: owner)

  Other Synonyms: Freeholder, host, hotelier, hotelkeeper, innkeeper, property owner, proprietor, saw, slumlord, squire.

  Antonyms: Addressee, boarder, dweller, holder, householder, indweller, inhabitant, leaseholder, lessee, lodger, occupant, occupier, possessor, rent payer, renter, resident, roomer.

- **Word:** Large (Synonym denoting Meaning: big)

  Other Synonyms: Ample, barn door, blimp, booming, broad, bulky, capacious, colossal, comprehensive, considerable, copious, enormous, excessive, exorbitant, extensive, extravagant, full, generous, giant, gigantic, goodly, grand, grandiose, great, gross, hefty, huge, humongous, immeasurable, immense, jumbo, king-size, liberal.

  Antonyms: Baby, bantam, bitty, cramped, diminutive, dwarf, humble, immature, inadequate, inconsequential, inconsiderable, insufficient, limited, little, meagre, microscopic, mini, miniature, minuscule, minute, modest, monkey, narrow, paltry, petite, petty, picayune, piddling, pint-sized, pitiful, pocket-sized, poor, puny, pygmy, runty.

- **Word:** Last (Synonym denoting Meaning: final)

  Other Synonyms: Aftermost, antipodal, bitter end, climactic, closing, concluding, conclusive, crowning, curtains, definitive, determinate, determinative, end, ending, eventual, extreme, far, far-off, farthest, finishing, furthest, hindmost, lag, latest, least, lowest.

Antonyms: Abutting, adjacent, adjoining, after, alongside, attached, beside, close, closest, coming, consequent, coterminous, ensuing, following, hard by, later, meeting, nearest, neighbouring, proximate, subsequent, succeeding, touching.

- **Word:** Late (Synonym denoting Meaning: slow)

  Other Synonyms: Backward, behind, behind time, behindhand, belated, blown, delayed, dilatory, eleventh hour, gone, held up, hung up, jammed, lagging, last-minute, overdue, postponed, put off, remiss, stayed, strapped, tardy, too late, unpunctual.

  Antonyms: Aboriginal, ancient, antecedent, antediluvian, antiquated, brand-new, budding, early bird, fresh, initial, maiden, new, original, preceding, premier, previous, primal, prime, primeval, primitive, primordial, prior, pristine, raw, recent, undeveloped, virgin, young.

- **Word:** Laughter (Synonym denoting Meaning: amusement)

  Other Synonyms: Amusement, cachinnation, cackle, chortle, chortling, chuckle, chuckling, crack-up, crow, crowing, fit, gesture, giggle, giggling, glee, guffaw, guffawing, hilarity, howling, laugh, merriment, mirth, peal, rejoicing, roar, roaring, shout, shouting, shriek.

  Antonyms: Anguish, blahs, bleakness, blue devils, blue funk, broken heart, bummer, cheerlessness, dejection, depression, despondency, disconsolateness, dismals, dispiritedness, distress, dolefulness, down trip, downer, forlornness, funk, gloominess, grief, grieving, heartache, heartbreak, heavy heart.

- **Word:** Labourious (Synonym denoting Meaning: toilsome)

  Other Synonyms: Difficult, tiresome, onerous, wearisome, fatiguing, arduous, hard, burdensome, tedious, irksome, industrious, diligent, toiling, assiduous, hard-working, painstaking, sedulous, indefatigable, active.

Antonyms: Easy, light, simple, facile, feasible, lazy, indolent, idle.

- **Word:** Lack (Synonym denoting Meaning: deficiency)

  Other Synonyms: Want, need, destitution, failure, scantiness, dearth, scarcity, fault, deficit, shortness, insufficiency.

  Antonyms: Plenty, fullness, sufficiency, competence, satisfaction.

- **Word:** Lame (Synonym denoting Meaning: hobbling)

  Other Synonyms: Crippled, limping, inefficient, imperfect, defective, weak, feeble, poor, unsatisfactory, insufficient, halt, faltering, impotent.

  Antonyms: Robust, strong, potent, efficient, cogent, effective, convincing, telling, satisfactory.

- **Word:** Language (Synonym denoting Meaning: idiom)

  Other Synonyms: Speech, dialect, tongue, patois, barbarism, diction, expression, vernacular, vocabulary, mother tongue, phraseology, discourse, conversation, talk, articulation, accents, style, utterance, voice.

  Antonyms: Jargon, gibberish, cry, howl, roar, in- articulateness, muteness, dumbness.

- **Word:** Languid (Synonym denoting Meaning: drooping)

  Other Synonyms: Indisposed, inanimate, feeble, weak, faint, sickly, pining, weary, listless, heavy, dull, exhausted, heartless, enervated, flagging, spiritless, unnerved.

  Antonyms: Strong, vigorous, robust, active, braced, healthy, energetic, animated, alert.

- **Word:** Large (Synonym denoting Meaning: colossal)

  Other Synonyms: Ample, broad, bulky, extensive, vast, massive, spacious, wide, commodious, enormous, coarse, grand, long, gigantic, immense, huge, great, big, capacious, considerable, abundant, diffuse, comprehensive, profuse, plentiful, populous, copious, liberal, enlightened, catholic.

Antonyms: Circumscribed, illiberal, contracted, niggardly, sordid, bigoted, small, little, microscopic, mean, minute, tiny, slender, trifling, trivial, diminutive, inconsiderable, slight, infinitesimal, limited, short, insignificant, scanty, petty, narrow, paltry.

- **Word:** Law (Synonym denoting Meaning: code)

  Other Synonyms: Canon, edict, decree, order, mandate, legislation, ordinance, rule, regulation, jurisprudence, enactment, command, commandment, economy, formula, polity, principle, statute, mode, method, sequence, adjudication, jurisdiction.

  Antonyms: Misrule, anarchy, disorder, insubordination, rebellion, caprice, chance, irregularity, accident, casualty.

- **Word:** League (Synonym denoting Meaning: alliance)

  Other Synonyms: Compact, coalition, confederacy, confederation, bond, combination, union.

  Antonyms: Neutrality, divorce, disruption, disunion, secession, disconnection, alienation, dissolution.

- **Word:** Licentious (Synonym denoting Meaning: excessive)

  Other Synonyms: Abusive, unrestrained, uncurbed, unruly, lawless, immoral, lewd, riotous, ungovernable, wanton, lax, dissolute, profligate, loose, sensual, impure, unchaste, lascivious.

  Antonyms: Temperate, strict, moderate, controlled, self-controlled, ascetic, austere, sober, self-denying.

- **Word:** Light (Synonym denoting Meaning: gleam)

  Other Synonyms: Shine, glitter, flame, blaze, illumination, incandescence, glow, flash, flare, sparkle, twinkle, flicker, glare, glimmer, glistening, sheen, luster, shimmer, shining, scintillation, day, open view, publicity, enlightenment, knowledge, information, prosperity, joy, happiness, felicity.

  Antonyms: Dark, gloom, darkness, dimness, blackness, dusk, shade, shadow, gloominess, obscurity, extinction, night, death, confusion, ignorance, misunderstanding, illiteracy, blindness, nescience.

- **Word:** Liberty (Synonym denoting Meaning: emancipation)

  Other Synonyms: Choice, freedom, license, independence, leave, permission, exemption, privilege, franchise, immunity.

  Antonyms: Slavery, captivity, servitude, serfdom, compulsion, necessity, constraint, imprisonment, oppression, superstition, obligation.

- **Word:** Likeness (Synonym denoting Meaning: resemblance)

  Other Synonyms: Similarity, guise, portrait, similitude, correspondence, copy, imitation, image, representation, picture.

  Antonyms: Unlikeness, disparity, dissimilarity, inequality.

- **Word:** Line (Synonym denoting Meaning: thread)

  Other Synonyms: Cord, hawser, rope, boundary, contour, outline, family, race, track, rail-road, course, method, continuity, sequence, succession.

  Antonyms: Breadth, expanse, space, deviation, variation, discontinuance.

- **Word:** Little (Synonym denoting Meaning: small)

  Other Synonyms: Diminutive, insignificant, contemptible, short, brief, inefficient, weak, slight, narrow, mean, illiberal, pigmy, scanty, unimportant, inconsiderable, trivial, petty, paltry, dwarf, puny.

  Antonyms: Great, big, large, huge, monstrous, enormous, long, developed, bulky, full, important, momentous, grave, serious, considerable, significant, colossal.

- **Word:** Live (Synonym denoting Meaning: have life)

  Other Synonyms: Abide, dwell, reside, survive, remain, last, enjoy, feed, subsist, vegetate, grow, continue, behave, act, exist, breathe.

  Antonyms: Die, perish, depart, decay, wither, fade, vanish, fail, demise, drop, languish, expire, decline, faint, sink, fall.

- **Word:** Lively (Synonym denoting Meaning: quick)

  Other Synonyms: Nimble, smart, active, alert, sprightly, brisk, animated, prompt, earnest, energetic, strong, vivacious, gleeful, blithe, airy, gay, jocund, keen, eager, vivid, spirited, vigorous.

  Antonyms: Lifeless, dull, torpid, inanimate, inert, insensate, listless, languid, indifferent.

- **Word:** Logical (Synonym denoting Meaning: dialectical)

  Other Synonyms: Reasonable, coherent, consistent, sound, argumentative, close, discriminating.

  Antonyms: Illogical, unsound, inconsistent, unreasonable, incoherent, undiscriminating, fallacious, inconclusive.

- **Word:** Look (Synonym denoting Meaning: behold)

  Other Synonyms: See, stare, scan, contemplate, view, glance, descry, watch, discern, gaze, regard, inspect, survey, consider, seem, appear, face, front, take notice, expect, anticipate.

  Antonyms: Be blind or unseeing, overlook, miss, pass, neglect.

- **Word:** Loose (Synonym denoting Meaning: unbound)

  Other Synonyms: Untied, free, unattached, unfastened, unconstrained, vague, liberal, unchaste, dissolute, unconnected, rambling, lax, detached, flowing, scattered, sparse, inexact.

  Antonyms: Tight, close, bound, tied, fastened, secured, thick, compact, dense, accurate, exact, strict, logical, scientific, conscientious, self-controlled, firm, rigorous.

- **Word:** Loss (Synonym denoting Meaning: failure)

  Other Synonyms: Destruction, privation, defect, harm, squandering, deprivation, forfeiture, detriment, ruin, defeat, injury, damage, disadvantage.

  Antonyms: Restoration, recovery, reimbursement, retention, preservation, hoarding, guarding, utilization, gain, aggrandizement, augmentation, advantage, acquisition, profit, benefit, increment, earnings.

- **Word:** Love (Synonym denoting Meaning: friendship)

  Other Synonyms: Liking, tenderness, regard, fondness, devotion, affection, attachment, attraction, charity, courtship, good will, kindness, delight, inclination, benevolence.

  Antonyms: Antipathy, hatred, enmity, alienation, dislike, disaffection, estrangement, bitterness, coldness, repugnance, infidelity, desertion.

- **Word:** Lovely (Synonym denoting Meaning: beautiful)

  Other Synonyms: Charming, delightful, delectable, enchanting, lovable, amiable, pleasing, winning, sweet, admirable.

  Antonyms: Hateful, hideous, ugly, homely, unattractive, unlovely, plain, gawky, unlovable.

- **Word:** Low (Synonym denoting Meaning: sunken)

  Other Synonyms: Quiet, small, submissive, humble, mean, vulgar, base, ignoble, dishonourable, moderate, feeble, weak, plain, simple, reasonable, cheap, abject, servile, slavish, degraded, vile, groveling, deep, reverent, dejected, depressed, dispirited.

  Antonyms: High, tall, lofty, elevated, exalted, eminent, noble, illustrious, rising, strong, influential, honourable, elaborate, ornate, notable, costly, expensive, precious, dear, arrogant, haughty, proud, masterly, lordly, high, loud, violent.

- **Word:** Lucid (Synonym denoting Meaning: luminous)

  Other Synonyms: Transparent, sane, reasonable, shining, resplendent, bright, clear, radiant, brilliant, limpid, lucent, distinct, intelligible, perspicuous, sober, sound.

  Antonyms: Dark, opaque, muddy, black, somber, turbid, obscure, indistinct, unintelligible, mystifying, insane, unsound, confused, involved, illegible.

- **Word:** Luster (Synonym denoting Meaning: brilliancy)

  Other Synonyms: Brightness, splendour, glitter, renown,

distinction, glory, gleam, radiance, resplendence, eminence, repute, celebrity, honour.

Antonyms: Darkness, blackness, gloom, obscuration, detraction, derogation, infamy, disrepute, dishonour, notoriety.

- **Word:** Luxury (Synonym denoting Meaning: lavish)

  Other Synonyms: Voluptuousness, effeminacy, sensuality, dainty, delicacy, gratification, pleasure, enjoyment, delight, treat, animalism.

  Antonyms: Stoicism, asceticism, self-denial, austerity, hardship, spirituality.

M

- **Word:** Major (Synonym denoting Meaning: bigger)

  Other Synonyms: Above, better, big, chief, considerable, dominant, elder, exceeding, extensive, extreme, greater, hefty, higher, large, large-scale, larger, leading, main, most, over, primary, senior, sizable, superior, supreme, ultra, upper, uppermost.

  Antonyms: Accessory, bush, bush-league, casual, dependent, dinky, inconsequential, inconsiderable, inferior, junior, lesser, light, low, minor-league, minus, negligible, paltry, petty, piddling, second-string, secondary, shoestring, slight, small, small-fry, small-time.

- **Word:** Machination (Synonym denoting Meaning: plot)

  Other Synonyms: Conspiracy, intrigue, cabal, stratagem, design, trick, artifice, contrivance, scheme.

  Antonyms: Detection, counter-action, overthrow, baffling, defeat, exposure, defiance, challenge, conflict, competition.

- **Word:** Maculate (Synonym denoting Meaning: blotched)

  Other Synonyms: Defiled, impure, spotted, blurred, corrupt, unclean, mottled.

  Antonyms: Unspotted, spotless, pure, clean, immaculate.

- **Word:** Mad (Synonym denoting Meaning: crazy)

  Other Synonyms: Insane, excited, inflamed, furious, rabid, angry, distracted, lunatic, delirious, crazed, deranged, demented, maniac, enraged, raging, exasperated, provoked, incensed, wrathful, wild, infatuated, frenzied, frantic, raving.

  Antonyms: Sane, sound, sensible, quiet, composed, sober, unexcited.

- **Word:** Magisterial (Synonym denoting Meaning: stately)

  Other Synonyms: Pompous, august, lordly, dignified, lofty, official, imperious, proud, domineering, haughty, despotic, arrogant, dictatorial, consequential, imposing, authoritative.

  Antonyms: Submissive, docile, un-dignified, unimposing, unassuming, modest.

- **Word:** Magnificent (Synonym denoting Meaning: glorious)

  Other Synonyms: Grand, majestic, splendid, admirable, superb, sublime, imposing, gorgeous, stately, showy, august, dignified.

  Antonyms: Petty, mean, paltry, little, flat, beggarly, ordinary, small-minded, tawdry, unimposing, tame.

- **Word:** Magniloquent (Synonym denoting Meaning: pompous)

  Other Synonyms: Grandiloquent, bombastic, declamatory, stilted, high-flown, turgid, inflated, boastful.

  Antonyms: Simple, vernacular, unaffected, plain-spoken.

- **Word:** Magnitude (Synonym denoting Meaning: extent)

  Other Synonyms: Size, grandeur, greatness, importance, volume, dimension, mass, consequence, sublimity, loftiness.

  Antonyms: Smallness, diminutiveness, littleness, meagerness, insignificance, meanness, unimportance.

- **Word:** Main (Synonym denoting Meaning: bulk)

  Other Synonyms: Majority, body, principal, trunk, chief, leading, most important, first, cardinal, capital, necessary, vital, essential, indispensable, requisite, huge, enormous, absolute, entire, mere, direct.

Antonyms: Subordinate, non-essential, auxiliary, minor, tributary, inferior.

- **Word:** Main (Synonym denoting Meaning: ocean)

  Other Synonyms: Mainland, continent, main conduit or pipe, force, power, might, strength, gross, majority.

  Antonyms: Bay, gulf, island, inability, weakness, tributaries, minority.

- **Word:** Mainly (Synonym denoting Meaning: chiefly)

  Other Synonyms: Principally, largely, greatly, mightily, absolutely, primarily, entirely.

  Antonyms: Secondarily, subordinately, partially, somewhat, slightly.

- **Word:** Majestic (Synonym denoting Meaning: august)

  Other Synonyms: Sublime, magnificent, regal, royal, pompous, stately, dignified, elevated, imperial, princely, grand, imposing.

  Antonyms: Low, humble, groveling, plebeian, vulgar, common, unassuming.

- **Work:** Make up (Synonym denoting Meaning: collect)

  Other Synonyms: Constitute, form, reconcile, settle, adjust, compose, make good, compensate, supply, furnish, provide, determine.

  Antonyms: Distribute, disperse, scatter, pi, default.

- **Word:** Malice (Synonym denoting Meaning: spite)

  Other Synonyms: Ill-will, malevolence, grudge, pique, bitterness, animosity, malignity, rancor, maliciousness, virulence.

  Antonyms: Goodwill, benevolence, kindliness.

- **Word:** Manage (Synonym denoting Meaning: direct)

  Other Synonyms: Govern, control, wield, order, contrive, concert, conduct, transact, administer, regulate, supervise, superintend, handle, rule.

Antonyms: Mismanage, misgovern, misconduct, upset, misuse, derange, let go.

- **Word:** Management (Synonym denoting Meaning: conduct)

  Other Synonyms: Administration, government, guidance, direction, care, charge, contrivance, intrigue, skill, address, economy, treatment, superintendence, surveillance, negotiations, dealings, transactions.

  Antonyms: Misconduct, maladministration, mismanagement.

- **Word:** Management (Synonym denoting Meaning: stratagem)

  Other Synonyms: Artifice, scheme, plan, trick, ruse, intrigue, evolution, movement, operation, tactics, contrivance.

  Antonyms: Countermovement, defeat, check, bafflement, counteraction, detection, neutralization.

- **Word:** Manhood (Synonym denoting Meaning: virility)

  Other Synonyms: Maturity, humanity, courage, resolution, bravery, hardihood, fortitude, manliness.

  Antonyms: Womanhood, femininity, effeminacy, delicacy.

- **Word:** Manifest (Synonym denoting Meaning: open)

  Other Synonyms: Clear, evident, apparent, visible, conspicuous, plain, obvious, patent, palpable, unmistakable, distinct.

  Antonyms: Hidden, indistinct, inconspicuous, occult, latent, obscure, confused, hazy, foggy.

- **Word:** Manly (Synonym denoting Meaning: bold)

  Other Synonyms: Daring, valorous, courageous, undaunted, hardy, dignified, intrepid, heroic, vigorous, firm, noble, chivalrous, mature, masculine, manlike.

  Antonyms: Womanly, childlike, timid, womanish, childish, unmanly, boyish, weak, dastardly, cowardly, effeminate.

- **Word:** Manner (Synonym denoting Meaning: mode)

  Other Synonyms: Custom, habit, deportment, fashion, air, look, mien, aspect, appearance, conduct, method, form, style.

  Antonyms: Being, action, proceeding, life, work, performance, project, business.

- **Word:** Mannerism (Synonym denoting Meaning: characteristic)

  Other Synonyms: Peculiarity, uniformity, self-repetition, self-consciousness, affectation, idiosyncrasy, specialty.

  Antonyms: Unaffectedness, simplicity, naturalness, character, genuineness.

- **Word:** Mannerly (Synonym denoting Meaning: civil)

  Other Synonyms: Complaisant, respectful, courteous, polite, urbane, refined, well-behaved, ceremonious, well-bred.

  Antonyms: Rude, coarse, unmannerly, rough, impolite, uncivil, boorish.

- **Word:** Many (Synonym denoting Meaning: frequent)

  Other Synonyms: Manifold, diverse, divers, sundry, numerous, multiplied, various, abundant, multifarious.

  Antonyms: Few, rare, scarce, in- frequent, scanty.

- **Word:** Marauder (Synonym denoting Meaning: plunderer)

  Other Synonyms: Robber, ravager, pillager, outlaw, bandit, brigand, freebooter, rover, invader.

  Antonyms: Guard, sentry, keeper, steward, ranger, outpost.

- **Word:** Margin (Synonym denoting Meaning: border)

  Other Synonyms: Edge, brim, lip, rim, brink, verge, confine, limit, skirt, extremity, loophole, profit, interest, lee-way.

  Antonyms: Centre, main, space, limitation, stringency, restriction.

- **Word:** Mark (Synonym denoting Meaning: impress)

  Other Synonyms: Stamp, vestige, impression, imprint, track, evidence, proof, characteristic, badge, indication, distinction, eminence, importance.

Antonyms: Effacement, obliteration, erasure, plainness.

- **Word:** Marvelous (Synonym denoting Meaning: wonderful)

  Other Synonyms: Astonishing, surprising, strange, improbable, incredible, miraculous, stupendous, extraordinary, wondrous, supernatural, portentous, prodigious.

  Antonyms: Commonplace, every- day, regular, normal, customary, natural, anticipated, current, calculated, expected.

- **Word:** Mask (Synonym denoting Meaning: cover)

  Other Synonyms: Disguise, pretext, subterfuge, screen, revel, frolic, evasion, pretense, ruse, plea, redoubt, domino, blind, veil, hypocrisy.

  Antonyms: Truth, nakedness, candor, verity, openness, exposure, detection, unmasking.

- **Word:** Mass (Synonym denoting Meaning: quantity)

  Other Synonyms: Sum, bulk, magnitude, body, size, main part, majority, aggregate, whole, totality, heap, assemblage, combination, concretion.

  Antonyms: Fragment, section, portion, bit, morsel, minority, segment.

- **Word:** Master (Synonym denoting Meaning: ruler)

  Other Synonyms: Director, manager, leader, employer, owner, governor, superintendent, commander, captain, teacher, instructor, tutor, adept, possessor, proprietor, professor, head, chief.

  Antonyms: Servant, slave, pupil, employee, subject, learner, student.

- **Word:** Masterly (Synonym denoting Meaning: imperious)

  Other Synonyms: Domineering, arbitrary, despotic, skilful, clever, expert, dexterous, adroit, finished, excellent, artistic, consummate.

Antonyms: Humble, obedient, compliant, rude, clumsy, bungling.

- **Word:** Matchless (Synonym denoting Meaning: unequaled)

  Other Synonyms: Peerless, unparalleled, incomparable, inimitable, consummate, exquisite, excellent, surpassing, unrivaled.

  Antonyms: Common, ordinary, mediocre, everyday, commonplace, general.

- **Word:** Matter (Synonym denoting Meaning: substance)

  Other Synonyms: Body, material, constituency, concern, affair, business, trouble, difficulty, amount, portion, space, sense, significance, moment, import, importance, topic, subject, question, thing, event.

  Antonyms: Immateriality, spirituality, mind, soul, spirit, intellect, animus, zeal, temper.

- **Word:** Mean (Synonym denoting Meaning: ignoble)

  Other Synonyms: Abject, beggarly, degraded, degenerate, vulgar, vile, servile, menial, groveling, slavish, dishonourable, disgraceful, shameful, despicable, contemptible, paltry, sordid.

  Antonyms: Noble, kingly, heroic, princely, exalted, generous, eminent, honourable, spirited, liberal, masterly, worthy, bountiful, munificent.

- **Word:** Measurement (Synonym denoting Meaning: dimension)

  Other Synonyms: Capacity, quantity, amount, moderation, restraint, extent, limit, proportion, degree, rule, gage, standard, metre.

  Antonyms: Bulk, mass, segment, section, portion, immensity, infinity.

- **Word:** Mechanical (Synonym denoting Meaning: approximate)

  Other Synonyms: Empirical, machine-made, automatic, involuntary, blind, habitual, spontaneous, effortless, unimpassioned.

Antonyms: Laboured, feeling, selfconscious, forced, spirited, appreciative, lifelike, lively, animated, impassioned.

- **Word:** Mediocrity (Synonym denoting Meaning: inferiority)

  Other Synonyms: Average, moderate or middle state, medium, moderation, commonplace, mean, sufficiency.

  Antonyms: Excellence, superiority, distinction, brilliance, rarity.

- **Word:** Melancholy (Synonym denoting Meaning: sad)

  Other Synonyms: Dispirited, low-spirited, down-hearted, unhappy, hypochondriac, heavy, doleful, afflictive, dejected, depressed, disconsolate, gloomy, sorrowful, moody, desponding, grave, somber, dark.

  Antonyms: Happy, cheerful, gladsome, sprightly, lively, merry, mirthful, blithesome, gleeful.

- **Word:** Melody (Synonym denoting Meaning: harmony)

  Other Synonyms: Rhythm, air, tune, music, song, sweetness of sound, descant, theme, unison, symphony.

  Antonyms: Discord, jarring, dissonance, harshness, discordance.

- **Word:** Memorable (Synonym denoting Meaning: important)

  Other Synonyms: Illustrious, remarkable, extraordinary, signal, distinguished, famous, celebrated, great, conspicuous, prominent.

  Antonyms: Ordinary, trivial, commonplace, insignificant, mediocre.

- **Word:** Memory (Synonym denoting Meaning: remembrance)

  Other Synonyms: Recollection, reminiscence, fame, renown, reputation, monument, retrospection, retrospect, perpetuation, retention.

  Antonyms: Oblivion, oversight, un mindfulness, obliviousness, forgetfulness.

- **Word:** Mendacity (Synonym denoting Meaning: lying)

  Other Synonyms: Deceit, falsehood, untruth, duplicity, lie, untruthfulness, deception, prevarication.

  Antonyms: Truth, honesty, rectitude, uprightness, veracity, accuracy, exactness.

- **Word:** Merciful (Synonym denoting Meaning: compassionate)

  Other Synonyms: Tender, humane, gracious, kind, mild, clement, benignant, lenient, pitiful, forgiving, tender-hearted.

  Antonyms: Remorseless, pitiless, inexorable, unrelenting, severe, cruel, hard, illiberal.

- **Word:** Mercy (Synonym denoting Meaning: compassion)

  Other Synonyms: Grace, favour, helpfulness, clemency, forbearance, tenderness, forgiveness, gentleness, pardon, blessing, pity, kindness, mildness, lenity, benevolence, benignity, lenience, leniency.

  Antonyms: Harshness, rigor, severity, sternness, penalty, justice, vengeance, revenge, punishment, hardness, cruelty, implacability, ruthlessness, inhumanity, brutality, exaction.

- **Word:** Metaphysical (Synonym denoting Meaning: mental)

  Other Synonyms: Intellectual, psychological, abstract, general, ideal, psychical, subjective, rational, abstruse, conceptual.

  Antonyms: Physical, substantial, physiological, material, practical, objective, palpable, external.

- **Word:** Might (Synonym denoting Meaning: force)

  Other Synonyms: Energy, power, means, resources, strength, capacity, ability.

  Antonyms: Weakness, feebleness, infirmity, impotence, inability, inefficiency, incapability, leant, lack.

- **Word:** Mind (Synonym denoting Meaning: understanding)

  Other Synonyms: Intellect, soul, opinion, judgement, belief, choice, inclination, liking, intent, will, courage, spirit, remembrance, memory, recollection, reason, brain, sense, consciousness, disposition, intelligence, thought, instinct.

Antonyms: Body, matter, brute force, limbs, material substance, members, feelings, emotions, heart, affections, sensibilities, conduct, forgetfulness, obliviousness.

- **Word:** Minute (Synonym denoting Meaning: small)

  Other Synonyms: Tiny, slender, diminutive, slight, little, precise, particular, detailed, critical, circumstantial, exact, fine, comminuted, specific, inconsiderable, microscopic.

  Antonyms: Monstrous, great, enormous, grand, huge, general, abstract, broad, comprehensive, inexact, superficial.

- **Word:** Misfortune (Synonym denoting Meaning: adversity)

  Other Synonyms: Failure, ill luck, hardship, harm, ill, affliction, calamity, blow, disaster, disappointment, trial, tribulation, sorrow, ruin, distress, stroke, misery, reverse, mischance, visitation, chastening, trouble, chastisement, misadventure, bereavement, mishap.

  Antonyms: Consolation, blessing, boon, happiness, joy, prosperity, relief, triumph, success, comfort, good fortune, gratification, good luck, pleasure.

- **Word:** Moderate (Synonym denoting Meaning: sparing)

  Other Synonyms: Temperate, frugal, calm, mild, limited, restrained, reasonable, dispassionate, controlled, abstinent, sober, austere, ascetic.

  Antonyms: Immoderate, intemperate, luxurious, excessive, extravagant.

- **Word:** Modesty (Synonym denoting Meaning: humility)

  Other Synonyms: Lowliness, humbleness, meekness, shyness, reserve, coldness, bashfulness, backwardness, constraint, timidity, unobtrusiveness, coyness.

  Antonyms: Frankness, freedom, impudence, indiscretion, sauciness, abandon, arrogance, confidence, egoism, assumption, assurance, boldness, haughtiness, loquacity, pertness, pride, vanity, self-sufficiency, openness, effrontery.

- **Word:** Monstrous (Synonym denoting Meaning: abnormal)

  Other Synonyms: Extraordinary, prodigious, portentous, marvelous, unnatural, vast, immense, colossal, stupendous, shocking, horrible, hateful, terrible, hideous.

  Antonyms: Beautiful, small, reasonable, little, shapely, regular, fair, pretty, comely, ordinary, familiar, natural, charming, lovely.

- **Word:** Mysterious (Synonym denoting Meaning: abstruse)

  Other Synonyms: Enigmatical, dark, mystical, occult, obscure, secret, transcendental, unknown, unfathomable, mystic, hidden, inexplicable, inscrutable, cabalistic, incomprehensible, recondite.

  Antonyms: Clear, plain, apparent, manifest, bright, light, explainable, simple, comprehensible, obvious, easy, revealed, understood.

- **Word:** Mystic (Synonym denoting Meaning: unknowable)

  Other Synonyms: Obscure, mysterious, allegorical, enigmatical, transcendental, cabalistic, symbolical.

  Antonyms: Familiar, simple, ordinary, commonplace, obvious, plain.

N

- **Word:** Native (Synonym denoting Meaning: home)

  Other Synonyms: Aboriginal, autochthonous, belonging, domestic, endemic, from, home-grown, homemade, indigenous, inland, internal, local, mother, municipal, national, original, primary, primeval, primitive, regional, related, vernacular.

  Antonyms: Face, floater, foreigner, greenhorn, gringo, guest, immigrant, incomer, interloper, intruder, invader, migrant, newcomer, non-citizen, outsider, refugee, settler, squatter, strange weed, stranger, visitor, weed, wetback.

- **Word:** Natural (Synonym denoting Meaning: normal)

  Other Synonyms: Accustomed, anticipated, characteristic, common, commonplace, congenital, connatural, consistent, constant, counted on, customary, essential, everyday, familiar, general, habitual, inborn, indigenous, ingenerate, inherent, innate, instinctive, intuitive, involuntary, legitimate, logical, looked for, matter-of-course, natal, native, ordinary.

  Antonyms: Abnormal, amazing, astonishing, atypical, awe-inspiring, awesome, bizarre, conspicuous, curious, different, distinguished, eminent, exceptional, extraordinary, far out, important, inconceivable, incredible, memorable, noteworthy, odd, outstanding, phenomenal, prodigious, prominent, queer, rare, refreshing, remarkable, significant.

- **Word:** Nauseous (Synonym denoting Meaning: disgusting)

  Other Synonyms: Abhorrent, brackish, detestable, distasteful, ill, loathsome, nauseated, nauseating, offensive, queasy, repugnant, repulsive, rocky, seasick, sick, sickening, squeamish.

  Antonyms: Ably, accurately, adeptly, adequately, admirably, agreeably, attentively, capably, capitally, carefully, closely, commendably, competently, completely, conscientiously, correctly, effectively, efficiently, excellently, expertly, famously, favourably, fully, irreproachably, nicely, pleasantly, proficiently, profoundly, properly.

- **Word:** Near (Synonym denoting Meaning: close by)

  Other Synonyms: Abreast, abutting, adjacent, adjoining, along toward, alongside, around, available, beside, bordering, burning, close, close by, close shave, conterminous, contiguous, convenient, hair's breadth, handy, hot, immediate, near miss, near-at-hand, nearby, neighbouring, next door, nigh, not remote, practically, proximal, proximate, ready, touching, vicinal, warm.

  Antonyms: Distant, far away, far off, remote.

- **Word:** Naked (Synonym denoting Meaning: nude)

  Other Synonyms: Bare, defenceless, unprotected, destitute, manifest, undisguised, simple, mere, plain, unclothed, undraped, denuded, uncoloured, unvarnished.

Antonyms: Robed, draped, veiled, dressed, shrouded, muffled, protected, sheltered, coloured, varnished, qualified.

- **Word:** Narrow (Synonym denoting Meaning: not wide)

  Other Synonyms: Straitened, limited, without margin, bigoted, illiberal, parsimonious, niggardly, selfish, close, scrutinizing, exact, slender, spare, thin, contracted, cramped.

  Antonyms: Wide, broad, ample, expanded, thick, generous, benevolent, unlimited, liberal.

- **Word:** Nature (Synonym denoting Meaning: creation)

  Other Synonyms: Universe, essence, constitution, kind, sort, character, quality, temper, disposition, mood, mind, intelligence, vitality.

  Antonyms: Thing, subject, object, man, being, creature, monstrosity, unnaturalness, art, fiction, romance, invention.

- **Word:** Near (Synonym denoting Meaning: nigh)

  Other Synonyms: Nigh, close, adjacent, adjoining, approximate, imminent, impending, forthcoming, approaching, familiar, dear, intimate, immediate, literal, accurate, narrow, parsimonious, short, proximate, contiguous, present, ready.

  Antonyms: Distant, remote, far, reserved, cool, stiff, indistinct, obscure, future.

- **Word:** Necessary (Synonym denoting Meaning: essential)

  Other Synonyms: Inevitable, needful, infallible, undeniable, indispensable, required, requisite, unavoidable, Force, compel, coerce, make necessary, oblige, constrain, make, drive, impel.

  Antonyms: Optional, useless, contingent, worthless, casual, non-essential, needless.

- **Word:** Neglect (Synonym denoting Meaning: negligence)

  Other Synonyms: Failure, omission, disregard, oversight, indifference, remissness, slight, thoughtlessness, slackness, default, carelessness, disrespect, inadvertence, inattention, scorn.

Antonyms: Care, attention, notice, regard, esteem, consideration, respect.

- **Word:** Neighbourly (Synonym denoting Meaning: kind)

  Other Synonyms:, Civil, social, friendly, near, adjoining, adjacent, neighbouring, friendly, attentive.

  Antonyms: Individual, solitary, personal, distant, remote, unkind, uncivil, unfriendly.

- **Word:** Nervous (Synonym denoting Meaning: excitable)

  Other Synonyms: Agitated, annoyed, irritable, weak, fearful, strong, vigorous, spirited, nervy, forceful.

  Antonyms: Self-possessed, self-controlled, poised, calm, composed, dull, inert, phlegmatic, sluggish.

- **Word:** New (Synonym denoting Meaning: fresh)

  Other Synonyms: Modern, novel, late, recent, juvenile, upstart, young, new-fangled, youthful, new-fashioned.

  Antonyms: Old, antique, ancient, old-fashioned, aged, elderly.

- **Word:** News (Synonym denoting Meaning: information)

  Other Synonyms: Tidings, intelligence, advice, word, report, account, announcement, rumour.

  Antonyms: Ignorance, silence, non-publication, misreport.

- **Word:** Nice (Synonym denoting Meaning: exquisite)

  Other Synonyms: Accurate, correct, precise, particular, punctilious, squeamish, effeminate, silly, exact, critical, definite, strict, fastidious, cautious, scrupulous, discerning, discriminating, fine, minute, refined, delicate, dainty, pleasant, agreeable.

  Antonyms: Coarse, rude, rough, inaccurate, blind, undiscriminating, unscrupulous, incautious, undiscerning, careless, negligent, disagreeable, nauseous.

- **Word:** Nicety (Synonym denoting Meaning: fastidiousness)

  Other Synonyms: Accuracy, scrupulousness, delicacy, precision, daintiness, subtlety, distinction, exactness.

  Antonyms: Coarseness, roughness, inaccuracy, rudeness.

- **Word:** Nobility (Synonym denoting Meaning: greatness)

  Other Synonyms: Dignity, superiority, nobleness, eminence, elevation, worthiness, family, rank, title, birth, aristocracy, peerage, patrician class.

  Antonyms: Obscurity, meanness, serfdom, paltriness.

- **Word:** Noble (Synonym denoting Meaning: honourable)

  Other Synonyms: Worthy, dignified, elevated, superior, sublime, great, eminent, stately, generous, liberal, free, aristocratic, patrician, illustrious, grand, lordly, renowned, magnificent, knightly.

  Antonyms: Ignoble, plebeian, paltry, vulgar, base-born, low-born, rustic, peasant, contemptible, unworthy, mean.

- **Word:** Noisome (Synonym denoting Meaning: noxious)

  Other Synonyms: Insalubrious, unwholesome, mischievous, destructive, nocuous, hurtful, pestilential, harmful.

  Antonyms: Wholesome, salutary, salubrious, beneficial.

- **Word:** Nominal (Synonym denoting Meaning: literal)

  Other Synonyms: Verbal, titular, formal, avowed, pretended, ostensible, supposititious.

  Antonyms: Veritable, essential, intrinsic, actual, substantial, important, real, serious, true.

- **Word:** Normal (Synonym denoting Meaning: regular)

  Other Synonyms: Ordinary, natural, standard, usual, typical, recognized, common.

  Antonyms: Exceptional, abnormal, uncommon, singular, unusual, monstrous, irregular, peculiar, rare, unprecedented, remarkable, unnatural.

- **Word:** Notable (Synonym denoting Meaning: plain)

  Other Synonyms: Evident, noted, noticeable, distinguished, memorable, extraordinary, conspicuous, manifest, notorious.

  Antonyms: Ordinary, mean, commonplace, everyday, undistinguished, unimpressive, insignificant.

- **Word:** Notice (Synonym denoting Meaning: observation)

  Other Synonyms: Regard, cognizance, information, advice, news, intelligence, intimation, announcement, premonition, instruction, warning, attention, consideration.

  Antonyms: Oversight, disregard, neglect, slight, ignorance, connivance, omission, misinformation.

- **Word:** Notion (Synonym denoting Meaning: idea)

  Other Synonyms: Conception, apprehension, sentiment, judgement, opinion, belief, impression, estimation, conceit, conviction.

  Antonyms: Misconception, misapprehension, frustration, falsification.

- **Word:** Novel (Synonym denoting Meaning: new)

  Other Synonyms: Recent, modern, fresh, uncommon, rare, unusual, fantastic, odd, upstart, new-fang.

  Antonyms: Ancient, old-fashioned, time.

- **Word:** Numb (Synonym denoting Meaning: enfeebled)

  Other Synonyms: Destitute, torpid, benumbed, insensible, paralyzed, deadened.

  Antonyms: Alive, alert, sensitive, keen, lively, animated, attentive.

- **Word:** Numerous (Synonym denoting Meaning: many)

  Other Synonyms: Abundant, diverse, multifarious, manifold, sundry.

  Antonyms: Few, scarce, rare, in-frequent.

- **Word:** Nurse (Synonym denoting Meaning: nourish)

  Other Synonyms: Cherish, foster, attend, manage, train, educate, teach, feed, nurture.

  Antonyms: Starve, kill, destroy, neglect.

- **Word:** Nimble (Synonym denoting Meaning: active)

  Other Synonyms: Alert, bustling, prompt, speedy, spry, agile, brisk, lively, quick, sprightly, swift.

  Antonyms: Clumsy, dull, heavy, inactive, inert, slow, sluggish, unready dilatory.

O

- **Word:** Objection (Synonym denoting Meaning: disagreement)

  Other Synonyms: Argument, beef, bellyache, bitch, boggling, cavil, censure, challenge, counter-argument, criticism, declination, demur, demurral, demurring, difficulty, disapprobation, disapproval, discontent, disesteem, disinclination, dislike, displeasure.

  Antonyms: Acquiescence, assent, bells, blessing, compliance, concurrence, confirmation, consent, countenance, endorsement, finest kind, go-ahead, green light, leave, license, mandate, ok, permission, ratification, recommendation, sanction, support, the nod, validation.

- **Word:** Oblige (Synonym denoting Meaning: require)

  Other Synonyms: Bind, coerce, command, compel, concuss, constrain, force, impel, make, necessitate, obligate, shotgun.

  Antonyms: Appeal, apply, beg, beseech, bespeak, bite, bum, burn, call for, demand, desire, entreat, hit, hustle, inquire, knock, make, mooch, nick, petition, pray, promote, requisition, score, seek, solicit, sponge, sue, supplicate, touch, whistle for.

- **Word:** Oblique (Synonym denoting Meaning: slanting)

  Other Synonyms: Angled, askance, askew, aslant, asymmetrical, awry, bent, cater-cornered, crooked, diagonal, distorted, diverging, inclined, inclining, leaning, pitched, pitching, sideways, skew, slanted, sloped, sloping, strained, tilted, tilting, tipped, tipping, turned, twisted.

Antonyms: cocked, end on, end up, erect, on end, perpendicular, plumb, raised, sheer, stand-up, standing, steep, straight, upended, upstanding, upward, vertical.

- **Word:** Oath (Synonym denoting Meaning: curse)

  Other Synonyms: Imprecation, profanity, swearing, adjuration, affidavit, anathema, ban, blasphemy, denunciation, execration, malediction, vow, reprobation, sworn statement.

  Antonyms: Blessing, benediction, benison.

- **Word:** Obdurate (Synonym denoting Meaning: firm)

  Other Synonyms: Unbending, inflexible, unyielding, obstinate, stubborn, impenitent, callous, unfeeling, insensible.

  Antonyms: Yielding, teachable, tender, docile, amenable.

- **Word:** Obligation (Synonym denoting Meaning: responsibility)

  Other Synonyms: Engagement, contract, agreement, bond, covenant, stipulation, necessity, debt, duty, compulsion.

  Antonyms: Choice, freedom, assurance, promise, declaration, intention.

- **Word:** Obscure (Synonym denoting Meaning: abstruse)

  Other Synonyms: Deep, involved, difficult, hidden, profound, mysterious, ambiguous, unintelligible, cloudy, complex, complicated, dark, darksome, dense, dim doubtful, intricate, dusky, indistinct, enigmatical, incomprehensible, muddy, turbid, shadowy.

  Antonyms: Clear, luminous, distinct, lucid, plain, plain-spoken, intelligible, prominent, eminent.

- **Word:** Obstinate (Synonym denoting Meaning: perverse)

  Other Synonyms: Obdurate, intractable, determined, stubborn, resolved, resolute, inflexible, unyielding, intractable, indomitable, unflinching, contumacious, decided, dogged, mulish, heady, headstrong, fixed, firm, immovable, opinionated, persistent, pertinacious.

Antonyms: Pliant, docile, submissive, dutiful, gentle, obedient, compliant, tractable, yielding, amenable, complaisant, irresolute, wavering, undecided, pliable, teachable.

- **Word:** Obsolete (Synonym denoting Meaning: disused)

  Other Synonyms: Ancient, neglected, antiquated, archaic, effete, past, old-fashioned, old, rare, obsolescent.

  Antonyms: Fashionable, modern, current, customary, new, novel, extant.

- **Word:** Operation (Synonym denoting Meaning: action)

  Other Synonyms: Effect, force, performance, result agency, execution, influence, procedure.

  Antonyms: Failure, ineffectiveness, inutility, powerlessness, uselessness inaction, inefficiency.

- **Word:** Obstruct (Synonym denoting Meaning: interrupt)

  Other Synonyms: Arrest, check, embarrass, stay, bar, choke, hinder, oppose, stop barricade, clog, impede, retard.

  Antonyms: Accelerate, aid, facilitate, free, open, promote advance, clear, forward, further, pave the way for.

- **Word:** Old (Synonym denoting Meaning: aged)

  Other Synonyms: Ancient, primitive, pristine, antique, antiquated, old-fashioned, obsolete, senile, gray, hoary, olden, immemorial, time-honoured, decrepit, elderly, patriarchal, remote, venerable, time-worn.

  Antonyms: Youthful, childlike, young, recent, modern, fresh,, new-fashioned, current.

- **Word:** Ominous (Synonym denoting Meaning: significant)

  Other Synonyms: Portentous, unpropitious, threatening, inauspicious, foreboding, premonitory, suggestive.

  Antonyms: Encouraging, auspicious, propitious.

- **Word:** Order (Synonym denoting Meaning: arrangement)

  Other Synonyms: System, procedure, method, rule, regulation, command, mandate, rank, direction, grade, class, kind, management, prohibition, requirement, instruction.

  Antonyms: consent, leave, permission, permit, liberty, license.

- **Word:** Outstanding (Synonym denoting Meaning: not paid)

  Other Synonyms: Uncollected, unpaid, projecting, opposing.

  Antonyms: Collected, appropriated, gathered, paid, supporting, reentrant.

- **Word:** Outward (Synonym denoting Meaning: out)

  Other Synonyms: Outer, external, exterior, public, visible, sensible, extraneous, superficial, apparent, extrinsic, ostensible.

  Antonyms: internal, intrinsic, inward, withdrawn.

- **Word:** Overcome (Synonym denoting Meaning: vanquish)

  Other Synonyms: Conquer, surmount, excel, overthrow, subjugate, rule, domineer over.

  Antonyms: Lose, forfeit, surrender, fail, submit, retreat, succumb.

- **Word:** Oversight (Synonym denoting Meaning: charge)

  Other Synonyms: Superintendence, management, supervision, command, care, watchfulness, surveillance, control, inspection, direction, watch, omission, error, inadvertence.

  Antonyms: Mismanagement, negligence, disregard, slight, particularity.

- **Word:** Overwhelm (Synonym denoting Meaning: submerge)

  Other Synonyms: Engulf, immerse, overpower, extinguish, bury, crush, sink, subdue, vanquish, conquer, defeat.

  Antonyms: Raise, reinstate, reestablish, rescue, extricate.

- **Word:** Ostentation (Synonym denoting Meaning: boast)

  Other Synonyms: Flourish, parade, pompousness, vaunt,

boasting, pageant, pomp, show, vaunting display, pageantry, pomposity.

Antonyms: Diffidence, quietness, retirement, timidity, modesty, reserve, shrinking, unobtrusiveness.

- **Word:** Obvious (Synonym denoting Meaning: opposing)

  Other Synonyms: Plain, evident, clear, manifest, apparent, discovered, perceived, open, explicit, patent.

  Antonyms: Remote, obscure, far- fetched, involved, latent.

- **Word:** Occult (Synonym denoting Meaning: secret)

  Other Synonyms: Concealed, hidden, unknown, invisible, latent, eclipsed, unrevealed, mysterious.

  Antonyms: Developed, plain, exposed, patent, clear, familiar, open.

- **Word:** Odious (Synonym denoting Meaning: hateful)

  Other Synonyms: Detestable, disgusting, abominable, repulsive, forbidding, unpopular, invidious, loathsome.

  Antonyms: Pleasing, pleasant, acceptable, agreeable, grateful, delectable, bewitching, charming.

- **Word:** Offensive (Synonym denoting Meaning: disagreeable)

  Other Synonyms: Obnoxious, distasteful, impertinent, disgusting, rude, saucy, approbrious, insulting, insolent, attacking, abusive, invading, assailant.

  Antonyms: Defensive, pleasing, grateful, savory.

- **Word:** Open (Synonym denoting Meaning: unclose)

  Other Synonyms: Disclose, expose, explain, begin, commence, initiate, uncovered, unprotected, exposed, plain, obvious, evident, public, artless, candid, free, available, accessible, undisguised, ingenuous.

  Antonyms: Close, shut, cover, conceal, conclude, terminate, misinterpret, mystify, barred, inaccessible, unavailable, reserved, shut, secreted.

- **Word:** Opinion (Synonym denoting Meaning: advice)

  Other Synonyms: Persuasion, idea, sentiment, view, conviction, judgement, notion, impression, estimation.

  Antonyms: Evidence, argument, inquiry, speculation, investigation, pleading.

- **Word:** Oppose (Synonym denoting Meaning: combat)

  Other Synonyms: Withstand, contradict, deny, gainsay, oppugn, contravene, check, obstruct.

  Antonyms: Aid, abet, support, advance, expedite.

- **Word:** Opposite (Synonym denoting Meaning: facing)

  Other Synonyms: Contrary, repugnant, antagonistic, adverse, counter, contradictory, opposed.

  Antonyms: Agreeing, coincident, harmonious, conformable, suiting, fitting, accordant.

- **Word:** Oracular (Synonym denoting Meaning: prophetic)

  Other Synonyms: Ominous, portentous, authoritative, positive, wise, grave, sage, obscure, equivocal, ambiguous.

  Antonyms: Cautious, modest, vacillating, diffident.

- **Word:** Ordeal (Synonym denoting Meaning: test)

  Other Synonyms: Trial, experiment, probation, proof, scrutiny, assay, investigation.

  Antonyms: Result, event, argument, evidence, plea, discussion.

- **Word:** Ordinary (Synonym denoting Meaning: normal)

  Other Synonyms: Usual, common, customary, settled, frequent, wonted, habitual, indifferent, mediocre, plain, commonplace.

  Antonyms: Extraordinary, superior, unusual, uncommon.

- **Word:** Organic (Synonym denoting Meaning: inherent)

  Other Synonyms: Fundamental, essential, constitutional, radical, vital, organized, systematised.

Antonyms: Non-essential, circumstantial, provisional, contingent, inorganic, secondary.

- **Word:** Origin (Synonym denoting Meaning: source)

  Other Synonyms: Rise, commencement, spring, fountain, derivation, cause, root, foundation.

  Antonyms: Termination, conclusion, extinction.

- **Word:** Original (Synonym denoting Meaning: primitive)

  Other Synonyms: New, primary, pristine, genuine, inventive, peculiar, initiatory, primordial, ancient, former, first.

  Antonyms: Subsequent, later, derivative, modern, terminal.

- **Word:** Ostensible (Synonym denoting Meaning: exhibited)

  Other Synonyms: Avowed, professed, apparent, pretended, declared, manifest, specious, plausible, outward.

  Antonyms: Real, actual, genuine, veritable, concealed, hidden.

- **Word:** Outrageous (Synonym denoting Meaning: violent)

  Other Synonyms: Furious, excessive, exorbitant, wanton, atrocious, monstrous, nefarious, heinous.

  Antonyms: Moderate, reasonable, justifiable.

P

- **Word:** Pack (Synonym denoting Meaning: group)

  Other Synonyms: Assemblage, band, barrel, bunch, bundle, circle, collection, company, crew, crowd, deck, drove, flock, gang, great deal, heap, herd, horde, lot, lump, mess, mob, much, multiplicity, number, peck, pile, press, set, swarm, troop.

  Antonyms: Ache for, be deficient, be deprived, be inadequate, be needy, be poor, be short, be without, call for, claim, covet, crave, demand, desire, die for, do without, drive for, exact, go hungry, hanker, hunger, hurting for, lack, letch for, long, miss, necessitate, pine, require, suffer privation, thirst, wish, yearn, yen for.

- **Word:** Paltry (Synonym denoting Meaning: worthless)

  Other Synonyms: Base, beggarly, cheap, common, contemptible, derisory, despicable, inconsiderable, ineffectual, insignificant, limited, low, low-down, meagre, mean, measly, Mickey Mouse, minor, miserable, narrow, pettifogging, petty, picayune, piddling, pitiful.

  Antonyms: Abundant, ample, big, big deal, big league, bulky, consequential, considerable, durable, extraordinary, firm, generous, goodly, heavy, heavyweight, hefty, key, large, major league, massive, material, meaningful, momentous, plentiful, principal.

- **Word:** Pandemonium (Synonym denoting Meaning: craziness)

  Other Synonyms: Anarchy, bedlam, bloody mess, bluster, chaos, clamour, clatter, commotion, confusion, din, hassle, hubhullabaloo, jangle, noise, racket, riot, ruckus, rumpus.

  Antonyms: Amity, calmness, composure, concord, congeniality, contentment, equanimity, harmony, hush, lull, peacefulness, placidity, quiet, quietude, relaxation, repose, reserve, rest, serenity, silence, stillness, sympathy, tranquility.

- **Word:** Pain (Synonym denoting Meaning: ache)

  Other Synonyms: Agony, ache, distress, suffering, torture, anguish, torment, pang, throe, paroxysm, twinge, woe, grief.

  Antonyms: Ease, peace, rapture, enjoyment, relief, solace, comfort, delight.

- **Word:** Pardon (Synonym denoting Meaning: absolution)

  Other Synonyms: Mercy, forgiveness, forbearance, remission, acquittal, indulgence, condone, forgive, absolve, excuse, overlook, remit, pass over or by, acquit.

  Antonyms: Penalty, punishment, vengeance, retribution, retaliation Inexcusable, unpardonable.

- **Word:** Particular (Synonym denoting Meaning: sole)

  Other Synonyms: Single, individual, respective, appropriate, personal, singular, important, peculiar, especial, specific, precise, critical, circumstantial.

Antonyms: Universal, general, comprehensive, indiscriminate, abstract, inaccurate, inexact, undiscriminating.

- **Word:** Partition (Synonym denoting Meaning: division)

  Other Synonyms: Distribution, separation, allotment, apportionment, compartment, barrier.

  Antonyms: Combination, inclusion, comprehension, collection, union.

- **Word:** Pass (Synonym denoting Meaning: go)

  Other Synonyms: Move, proceed, disappear, vanish, depart, take place, occur, elapse, spend, live, experience, transcend, exceed, send, transmit, deliver, utter, promise, pledge, finish.

  Antonyms: Hold up, abide, wait, halt, continue, endure.

- **Word:** Passion (Synonym denoting Meaning: feeling)

  Other Synonyms: Emotion, susceptibility, sentiment, ardour, excitement, desire, anger, warmth, vehemence.

  Antonyms: Indifference, apathy, coldness, coolness, frigidity.

- **Word:** Patience (Synonym denoting Meaning: composure)

  Other Synonyms: Calmness, leniency, fortitude, sufferance, submission, endurance, forbearance, resignation, long-suffering.

  Antonyms: Anger, impatience, ire, passion, fury, frenzy, rage, temper, vexation, petulance, wrath, fretfulness, peevishness.

- **Word:** Pay (Synonym denoting Meaning: earnings)

  Other Synonyms: Stipend, salary, wages, allowance, retainer, remuneration, payment, compensation, hire, fee, requital.

  Antonyms: Deprive, defraud, retain, exact, hoard, invest.

- **Word:** Peace (Synonym denoting Meaning: quiet)

  Other Synonyms: Calm, repose, tranquility, stillness, silence, harmony, amity, concord, reconciliation, order, pacification.

Antonyms: Noise, disturbance, disorder, strife, discord, variance, tumult, agitation, hostility.

- **Word:** Perfect (Synonym denoting Meaning: finished)

  Other Synonyms: Complete, entire, faultless, consummate, accurate, ideal, finished, absolute, completed, correct, immaculate, sinless, blameless, holy, undefiled, stainless, spotless, unblemished.

  Antonyms: Imperfect, bad, deficient, blemished, faulty, corrupt, poor, inferior, incomplete, perverted, worthless, spoiled, insufficient, meager, defective, short, scant, marred, defaced, corrupted, deformed, fallible, ruined.

- **Word:** Perform (Synonym denoting Meaning: complete)

  Other Synonyms: Accomplish, execute, do, discharge, fulfil, represent, act, play, enact, consummate, achieve.

  Antonyms: Spoil, injure, harm, ruin, mar, fail of, misconduct.

- **Word:** Performance (Synonym denoting Meaning: completion)

  Other Synonyms: Consummation, execution, accomplishment, achievement, work, production, act, action, deed, exploit, feat.

  Antonyms: Failure, defeat, omission, abortion, undoing.

- **Word:** Period (Synonym denoting Meaning: time)

  Other Synonyms: Cycle, age, epoch, limit, end, conclusion, era, duration, date, term, continuance, termination, conclusion, bound.

  Antonyms: Eternity, infinity, perpetuity, endlessness, everlasting.

- **Word:** Permanent (Synonym denoting Meaning: enduring)

  Other Synonyms: Abiding, changeless, constant, durable, steadfast, unchangeable, immutable, invariable, fixed, unchanging, stable, lasting, persistent, perpetual.

  Antonyms: Transient, brief, fleeting, evanescent, passing, transitory, momentary, temporary, ephemeral.

- **Word:** Pernicious (Synonym denoting Meaning: mischievous)

  Other Synonyms: Baneful, destructive, noisome, deleterious, harmful, hurtful, poisonous, noxious, pestilential, unhealthful, unwholesome, detrimental, deadly, evil, foul, injurious, insalubrious, pestiferous, perverting, ruinous.

  Antonyms: Helpful, invigorating, salutary, advantageous, good, favourable, life-giving, rejuvenating, useful, serviceable, beneficent, wholesome, beneficial, healthful.

- **Word:** Perplex (Synonym denoting Meaning: entangle)

  Other Synonyms: Involve, complicate, embarrass, puzzle, bewilder, confuse, distract, annoy, confound, trouble, worry, disturb, pester, bother, mystify.

  Antonyms: Enlighten, clear, simplify, elucidate, illumine, unfold, explain, manifest, calm, quiet, control, please, instruct, solve, illustrate, make intelligible, account for.

- **Word:** Perspicacity (Synonym denoting Meaning: acuteness)

  Other Synonyms: Keenness, discernment, penetration, insight, sagacity, astuteness, distinctness, explicitness.

  Antonyms: Dullness, stupefaction, obtuseness, stolidity, inobservance, insensibility.

- **Word:** Philosopher (Synonym denoting Meaning: theorist)

  Other Synonyms: Student, theorist, speculator, teacher, master, savant, schoolman, doctor, adept.

  Antonyms: Learner, pupil, beginner, ignoramus, dunce.

- **Word:** Pitiful (Synonym denoting Meaning: lamentable)

  Other Synonyms: Mournful, base, contemptible, piteous, pathetic, pitiable, touching, sorrowful, wretched, despicable, moving, paltry.

  Antonyms: Exalted, glorious, helpful, great, grand, sublime, superior, beneficent, commanding, august, dignified, noble, lofty, mighty, superb.

- **Word:** Plain (Synonym denoting Meaning: artless)

  Other Synonyms: Undisguised, sincere, frank, honest, ingenuous, candid, unembellished, simple, downright, blunt, distinct, apparent, manifest, open, clear, evident, visible, obvious, unmistakable, conspicuous, level, flat, smooth, easy, natural, homely, ugly, simple, frugal.

  Antonyms: Unnatural, pretended, affected, assumed, feigned, artificial, insincere, vain, pretentious, conceited, ornate, ornamented, decorated, embellished, involved, obscure, hidden, invisible, inconspicuous, uneven, undulating, rugged, broken, ambiguous, abrupt, obstructed, uncertain, enigmatical, abstruse, beautiful, sophisticated, artful.

- **Word:** Pleasure (Synonym denoting Meaning: satisfaction)

  Other Synonyms: Comfort, solace, joy, gladness, delight, will, chdice, purpose, command, kindness, enjoyment, gratification, happiness, self-indulgence, voluptuousness.

  Antonyms: Suffering, affliction, pain, sorrow, sadness, distress, misery, compulsion, force, coercion, mourning, depression, dejection, melancholy, misfortune, poverty, want.

- **Word:** Plenitude (Synonym denoting Meaning: fullness)

  Other Synonyms: Acompleteness, plenty, repletion, plethora, luxury, affluence, exuberance, wealth, richness, profusion, amplitude, enough, supply, sufficiency.

  Antonyms: Want, need, scarcity, scantiness, dearth, insufficiency, restriction, poverty, partiality, stint, reserve, narrowness, penury.

- **Word:** Plentiful (Synonym denoting Meaning: bountiful)

  Other Synonyms: Generous, large, abundant, adequate, copious, enough, full, profuse, rich, sufficient, complete, exuberant, plenteous, replete, teeming, affluent, ample, lavish, liberal, luxuriant, overflowing, abounding.

  Antonyms: Deficient, drained, impoverished, scanty, insufficient, small, sparing, stingy, straitened, poor, scant, exhausted, inadequate, mean, miserly, narrow, niggardly, scarce, short, scrimped.

- **Word:** Poisonous (Synonym denoting Meaning: venomous)

  Other Synonyms: Baneful, corrupting, noxious, pestilential, malignant, virulent, pestiferous, deleterious, mephitic.

  Antonyms: Salubrious, healthful, beneficial, sanative, genial, remedial, hygienic.

- **Word:** Polite (Synonym denoting Meaning: courteous)

  Other Synonyms: Civil, courtly, obliging, gracious, polished, accomplished, complaisant, cultivated, cultured, elegant, genteel, urbane, well-behaved, well- mannered, well-bred.

  Antonyms: Awkward, clownish, unmannerly, uncouth, boorish, blunt, impertinent, bluff, impolite, insolent, ill-behaved, rude, rustic, impudent, ill-mannered, untutored, uncivil, untaught, discourteous, unpolished, insulting.

- **Word:** Poor (Synonym denoting Meaning: needy)

  Other Synonyms: Indigent, destitute, lean, emaciated, feeble, dejected, shabby, mean, unfavourable, uncomfortable, barren, sterile, inadequate, insignificant, insufficient, meek.

  Antonyms: Rich, wealthy, affluent, opulent, splendid, costly, valuable, estimable, fruitful, abundant, luxuriant, productive, prolific, copious, abounding, ample, well- supplied, comfortable, favourable, adequate, sufficient, important, significant, arrogant, self-assertive.

- **Word:** Popular (Synonym denoting Meaning: cheap)

  Other Synonyms: Common, ordinary, inferior, familiar, plain, easy, comprehensible, favourite, liked, approved, accepted, accredited, current, prevalent, general, prevailing, pertaining to the people, vulgar, plebeian, mediocre.

  Antonyms: Unpopular, exclusive, aristocratic, snobbish, special, excellent, unique, superior, eminent, selfish, narrow, illiberal, uncharitable, sole, only.

- **Word:** Positive (Synonym denoting Meaning: real)

  Other Synonyms: Actual, absolute, explicit, definite, confident, certain, dogmatic, defined, precise, clear, veritable, substantial, true, indisputable, incontrovertible, indubitable, decisive, unconditional, imperative, un- equivocal, settled, assured, express.

  Antonyms: Negative, denying, indirect, disavowing, disclaiming, privative, relative, unreal, fictitious, imaginative, contingent, dependent, implied, conditional, dubious, unsubstantial, indefinite, equivocal.

- **Word:** Power (Synonym denoting Meaning: ability)

  Other Synonyms: Competency, capacity, faculty, aptitude, dexterity, efficiency, might, talent, energy, skill, strength, readiness, capability, cleverness, expertness, efficacy, force, qualification, cogency, susceptibility.

  Antonyms: Feebleness, weakness, helplessness, impotence, incompetence, inability, inaptitude, dullness, awkwardness, imbecility, incapacity, inefficiency, unskillfulness, stupidity.

- **Word:** Praise (Synonym denoting Meaning: applause)

  Other Synonyms: Approval, cheering, compliment, acclaim, adulation, acclamation, approbation, cheers, plaudit, eulogy, encomium, flattery, laudation, panegyric, sycophancy.

  Antonyms: Abuse, blame, censure, contempt, reproach, ignominy, slander, scorn, obloquy, animadversion, condemnation, denunciation, disapprobation, disparagement, vituperation, reproof, disapproval, repudiation, hissing, vilification.

- **Word:** Precarious (Synonym denoting Meaning: doubtful)

  Other Synonyms: Dubious, hazardous, perilous, risky, insecure, uncertain, unsettled, unsteady, unstable.

  Antonyms: Firm, settled, stable, sure, certain, real, undoubted, unquestionable, actual, assured, immutable, incontestable, undeniable, infallible, strong, steady.

- **Word:** Prefer (Synonym denoting Meaning: choose)

  Other Synonyms: Elect, select, desire, pick out, fancy, single out, fix upon, elevate, advance, promote, offer, proffer, present, address.

  Antonyms: Reject, discard, decline, refuse, repudiate, degrade, depress, postpone, defer, withhold.

- **Word:** Presumption (Synonym denoting Meaning: assumption)

  Other Synonyms: Arrogance, effrontery, audacity, assurance, presupposition, hypothesis, guess, conjecture, belief, opinion, judgement, under- standing, concession, condition.

  Antonyms: Modesty, deference, diffidence, bashfulness, hesitation, proof,. deduction, demonstration, verification, certainty fact.

- **Word:** Pretense (Synonym denoting Meaning: disguise)

  Other Synonyms: Excuse, affectation, mask, show, pretension, semblance, wile, trick, subterfuge, simulation, ruse, assumption, pretext, seeming, dissimulation, air, cloak, colour.

  Antonyms: Candor, sincerity, ingenuousness, frankness, honesty, truth, openness, reality, simplicity, guilelessness, fact, actuality.

- **Word:** Prevalence (Synonym denoting Meaning: success)

  Other Synonyms: Superiority, predominance, preponderance, influence, force, power, strength, efficacy, universality, extension, acceptation, custom, operation.

  Antonyms: Decay, desuetude, disappearance, evanescence, subordination, collapse, destruction, abolition, subsidence, subjection, diminution.

- **Word:** Pride (Synonym denoting Meaning: arrogance)

  Other Synonyms: Insolence, reserve, haughtiness, self-esteem, presumption, superciliousness, vanity, ostentation, conceit, self-respect, self-exaltation, disdain, vainglory, self-conceit, self-complacency.

Antonyms: Humility, lowliness, modesty, self-distrust, meekness, self-abasement.

- **Word:** Primeval (Synonym denoting Meaning: immemorial)

  Other Synonyms: Original, old, primal, patriarchal, native, primitive, pristine, uncreated, ancient, aboriginal, autochthonic, indigenous, prime, primary, primordial.

  Antonyms: Foreign, fresh, late, modern, new, novel, recent, exotic, adventitious.

- **Word:** Principle (Synonym denoting Meaning: source)

  Other Synonyms: Cause, origin, faculty, endowment, postulate, truth, maxim, axiom, rule, law, element, doctrine, dogma, opinion, ground, motive, reason, integrity, rectitude, uprightness, probity, virtue, worth, honour.

  Antonyms: Result, sequence, development, issue, application, action, operation, exercise, manifestation, exhibition, iniquity, immorality.

- **Word:** Profession (Synonym denoting Meaning: business)

  Other Synonyms: Avowal, declaration, claim, occupation, vocation, employment, law, theology, or medicine, assertion, acknowledgment, representation, pretense, protestation.

  Antonyms: Denial, concealment, suppression, retraction, recantation, disavowal, leisure, fad, hobby, avocation, trade.

- **Word:** Profit (Synonym denoting Meaning: gain)

  Other Synonyms: Advantage, benefit, emolument, improvement, proceeds, utility, usefulness, returns, value, receipts, avail, expediency, good, service.

  Antonyms: Damage, destruction, harm, hurt, loss, injury, waste, ruin, detriment, disadvantage.

- **Word:** Prominent (Synonym denoting Meaning: projecting)

  Other Synonyms: Manifest, protuberant, conspicuous, eminent, distinguished, famous, celebrated, important, main, principal, leading, characteristic.

Antonyms: Receding, hollowed, concave, indented, engraved, insignificant, secondary, unimportant, minor, indistinguishable, indistinct, subordinate, inconspicuous, trivial, immaterial, unessential.

- **Word:** Proud (Synonym denoting Meaning: arrogant)

  Other Synonyms: Haughty, presumptuous, lordly, worthy, admirable, grand, splendid, magnificent, ostentatious, lofty, supercilious, boastful, elated, imposing, vainglorious.

  Antonyms: Humble, unassuming, unobtrusive, meek, lowly, mild, submissive, unpretending, deferential, affable.

- **Word:** Pure (Synonym denoting Meaning: innocent)

  Other Synonyms: Unsullied, spotless, unspotted, stainless, true, guiltless, incorrupt, clean, genuine, chaste, guileless, classic, classical, holy, immaculate, virtuous, real, sheer, mere, simple, unmixed, unpolluted, unadulterated, unmingled, undefiled, unblemished, uncorrupted, unstained, untainted, untarnished, upright, perfect.

  Antonyms: Impure, indecent, polluted, foul, tainted, unchaste, immodest, lewd, obscene, indelicate, defiled, dirty, filthy, gross, mixed, stained, sullied, unclean, tarnished, adulterated.

Q

- **Word:** Qualified (Synonym denoting Meaning: skilful)

  Other Synonyms: Able, accomplished, adept, adequate, all around, au fait, capable, certified, competent, disciplined, efficient, equipped, examined, experienced, expert, fit, fitted, good, instructed, know beans, know onions, knowledgeable, licensed, practiced.

  Antonyms: Amateur, amateurish, awkward, bungling, bush, bush league, clumsy, disqualified, floundering, helpless, inadequate, incapable, incapacitated, ineffectual, inefficient, ineligible, inept, inexperienced, inexpert, insufficient, maladroit, raw.

- **Word:** Qualify (Synonym denoting Meaning: prepare)

  Other Synonyms: Authorise, capacitate, certify, check out, commission, condition, cut it, empower, enable, endow, entitle, equip, fit, get by, ground, hack it, make it, make ready.

  Antonyms: Abort, backslide, be defeated, be demoted, be ruined, blunder, break down, decline, deteriorate, fall, fall flat, fall short, fall through, fizzle, flop, flounder, fold.

- **Word:** Quality (Synonym denoting Meaning: status)

  Other Synonyms: Calibre, capacity, character, class, condition, distinction, excellence, footing, grade, group, kind, merit, perfection, place, position, pre-eminence, rank, repute, standing, state, station, stature, step, superiority, value, variety, virtue, worth.

  Antonyms: Abasement, decadence, degradation, depravity, dissoluteness, downfall, immorality, inferiority, meanness, poorness.

- **Word:** Queasy (Synonym denoting Meaning: uncomfortable)

  Other Synonyms: Anxious, bilious, concerned, fidgety, groggy, ill, indisposed, nauseated, queer, restless, rocky, sick, sickly, squeamish, trouble, uncertain, uncomfortable, uneasy, unwell, upset, worried.

  Antonyms: Ably, accurately, adeptly, adequately, admirably, agreeably, attentively, capably, capitally, carefully, closely, commendably, competently, completely, conscientiously, correctly, effectively, efficiently, excellently, expertly, famously.

- **Word:** Question (Synonym denoting Meaning: ask)

  Other Synonyms: Ask about, challenge, cook, cross-examine, enquire, examine, go over, grill, hit, hit up, inquire, interrogate, interview, investigate, knock, make inquiry, petition, probe, pry, pump, query, quest, quiz, raise question, roast, search, seek, show.

  Antonyms: Acknowledgement, antiphon, back talk, band-aid, clause, comeback, comment, cooler, counterclaim, crack, disclosure, echo, elucidation, explanation, feedback, guff, interpretation, justification, key, lip, observation, parting shot, pay dirt, plea, quick.

- **Word:** Quick (Synonym denoting Meaning: fast)

  Other Synonyms: Abrupt, accelerated, active, agile, alert, animated, ASAP, breakneck, brief, brisk, cursory, curt, double time, energetic, expeditious, express, fleet, flying, get going, hasty, headlong, hurried, immediate, impatient, impetuous, instantaneous, keen, lively.

  Antonyms: Apathetic, crawling, creeping, dawdling, delaying, deliberate, dilatory, disinclined, dreamy, drowsy, easy, gradual, heavy, idle, imperceptible, inactive, indolent, inert, lackadaisical, laggard, lagging, lazy, leaden, leisurely, lethargic, listless, loitering.

- **Word:** Quicken (Synonym denoting Meaning: invigorate)

  Other Synonyms: Accelerate, activate, actuate, animate, arouse, awaken, dispatch, energise, excite, expedite, goad, grow, hasten, hurry, impel, incite, increase, innervate, innerve, inspire, kindle, liven, make haste, move, pique, precipitate, promote.

  Antonyms: Arrest, baffle, bar, bit, bottleneck, bridle, checkmate, choke, circumvent, constrain, control, counteract, curb, cut short, delay, discourage, foil, frustrate, halt, harness, hold, hold back, hold down, hold in, impede, inhibit, interrupt, keep back, limit, moderate, obstruct, obviate, pause, preclude, prevent, rebuff, reduce, rein in.

- **Word:** Quiet (Synonym denoting Meaning: low-sounding)

  Other Synonyms: Buttoned up, clammed up, close, close-mouthed, dumb, dummied up, hushed, iced, inaudible, low, low-pitched, muffled, mute, muted, noiseless, peaceful, pin drop, quiescent, quieted, reserved, reticent, secretive, silent, soft, soundless, speechless, still.

  Antonyms: Audibly, clearly, distinctly, intelligibly, loudly, lustily, noisily, out loud, plainly, vociferously.

- **Word:** Quaint (Synonym denoting Meaning: odd

  Other Synonyms: Antique, curious, fanciful, affected, whimsical, archaic, singular, unusual, antiquated, extraordinary, droll.

  Antonyms: Commonplace, usual, ordinary, common, fashionable, modish, modern.

- **Word:** Quantity (Synonym denoting Meaning: greatness)

  Other Synonyms: Measure, amount, bulk, extent, size, aggregate, length, duration, content, comprehensiveness.

  Antonyms: Scantiness, want, deficiency, margin, deterioration, diminution, waste, wear, loss.

- **Word:** Queer (Synonym denoting Meaning: curious)

  Other Synonyms: Bizarre, droll, comical, odd, peculiar, quaint, strange, uncommon, unusual, whimsical, singular, ridiculous, anomalous, fantastic, funny, erratic, extraordinary, ludicrous, grotesque, laughable, preposterous, unique, unmatched, eccentric, crotchety.

  Antonyms: Common, customary, normal, ordinary, usual, regular, familiar, natural.

- **Word:** Query (Synonym denoting Meaning: question)

  Other Synonyms: Inquiry, doubt, point, topic, subject.

  Antonyms: Solution, explanation, answer, reply, response, concession, admission.

R

- **Word:** Raise (Synonym denoting Meaning: lift)

  Other Synonyms: Boost, bring up, build, build-up, construct, elevate, erect, establish, exalt, heave, hoist, hold up, lever, lift, lift up, mount, move up, place up, prise, promote, pry, pull up, put up, rear, run up, setup, set upright, shove, stand up, take up, throw up, upcast, uplift, upraise .

Antonyms: Bead, bit, bubble, crumb, dab, dash, dewdrop, driblet, drip, droplet, iota, molecule, morsel, nip, ounce, particle, pearl, pinch, sip, smidgen, speck, splash, spot, taste, tear, teardrop, trace, trickle.

- **Word:** Rancid (Synonym denoting Meaning: rotten)

  Other Synonyms: Bad, carious, contaminated, curdled, decomposing, disagreeable, disgusting, evil-smelling, feculent, fetid, foul, fusty, gamy, high, impure, loathsome, malodorous, musty, nasty, noisome, noxious, of, offensive, polluted.

  Antonyms: Beginning, brand-new, cherry, comer, crisp, crude, current, different, gleaming, glistening, green, immature, just out, late, latest, mint, modern, modernistic, natural, neoteric, newborn, newfangled, novel, now, original, original, radical, raw.

- **Word:** Rant (Synonym denoting Meaning: yell)

  Other Synonyms: Bellow, bluster, carry on, clamour, cry, declaim, fume, go on, harangue, huff, mouth, objurgate, orate, perorate, pop off, rag, rage, rail, rave, roar, scold, shout, sizzle, soapbox, sound off, spiel, spout, storm, stump, take on, vociferate.

  Antonyms: Abstain, avoid, bridle, cease, curb, decline, desist, escape, eschew, evade, forgo, go easy, hold back, inhibit, keep, keep from, omit, pause, refrain, restrain, sacrifice, shun, stop.

- **Word:** Rapture (Synonym denoting Meaning: delight)

  Other Synonyms: Altitudes, at-oneness, beatitude, bliss, buoyancy, cheer, cloud nine, communion, contentment, cool, delectation, delight, ecstasy, elation, Elysium, enchantment, enjoyment, enthusiasm, euphoria, exaltation, exhilaration, far out, felicity, gaiety, gladness, glory, gone, good spirits, gratification, happiness, heaven, inspiration.

  Antonyms: Anguish, bitterness, blue devils, blue funk, blues, catatonia, chagrin, cheerlessness, dejection, desolation, despair, despondency, disconsolateness, discouragement, dismals, distress, doldrums, downheartedness, dullness, dumps, foreboding, grief, heaviness, heavy-heartedness, horror, low spirits, malaise, melancholia.

- **Word:** Rarely (Synonym denoting Meaning: not often)

  Other Synonyms: Almost never, barely, exceptionally, extra, extraordinarily, extremely, finely, hardly, hardly ever, infrequently, little, notably, remarkably, scarcely ever, seldom, singularly, uncommon, uncommonly, infrequently, unusually.

  Antonyms: Generally, much, oftentimes, recurrently, regularly, repeatedly, usually.

- **Word:** React (Synonym denoting Meaning: respond)

  Other Synonyms: Acknowledge, act, answer, answer back, backfire, be affected, behave, boomerang, bounce back, conduct oneself, counter, echo, feel, feel for, function, give back, have vibes, operate, perform, proceed, rebound, reciprocate, recoil, recur, reply.

  Antonyms: Blink at, brush aside, brush away, brush off, cold-shoulder, contemn, despise, discount, disdain, disobey, disparage, fail, forget, laugh off, let go, let pass, live with, miss, neglect, omit, overlook, overpass, pass over, pooh pooh, scorn, slight, snub, tune.

- **Word:** Radiant (Synonym denoting Meaning: lustrous)

  Other Synonyms: Brilliant, splendid, gorgeous, glittering, glaring, radiating, beaming, resplendent, shining, sparkling, luminous, effulgent, glorious.

  Antonyms: Dull, dark, somber, murky, lusterless, non-luminous, sunless, shadowy, lurid, cloudy, gloomy, obscure, over-cast, ebon, black.

- **Word:** Radical (Synonym denoting Meaning: fundamental)

  Other Synonyms: Innate, essential, native, natural, original, organic, primitive, entire, complete, extreme, thorough, positive, perfect, thorough-going, total, ingrained, constitutional.

Antonyms: Superficial, tentative, trial, inadequate, incomplete, moderate, partial, palliative, conservative.

- **Word:** Random (Synonym denoting Meaning: chance)

  Other Synonyms: Haphazard, fortuitous, casual, wandering, stray, wild, aimless, purposeless, accidental, vague.

  Antonyms: Aimed, intended, controlled, purposed, deliberate, designed, intentional, regular, systematic, planned.

- **Word:** Reality (Synonym denoting Meaning: verity)

  Other Synonyms: Actuality, substance, truth, genuineness, authenticity, fact, substantiality, existence.

  Antonyms: Fiction, falsehood, untruth, myth, imagination, fabrication, fancy, supposition, unreality, chimera, vision, hypothesis, hollowness.

- **Word:** Realm (Synonym denoting Meaning: domain)

  Other Synonyms: Kingdom, region, province, country, department, empire, state, jurisdiction, sovereignty, dominion.

  Antonyms: Anarchy, insurrection, independence, democracy.

- **Word:** Rear (Synonym denoting Meaning: lift)

  Other Synonyms: Elevate, erect, raise, build, establish, exalt, foster, construct, breed, educate, instruct, train, discipline.

  Antonyms: Tear down, degrade, undermine, depress, overthrow, destroy, kill, demolish, subvert, stifle, extinguish.

- **Word:** Reason (Synonym denoting Meaning: cause

  Other Synonyms: Ground, aim, motive, account, argument, design, consideration, end, object, purpose, principle.

  Antonyms: Pretext, pretense, falsification, unreason, unreasonableness, irrationality, absurdity, fallacy.

- **Word:** Rebellious (Synonym denoting Meaning: intractable)

  Other Synonyms: Refractory, seditious, unmanageable, contumacious, disobedient, in-subordinate, mutinous, ungovernable, uncontrollable.

Antonyms: Deferential, compliant, docile, manageable, obedient, submissive, subservient, yielding, tractable, gentle, controllable, dutiful.

- **Word:** Recite (Synonym denoting Meaning: describe)

  Other Synonyms: Recapitulate, detail, number, repeat, deliver, rehearse, relate, narrate, recount, quote, count, enumerate, tell.

  Antonyms: Misquote, garble, falsify, misrepresent, pervert, forget, fail.

- **Word:** Reckless (Synonym denoting Meaning: mindless)

  Other Synonyms: Negligent, thoughtless, regardless, unconcerned, inattentive, remiss, improvident, rash, inconsiderate.

  Antonyms: Circumspect, careful, wary, thoughtful, mindful, attentive, considerate, provident, prudent, calculating.

- **Word:** Reconciliation (Synonym denoting Meaning: reconcilement,)

  Other Synonyms: Reunion, pacification, appeasement, propitiation, atonement, expiation, adjustment, restoration, harmony.

  Antonyms: Separation, estrangement, alienation, disaffection.

- **Word:** Recovery (Synonym denoting Meaning: repossession)

  Other Synonyms: Resumption, recruiting, healing, restoration, regaining, recuperation, convalescence, retrieval, redemption, resuscitation, revival, vindication, reinstatement, reestablishment.

  Antonyms: Loss, forfeiture, privation, damage, ruin, destruction, waste, illness, relapse, declension, incurableness, hopelessness.

- **Word:** Recreation (Synonym denoting Meaning: sport)

  Other Synonyms: Amusement, diversion, refreshment, reanimation, holiday, pastime, relaxation.

Antonyms: Toil, labour, work, industry, employment, fatigue, weariness, lassitude, exhaustion.

- **Word:** Rectitude (Synonym denoting Meaning: justice)

  Other Synonyms: Honesty, up-tightness, fairness, integrity, straightforwardness, conscientiousness, equity.

  Antonyms: Iniquity, wrong, injustice, immorality, corruption, dishonesty, duplicity, under-handedness.

- **Word:** Redemption (Synonym denoting Meaning: ransom)

  Other Synonyms: Release, rescue, retrieval, recovery, deliverance, liberation, salvation, discharge, fulfilment, atonement, compensation.

  Antonyms: Abandonment, forfeiture, sacrifice, betrayal, deprivation, desertion.

- **Word:** Reduce (Synonym denoting Meaning: decrease)

  Other Synonyms: Curtail, abate, shorten, impair, lower, subjugate, subject, diminish, attenuate, abridge, contract, subdue.

  Antonyms: Magnify, augment, expand, amplify, exalt, raise, invigorate, promote, restore, repair, renovate, transform.

- **Word:** Reflect (Synonym denoting Meaning: reproduced)

  Other Synonyms: Think, cogitate, meditate, contemplate, ruminate, ponder, muse, animadvert.

  Antonyms: Idle, dream, imagine, fancy, wander, rove, disregard, neglect.

- **Word:** Regard (Synonym denoting Meaning: consider)

  Other Synonyms: Observe, remark, heed, mind, respect, esteem, value, attend, notice, contemplate, revere, reverence.

  Antonyms: Overlook, disregard, miss, neglect, omit, dislike, hate, loathe, contemn.

- **Word:** Regret (Synonym denoting Meaning: grief)

  Other Synonyms: Concern, sorrow, lamentation, repentance, penitence, self-condemnation, compunction, remorse, contrition.

Antonyms: Joy, exultation, happiness, delight, approbation, praise, commendation, felicitation.

- **Word:** Regular (Synonym denoting Meaning: orderly)

  Other Synonyms: Methodical, conformable, agreeing, governed, subject, normal, constituted, selected, customary, systematic, stated, established, periodical, recognised, formal, recurrent, certain.

  Antonyms: Unusual, exceptional, rare, irregular, abnormal, eccentric, capricious, variable, uncertain, erratic.

- **Word:** Relation (Synonym denoting Meaning: recital)

  Other Synonyms: Rehearsal, account, narration, tale, narrative, detail, description, kindred, affinity, consanguinity, kinsman, kinswoman, connection, association, relevancy, agreement.

  Antonyms: Action, happening, occurrence, alien, stranger, foreigner, absoluteness, disagreement, dissociation, disconnection, irrelevancy.

- **Word:** Relief (Synonym denoting Meaning: alleviation)

  Other Synonyms: Mitigation, aid, help, succor, assistance, redress, remedy, indemnification, exemption, deliverance, refreshment, support, comfort.

  Antonyms: Oppression, persecution, aggravation, severity, cruelty, weariness, discomfort, exhaustion.

- **Word:** Religion (Synonym denoting Meaning: devotion)

  Other Synonyms: Faith, piety, righteousness, holiness, morality, godliness, pietism, worship, theology.

  Antonyms: Irreligion, atheism, unbelief, blasphemy, impiety, godlessness, profanity, sacrilege, ungodliness, wickedness.

- **Word:** Remarkable (Synonym denoting Meaning: observable)

  Other Synonyms: Rare, noticeable, extraordinary, unusual, strange, wonderful, notable, eminent: distinguished, famous, prominent, conspicuous, singular, peculiar, individual.

Antonyms: Ordinary, usual, commonplace, mediocre, everyday, common, general.

- **Word:** Remote (Synonym denoting Meaning: removed)

  Other Synonyms: Far, distant, irrelevant, not related, foreign, indirect, unconnected, alien, unallied, separate, abstract.

  Antonyms: Near, close, direct, related, connected, contiguous, immediate, present, pressing urgent, proximate, essential.

- **Word:** Render (Synonym denoting Meaning: return)

  Other Synonyms: Pay back, restore, requite, give up, yield, surrender, furnish, contribute, deliver, translate, interpret, set forth, exhibit, try out, apportion, give, present, assign.

  Antonyms: Keep, withhold, appropriate, retain, refuse, use, apply, employ, alienate.

- **Word:** Reproach (Synonym denoting Meaning: disrepute)

  Other Synonyms: Opprobrium, discredit, dishonour, invective, contumely, reviling, vilification, abuse, scurrility, insolence, insult, scorn, contempt, ignominy, shame, scandal, disgrace, infamy.

  Antonyms: Approbation, satisfaction, praise, encouragement, exaltation, commendation, honour, applause, eulogy, assent, acceptance, approval.

- **Word:** Reproof (Synonym denoting Meaning: comment)

  Other Synonyms: Criticism, disapproval, chiding, reproach, upbraiding, admonition, animadversion, censure, blame, condemnation, denunciation, reprehension, rebuke, reprimand, reflection, check.

  Antonyms: Commendation, panegyric, approbation, applause, approval, encomium, praise, eulogy.

- **Word:** Reprove (Synonym denoting Meaning: admonish)

  Other Synonyms: Blame, reproach, censure, condemn,

reprimand, warn, upbraid, chide, check, chasten, find fault with, expostulate with, rebuke, reprehend, remonstrate with, take to task.

Antonyms: Abet, applaud, encourage, cheer, countenance, incite, urge on, impel, instigate, approve.

- **Word:** Requite (Synonym denoting Meaning: avenge)

  Other Synonyms: Pay off, quit, punish, retaliate, revenge, satisfy, settle with, reward, return, repay, remunerate, recompense, compensate, reciprocate.

  Antonyms: Absolve, acquit, forgive, excuse, neglect, pardon, slight, forget, overlook, pass over.

- **Word:** Reserve (Synonym denoting Meaning: reservation)

  Other Synonyms: Retention, limitation, backwardness, coldness, shyness, coyness, modesty, taciturnity, restraint, repression, constraint.

  Antonyms: Profuseness, prodigality, diffusion, affability, geniality, cordiality, abandonment, surrender, openness, frankness, transparency, indiscretion, volubility.

- **Word:** Resignation (Synonym denoting Meaning: relinquishment)

  Other Synonyms: Forsaking, abandonment, abdication, renunciation, endurance, patience, long-suffering, forbearance, acquiescence, submission.

  Antonyms: Maintenance, grasp, resistance, retention, rebellion, contention, reservation, holding, keeping, retaining, detention, murmuring, dissatisfaction, discontent, protestation.

- **Word:** Resolute (Synonym denoting Meaning: determined)

  Other Synonyms: Decided, fixed, steadfast, constant, persevering, firm, bold, unshaken, steady, undaunted, unflinching, stout-hearted.

  Antonyms: Irresolute, timid, hesitating, doubtful, ivavering, vacillating, capricious, variable, weak, undetermined, undecided.

- **Word:** Restive (Synonym denoting Meaning: restless)

  Other Synonyms: Fidgety, fretful, fractious, refractory, intractable, impatient, rebellious, skittish, resentful, recalcitrant, balky, vicious, unruly, stubborn, mulish, mutinous, obstinate.

  Antonyms: Docile, gentle, submissive, passive, quiet, tractable, yielding, obedient, manageable, peaceable.

- **Word:** Restrain (Synonym denoting Meaning: constrain)

  Other Synonyms: Hold in, check, repress, circumscribe, confine, curb, hinder, hold, hold back, restrict, suppress, withhold, bridle, abridge, keep back, keep down, keep in, keep under.

  Antonyms: Let loose, set free, release, arouse, aid, emancipate, animate, incite, excite, encourage, free, impel.

- **Word:** Result (Synonym denoting Meaning: consequence)

  Other Synonyms: Issue, conclusion, effect, end, event, termination, product, outcome, inference, deduction, resolution, determination.

  Antonyms: Cause, beginning, commencement, rise, origin, antecedent, prognostic, initiation, premonition, indication.

- **Word:** Revolution (Synonym denoting Meaning: lawlessness)

  Other Synonyms: Insurrection, revolt, riot, sedition, anarchy, rebellion, mutiny, confusion, disorder, tumult, disintegration.

  Antonyms: Government, submission, obedience, authority, control, command, dominion, domination, law, empire, rule, loyalty, supremacy, order.

- **Word:** Rich (Synonym denoting Meaning: wealthy)

  Other Synonyms: Opulent, affluent, supplied, abounding, abundant, copious, bountiful, fertile, productive, valued, sumptuous, precious, costly, high-seasoned, luscious, vivid.

  Antonyms: Poor, indigent, needy, impoverished, destitute, impecunious, penniless, lacking, scanty, scarce, meager, barren, sterile, trivial, worthless, unproductive, fruitless, paltry, valueless, dull, tame, dry.

- **Word:** Righteous (Synonym denoting Meaning: holy)

  Other Synonyms: Uncorrupt, honest, equitable, rightful, upright, virtuous, just, good, conscientious.

  Antonyms: Unholy, corrupt, dishonest, unjust, wicked, evil, unscrupulous, vicious, false, unprincipled, profligate.

- **Word:** Robust (Synonym denoting Meaning: strong)

  Other Synonyms: Lusty, sinewy, muscular, hale, hearty, vigorous, forceful, healthy, sturdy, sound, violent, rude, rough.

  Antonyms: Puny, weak, delicate, frail, sickly, emaciated, thin, slender, gentle, mild, considerate, tender.

- **Word:** Rough (Synonym denoting Meaning: uneven)

  Other Synonyms: Uncut, boisterous, unpolished, coarse, disordered, shaggy, ragged, rude, uncivil, harsh, loud, offensive, tempestuous, stormy, rugged, knotty, craggy, gruff, incomplete, churlish, blunt.

  Antonyms: Smooth, plain, level, polished, flat, glossy, sleek, soft, mild, quiet, refined, tender, gentle, balmy.

- **Word:** Rude (Synonym denoting Meaning: rough)

  Other Synonyms: Uneven, shapeless, rugged, uncouth, inelegant, rustic, vulgar, raw, clownish, unskillful, untaught, illiterate, ignorant, uncivil, impolite, saucy, impudent, insolent, surly, uncivilised, brutal, barbarous, savage, violent, fierce, tumultuous, impetuous, boisterous, inclement, severe.

  Antonyms: Polite, urbane, accomplished, cultivated, courteous, refined, civil, affable, courtly, gracious, elegant, polished, obliging, modest, bashful, considerate, serene, placid, genial, calm, fashionable, modern, civilised, modish.

- **Word:** Rugged (Synonym denoting Meaning: rough)

  Other Synonyms: Uneven, rude, wrinkled, cragged, harsh, hard, crabbed, steep, precipitate, violent, sour, surly, boisterous, tumultuous, stormy, inclement, tempestuous, austere, severe, ruffled, blunt.

Antonyms: Smooth, even, gentle, soft, low, pleasant, kindly, balmy, soothing, complaisant, mild.

S

- **Word:** Sacred (Synonym denoting Meaning: holy)

  Other Synonyms: Angelic, blessed, cherished, consecrated, divine, enshrined, godly, hallowed, numinous, pious, pure, religious, revered, sacramental, saintly, sanctified, solemn, spiritual, venerable.

  Antonyms: Civil, earthly, laic, lay, material, materialistic, non-clerical, nonreligious, profane, state, temporal, unsacred, worldly.

- **Word:** Sad (Synonym denoting Meaning: unhappy)

  Other Synonyms: Bereaved, bitter, blue, cheerless, dejected, depressed, despairing, despondent, disconsolate, dismal, distressed, doleful, down, downcast, forlorn, gloomy, glum, grief-stricken, grieved, heartbroken, heartsick, heavy-hearted, hurting, in doldrums, in grief.

  Antonyms: August, beautiful, bright, brilliant, celebrated, dazzling, delightful, distinguished, effulgent, elevated, eminent, enjoyable, esteemed, exalted, excellent, famed, famous, fine, gorgeous, grand, gratifying, great, heavenly, heroic, honoured.

- **Word:** Saddle (Synonym denoting Meaning: encumber)

  Other Synonyms: Afflict, bother, crush, cumber, depress, dish out, dump on, encumber, hamper, handicap, hinder, impede, lade, load, make heavy, obligate, oppress, overcharge, overload, overwhelm, pile, press, burden with, snow, snow under, strain, tax, trouble, try, vex, weigh down, worry.

  Antonyms: Absolve, deliver, discharge, disembarrass, disencumber, dismiss, dispense, excuse, exempt, free, let off, privilege, pull, release, spare, throw out, unburden, yank.

- **Word:** Sadism (Synonym denoting Meaning: viciousness)

  Other Synonyms: Barbarism, barbarity, bestiality,

bloodthirstiness, brutality, brutishness, callousness, coarseness, coldness, depravity, despotism, ferocity, fiendishness, fierceness, hardheartedness, harshness, inhumanity, insensibility, insensitiveness, malice, malignity, masochism, mercilessness.

Antonyms: Affection, agape, altruism, amity, attachment, benevolence, benignity, bountifulness, bounty, caritas, clemency, compassion, fellow feeling, generosity, goodness, goodwill, grace, humaneness, humanity, indulgence, kindliness, lenity, love, magnanimity, mercy.

- **Word:** Safe (Synonym denoting Meaning: protected)

  Other Synonyms: Buttoned down, buttoned up, cherished, fostered, guarded, home free, impervious, impregnable, in safety, intact, inviolable, invulnerable, maintained, OK, preserved, safeguarded, secure, sheltered, shielded, sitting pretty, snug, tended.

  Antonyms: Exposed, fluctuant, frail, hazardous, immature, insubstantial, loose, perilous, precarious, rickety, rocky, rootless, shaky, unguarded, unprotected, unreliable, unsafe, unshielded, unsound, unstable, unsteady, vacillating, vulnerable.

- **Word:** Safeguard (Synonym denoting Meaning: protection)

  Other Synonyms: Aegis, armament, armour, buffer, bulwark, convoy, escort, guard, palladium, screen, security, shield, surety, ward.

  Antonyms: Be careless, chance, chance it, compromise, expose, hazard, imperil, jeopardy, lay open, leave make liable, menace, peril, risk, threaten, venture.

- **Word:** Safety (Synonym denoting Meaning: protection)

  Other Synonyms: Assurance, cover, freedom, immunity, impregnability, inviolability, invulnerability, refuge, safeness, sanctuary, security, shelter.

  Antonyms: Crisis, double trouble, dynamite, emergency, endangerment, exigency, exposure, hot potato, insecurity, instability, jeopardy, menace, peril, pitfall, possibility.

- **Word:** Sacrifice (Synonym denoting Meaning: offering)

  Other Synonyms: Propitiation, expiation, thanksgiving, destruction, devotion, surrender, oblation, atonement.

  Antonyms: Offense, transgression, retention, reservation, acceptance.

- **Word:** Sad (Synonym denoting Meaning: mournful)

  Other Synonyms: Dejected, gloomy, depressed, sedate, cheerless, downcast, grievous, dull, grave, dark, somber, afflicted, calamitous, serious, staid, melancholy.

  Antonyms: Happy, Cheerful, joyous, glad, mirthful, jubilant, joviall, light- hearted, exultant, gay, exhilarated, happy, blithe.

- **Word:** Sagacious (Synonym denoting Meaning: sage)

  Other Synonyms: Sensible, keen, discerning, clear-sighted, apt, acute, intelligent, sharp, wise, rational, shrewd, able, keen-sighted, keen-witted, perspicacious, quick-scented, sharp-witted.

  Antonyms: Obtuse, senseless, irrational, silly, stupid, simple, un- intelligent, undiscerning, dull, absurd, foolish, futile, ignorant.

- **Word:** Salient (Synonym denoting Meaning: leaping)

  Other Synonyms: Bounding, jumping, projecting, prominent, conspicuous, noticeable, significant, strategic.

  Antonyms: Retreating, retiring, low-lying, unimportant, inconspicuous, unnoticeable, minor, inconsiderable, subordinate, in- significant.

- **Word:** Sanction (Synonym denoting Meaning: authorization)

  Other Synonyms: Authority, countenance, ratification, confirmation, approbation, approval, support, seal, allowance.

  Antonyms: Discountenance, disallowance, unauthorization, cancellation, nullification, disapproval, non-support.

- **Word:** Savage (Synonym denoting Meaning: wild)

  Other Synonyms: Uncultivated, untamed, uncivilised, rude, brutish, brutal, barbarous, cruel, inhuman, fierce, pitiless, merciless, atrocious, ferocious, murderous, violent.

Antonyms: Tame, civilised, cultivated, domesticated, tender, refined, polished, gentle, humane, considerate, pitiful, merciful, protective, generous, subdued, chivalrous, clement, self-controlled.

- **Word:** Save (Synonym denoting Meaning: preserve)

  Other Synonyms: Rescue, deliver, lay up, reserve, keep, spare, prevent, protect, be economical, hoard, husband, obviate, snatch, catch.

  Antonyms: Lose, destroy, abandon, imperil, expose, endanger, risk, hazard, waste, lavish, spend, fling away.

- **Word:** Say (Synonym denoting Meaning: utter)

  Other Synonyms: Express, tell, speak, declare, repeat, rehearse, recite, assert, mention, suggest, suppose, answer, respond, reply, state, pronounce, affirm, deny, allege.

  Antonyms: Silence, hush, whisper, mumble, be taciturn, suppress, repress, mispronounce.

- **Word:** Scheme (Synonym denoting Meaning: plan)

  Other Synonyms: Project, contrivance, design, purpose, plot, device, system, outline, machination, intrigue, stratagem, cabal, conspiracy, theory.

  Antonyms: Blunder, derangement, Disarrangement, bungle, botch.

- **Word:** Science (Synonym denoting Meaning: study of facts)

  Other Synonyms: Literature, art, knowledge, truth, facts, skill, ex- pertness, comprehension, information, investigation, experimentation, learning, experience.

  Antonyms: Ignorance, error, smattering, fallacy, inexperience, unfamiliarity, incomprehension.

- **Word:** Scrupulous (Synonym denoting Meaning: cautious)

  Other Synonyms: Careful, conscientious, hesitating, exact, nice, questioning, unwilling, punctilious, precise, diffident, dubious.

Antonyms: Reckless, confident, careless, heedless, unwary, incautious, daring.

- **Word:** Secure (Synonym denoting Meaning: protective)

  Other Synonyms: Undisturbed, assured, heedless, inattentive, easy, un-anxious, trustful, insured, obtained, acquired, fast, firm, defended, guarded, protected, certain, sheltered, safe.

  Antonyms: Disturbed, endangered, imperiled, insecure, hazardous, anxious, distrustful, suspicious, careful, precarious, loose, drifting, doubtful, dubious.

- **Word:** Sedate (Synonym denoting Meaning: settled)

  Other Synonyms: Composed, calm, quiet, tranquil, still, serene, unruffled, undisturbed, contemplative, sober, serious, passive.

  Antonyms: Flighty, disturbed, uneasy, restless, excited, discomposed, agitated, indiscreet, active, moving, frivolous.

- **Word:** See (Synonym denoting Meaning: perceive)

  Other Synonyms: Behold, descry, view, observe, discern, understand, comprehend, watch, look after, interview, visit, associate, meet, accompany, escort, attend, heed, be attentive, gaze, glance at.

  Antonyms: Be blind, overlook, mistake, misunderstand, miscomprehend, pass, ignore, neglect, disregard, misconceive.

- **Word:** Send (Synonym denoting Meaning: sling)

  Other Synonyms: Throw, fling, hurl, lance, launch, propel, project, cast, dart, dispatch, discharge, drive, emit, forward, transmit, impel, dismiss, delegate, depute.

  Antonyms: Receive, keep, retain, hold, bring, carry, hand, get, give, convey.

- **Word:** Sense (Synonym denoting Meaning: understanding)

  Other Synonyms: Reason, cognition, apprehension, deduction, perception, feeling, recognition, discernment, reasoning, opinion, judgement, notion, meaning, import, signification.

Antonyms: Nonsense, misunderstanding, stupidity, non-apprehension, non-comprehension, stolidity, inertness, non-observance, fancy, folly, unsoundness.

- **Word:** Sentiment (Synonym denoting Meaning: thought)

  Other Synonyms: Opinion, notion, sensibility, feeling, susceptibility, impressibility, impression, conviction, emotion, maxim, saying, toast.

  Antonyms: Nonsense, conjecture, vacuity, assumption, prejudice, preconception.

- **Word:** Separate (Synonym denoting Meaning: disunite)

  Other Synonyms: Divide, sever, come between, part, disjoin, divorce, disengage, detach, sunder, withdraw, eliminate, remove, segregate.

  Antonyms: Unite, consolidate, integrate, connect, join, attach, link, weld, engage, wed, gather, convene, collect.

- **Word:** Set (Synonym denoting Meaning: place)

  Other Synonyms: Put, seat, fix, affix, attach, fasten, make stable or firm, obstruct, embarrass, determine upon, fix upon, plant, frame, stiffen, solidify, adjust, regulate, adapt, prepare, replace, spread, stud, variegate, value at, rate at, establish, furnish, prescribe, strengthen.

  Antonyms: Remove, uproot, transfer, eradicate, transplant, unsettle, weaken, soften, destroy, demolish, disperse, discard, denude, disarrange, divest, strip, under- or over-rate, abolish, frustrate.

- **Word:** Settle (Synonym denoting Meaning: regulate)

  Other Synonyms: Arrange, compose, decide, establish, still, calm, clear, restore, depress, sink, lower, make compact, harden, determine, adjust, make up, pacify, liquidate, balance, colonize, people.

Antonyms: Disturb, confuse, derange, agitate, unsettle, excite, uproot, overturn, obstruct, elevate, breakup, discompose, disorder, rise, ascend, move, aggravate.

- **Word:** Shade (Synonym denoting Meaning: shadow)

  Other Synonyms: Darkness, obscurity, screen, shelter, protection, body, spirit, ghost, umbrage, adumbration, degree, minuteness, seclusion.

  Antonyms: Light, illumination, sunshine, brightness, daylight, glare, radiance, exposure, publicity, quantity, amount.

- **Word:** Shame (Synonym denoting Meaning: disgrace)

  Other Synonyms: Reproach, dishonour, ignominy, degradation, contempt, infamy, diffidence, modesty, discredit, humiliation, abashment, decency, decorum.

  Antonyms: Fame, honour, glory, approval, renown, credit, impudence, indecency, immodesty, indecorum, impropriety.

- **Word:** Sharp (Synonym denoting Meaning: quick)

  Other Synonyms: Sagacious, witty, discerning, shrewd, ingenious, sour, acid, tart, acrid, biting, poignant, acrimonious, sarcastic, bitter, painful, afflictive, violent, fierce, ardent, fiery, acute, keen, trenchant, astute, subtle, penetrating, discriminating, inventive, piquant, se-vigilant, attentive, caustic, cutting, eager, hungry, thin, emaciated, shrill, high.

  Antonyms: Dull, blunt, slow, obtuse, undiscerning, sweet, honeyed, cloying, saccharine, mellow, soft, gentle, mild, tender, considerate, kindly, lenient, clement, uninventive, indifferent, sluggish, inactive, tame, characterless, spiritless, careless, inattentive, thick, generous, unexacting.

- **Word:** Short (Synonym denoting Meaning: brief)

  Other Synonyms: Contracted, inadequate, limited, scanty, insufficient, incomplete, imperfect, abrupt, petulant, quick, near, direct, straight, succinct, concise, condensed, compendious, terse, pithy, laconic, curt, sententious, severe, uncivil, narrow, destitute.

Antonyms: Long, protracted, extended, adequate, ample, sufficient, plentiful, abundant, copious, perfect, complete, civil, suave, complaisant, circuitous, indirect, tedious, prolix, verbose, extended, wordy, broad, provided for.

- **Word:** Show (Synonym denoting Meaning: exhibit)

  Other Synonyms: Present, display, tell, reveal, direct, conduct, clear, prove, manifest, explain, evince, bestow, confer, appear, look, seem, demonstrate, unfold, inform, teach, evidence.

  Antonyms: Conceal, hide, withhold, suppress, obscure, mystify, cloak, wrap, contradict, deny, refute, disprove, falsify, misinterpret.

- **Word:** Shrewd (Synonym denoting Meaning: keen)

  Other Synonyms: Critical, subtle, arch, astute, sagacious, acute, discerning, penetrating, malicious, evil, vicious, wily, artful, cunning, clever, sharp, able, discriminating, intelligent.

  Antonyms: Stolid, stupid, unintelligent, dull, thick, undiscerning, undiscriminating, plain, blank, blunt, frank, kindly, sincere, benevolent, fair, open.

- **Word:** Sight (Synonym denoting Meaning: vision)

  Other Synonyms: Show, representation, exhibition, faculty of seeing, view, visibility, spectacle, inspection, examination, opinion, judgement, perception, ken, cognizance, contemplation, survey, insight, appearance.

  Antonyms: Blindness, non-visibility, obscuration, non-appearance, oversight, neglect, disappearance, vanishing, impression, prejudice.

- **Word:** Significant (Synonym denoting Meaning: important)

  Other Synonyms: Suggestive, weighty, momentous, manifest, intimating, declarative, betokening, implying, meaning, denoting, telling, speaking, forcible, conspicuous.

  Antonyms: Insignificant, meaningless, inconspicuous, mute, inexpressive, expressionless, unsuggestive.

- **Word:** Simple (Synonym denoting Meaning: silly)

  Other Synonyms: Single, uncombined, plain, unadorned, mere, sincere, artless, unaffected, natural, direct, clear, perspicuous, credulous, foolish, humble, undistinguished, lowly, innocent, elementary.

  Antonyms: Complex, double, compound, combined, mixed, ornate, adorned, blended, fused, multiform, artful, affected, artificial, indirect, complicated, circuitous, skeptic, pragmatic, proud, haughty, distinguished, celebrated, various, organised, elaborate.

- **Word:** Sin (Synonym denoting Meaning: evil)

  Other Synonyms: Crime, guilt, offense, wickedness, fault, vice, criminality, misdeed, viciousness, ungodliness, wrong, wrong-doing, unrighteousness, iniquity, transgression, immorality, depravity, delinquency.

  Antonyms: Virtue, godliness, rectitude, uprightness, excellence, blamelessness, holiness, innocence, morality, integrity, purity, righteousness, right.

- **Word:** Singular (Synonym denoting Meaning: unexampled)

  Other Synonyms: Eminent, unprecedented, extraordinary, remarkable, uncommon, rare, unusual, peculiar, strange, odd, eccentric, fantastic, individual, unique, conspicuous, consummate, exceptional, particular, curious, queer.

  Antonyms: Common, everyday, ordinary, commonplace, general, universal, usual, regular, customary, frequent, numerous, unnoticeable, normal, typical, inconspicuous, humdrum.

- **Word:** Sink (Synonym denoting Meaning: subside)

  Other Synonyms: Drop, droop, decay, lower, lessen, submerge, immerse, engulf, depress, degrade, debase, diminish, fall, descend, decline, dwindle, decrease, weary, flag, abate, reduce, drown, attenuate.

  Antonyms: Rise, ascend, mount, increase, augment,

aggrandize, swell, flourish, exalt, heighten, promote, enhance, encourage, perpetuate.

- **Word:** Situation (Synonym denoting Meaning: site)

  Other Synonyms: Post, case, plight, state, location, position, place, office, condition, locality, seat, ground, spot, circumstance, predicament, category, employment, footing, aspect, birth, standing.

  Antonyms: Absence, dislodgment, displacement, non-assignment.

- **Word:** Skilful (Synonym denoting Meaning: expert)

  Other Synonyms: Dexterous, apt, handy, adroit, clever, deft, proficient, skilled, trained, accomplished, happy, ingenious, practiced, adept, masterly, cunning.

  Antonyms: Unskilled, clumsy, inexpert, unskillful, unintelligent, awkward, incompetent, unprepared, untrained, unable, un- taught, bungling, helpless, maladroit, shiftless.

- **Word:** Slippery (Synonym denoting Meaning: smooth)

  Other Synonyms: Glib, mutable, uncertain, fickle, inconstant, unstable, changeable, wanton, loose, unchaste, icy, glassy, insecure, perilous, unsafe, shifty, elusive, deceptive, evasive, unprincipled.

  Antonyms: Rough, firm, safe, secure, stable, constant, certain, dependable, upright, sincere, outright, trustworthy, sound.

- **Word:** Small (Synonym denoting Meaning: little)

  Other Synonyms: Diminutive, inconsiderable, inconsequential, trivial, insignificant, paltry, mean, incapable, unable, short, weak, slender, gentle, low, tiny, puny, unimportant, scanty, moderate, sordid, selfish, inferior, ungifted, unintelligent.

  Antonyms: Large, great, big, extensive, enormous, bulky, massive, weighty, ample, spacious, broad, strong, stout, generous, liberal, munificent, important, significant, notable, influential, distinguished, gifted, magnanimous, intelligent, intellectual, superior, competent.

- **Word:** Smart (Synonym denoting Meaning: acute)

  Other Synonyms: Quick, lively, brisk, clever, dashy, showy, pungent, pricking, keen, severe, poignant, vigorous, sharp, active, shrewd, efficient, witty, pretentious, spruce, fresh.

  Antonyms: Dull, heavy, blunt, obtuse, dense, stupid, aching, slow, inactive, sluggish, inefficient, shabby, dowdy, boorish, clownish.

- **Word:** Sober (Synonym denoting Meaning: abstinent)

  Other Synonyms: Abstemious, moderate, regular, steady, collected, quiet, cool, staid, somber, temperate, dispassionate, self-controlled, calm, self-possessed, solemn, sedate.

  Antonyms: Intemperate, intoxicated, drunk, impassioned, excited, heated, furious, passionate, unreasonable, immoderate, uncontrolled, agitated, extravagant, erratic, eccentric.

- **Word:** Solitude (Synonym denoting Meaning: loneliness)

  Other Synonyms: Solitariness, loneness, withdrawal, remoteness, destitution, absence, seclusion, retirement, desertion, retreat, wilderness, desert, privacy, isolation.

  Antonyms: Society, popularity, throng, crowd, intercourse, meeting, convening, populace, multitude.

- **Word:** Solution (Synonym denoting Meaning: disruption)

  Other Synonyms: Separation, breach, disentanglement, explanation, clearing up, resolution, disintegration, release, discharge, solvency, disconnection, discontinuance, key, answer.

  Antonyms: Union, amalgamation, conjunction, connection, combination, entanglement, complication, continuity, integration, obscurity, confusion, perplexity, mystification.

- **Word:** Soul (Synonym denoting Meaning: spirit)

  Other Synonyms: Life, courage, fire, ardor, vitality, animus, leader, inspirer, passion, fervour, affection, person, reason, intellect, emotions, ghost, specter.

Antonyms: Lifelessness, soullessness, body, coldness, irrationality.

- **Word:** Sound (Synonym denoting Meaning: noise)

  Other Synonyms: Note, tone, report, impulse, vibration Whole, unbroken, unharmed, free, perfect, healthy, firm, strong, solid, safe, correct, true, orthodox, deep, profound, undisturbed, right, legal, valid, entire, thorough, substantial, irrefutable.

  Antonyms: Silence, taciturnity, stillness, hush, lull, muteness, noise, Unsound, broken, partial, harmed, imperfect, soft, diseased, weak, mellow, unsafe, incorrect, untrue, heterodox, light, trivial, fragile, illegal, illegitimate, invalid, defective.

- **Word:** Spring (Synonym denoting Meaning: leap)

  Other Synonyms: Bound, jump, shoot, fly, dart, start, emerge, bend, warp, proceed, issue, result, burst, emanate, flow, rise, originate, germinate.

  Antonyms: Settle, alight, arrive, land, drop, end, terminate, debouch, finish, eventuate.

- **Word:** Stable (Synonym denoting Meaning: steady)

  Other Synonyms: Abiding, firm, strong, durable, fixed, established, constant, resolute, unwavering, secure, stanch, permanent, solid, lasting, perpetual, immobile, rigid.

  Antonyms: Vacillating, wavering, unsteady, toppling, weak, tottering, infirm, insecure, precarious, frail, unstable, transient, ephemeral, evanescent, vanishing, non-durable.

- **Word:** Stiff (Synonym denoting Meaning: rigid)

  Other Synonyms: Inflexible, strong, obstinate, pertinacious, rigorous, constrained, affected, unbending, starched, formal, ceremonious, difficult, punctilious, stately, austere, peremptory, inexorable, uncompromising.

  Antonyms: Flexible, pliant, un-affected, amenable, easy, yielding, affable, genial, unceremonious, informal, pliable, malleable, considerate, compromising.

- **Word:** Strange (Synonym denoting Meaning: outlandish)

  Other Synonyms: Wonderful, astonishing, marvelous, uncommon, irregular, queer, odd, eccentric; foreign, new, novel, unusual, reserved, distant, un- familiar, unaccustomed, inexperienced.

  Antonyms: Familiar, usual, common, general, universal, accustomed, ordinary, home, domestic, regular, customary, habitual, commonplace.

- **Word:** Strength (Synonym denoting Meaning: robustness)

  Other Synonyms: Toughness, hardness, stoutness, spirit, lustiness, puissance, authority, force, vigor, power, endurance, resistance, security, validity, firmness, invirtue, energy, nerve, sinew, fiber, soundness.

  Antonyms: Weakness, thinness, frailty, softness, delicacy, imbecility, feebleness, impotence, inability, insecurity, invalidity, wavering.

- **Word:** Studious (Synonym denoting Meaning: contemplative)

  Other Synonyms: Observant, sedulous, earnest, diligent, studied, absorbed, meditative, thoughtful, attentive, pondering, devoted, musing, cogitative, careful, literary, reflective, assiduous.

  Antonyms: Illiterate, unliterary, idle, indulgent, careless, inattentive, thoughtless, negligent, regardless, indifferent.

T

- **Word:** Tactile (Synonym denoting Meaning: real)

  Other Synonyms: Concrete, material, sensible, solid, substantial, palpable, tangible, touchable.

  Antonyms: Abstract, abstruse, airy, dim, eluding, elusive, ethereal, evading, evanescent, evasive, hypothetical, impalpable, imperceptible, imponderable, inappreciable, incorporeal, indeterminate, insensible, invisible, obscured, rare, shadowy, slender, slight.

- **Word:** Talkative (Synonym denoting Meaning: communicative)

  Other Synonyms: Articulate, big-mouthed, chattering, chatty, effusive, eloquent, fluent, gabbling, gabby, garrulous, gassy, glib, gossipy, long-winded, loose-lipped, loquacious.

  Antonyms: Bashful, clam, clammed up, close, close-mouthed, dried up, dummied up, hesitant, mum, quiet, reserved, restrained, shy, silent, taciturn, tight-lipped.

- **Word:** Tall (Synonym denoting Meaning: exaggerated)

  Other Synonyms: Absurd, demanding, difficult, embellished, exorbitant, far-fetched, hard, implausible, impossible, outlandish, overblown, preposterous, steep, unbelievable, unreasonable.

  Antonyms: Abbreviate, abbreviated, aphoristic, bare, boiled down, brief, compendious, compressed, concise, condensed, curtailed, cut short, decreased, diminished, epigrammatic, fleeting, laconic, lessened, little, momentary, not protracted.

- **Word:** Tally (Synonym denoting Meaning: add-up)

  Other Synonyms: Catalogue, compute, count, enumerate, inventory, keep score, mark, mark down, number, numerate, reckon, record, register, sum, tale, tell, total, write down.

  Antonyms: Abstract, allow, bate, cut back, decrease by, diminish, discount, drawback, knock off, lessen, rebate, reduce, remove, subtract, take, take off, withdraw.

- **Word:** Tame (Synonym denoting Meaning: domesticated)

  Other Synonyms: Amenable, biddable, bridled, broken, busted, civilised, compliant, cultivated, disciplined, docile, domestic, fearless, gentle, harmless, harnessed, housebroken, kindly, manageable, mastered, meek, mild, muzzled, obedient.

  Antonyms: Agrarian, barbarian, barbaric, barbarous, dense, desert, deserted, desolate, escaped, feral, ferocious, fierce, free, indigenous, lush, luxuriant, native, natural, neglected, overgrown, overrun, primitive, rampant, rude, savage, unbroken, uncivilized.

- **Word:** Tasty (Synonym denoting Meaning: delicious)

  Other Synonyms: Appetising, delectable, delish, divine, flavourful, flavoursome, flavoury, full-flavoured, good-tasting, heavenly, luscious, mellow, palatable, piquant, pungent, sapid.

  Antonyms: Abominable, bitter, detestable, disagreeable, dislikeable, displeasing, flat, flavourless, galling, grievous, gross, hateful, icky, insipid, loathsome, nauseous, objectionable, obnoxious, odious, offensive, painful, repellent, repugnant.

- **Word:** Tear (Synonym denoting Meaning: cut)

  Other Synonyms: Break, claw, cleave, crack, damage, divide, extract, fray, frazzle, gash, grab, impair, incise, injure, lacerate, mangle, mutilate, pluck, pull, pull apart, rend, ribbon, rift.

  Antonyms: Accompany, add, adhere, affix, agglutinate, annex, append, assemble, associate, attach, blend, bracket, cement, clamp, clasp, clip, coadunate, coalesce, combine, compound, concrete, conjoin, conjugate, connect, copulate, couple, entwine.

- **Word:** Taciturn (Synonym denoting Meaning: mute)

  Other Synonyms: Silent, speechless, reserved, close, dumb, un-communicative, reticent.

  Antonyms: Communicative, free, garrulous, loquacious, talkative, unreserved.

- **Word:** Take (Synonym denoting Meaning: lay hold)

  Other Synonyms: Seize, grasp, obtain, capture, fasten on, attack, gain, captivate, charm, choose, turn to, employ, use, demand, require, copy, delineate, assume, adopt, acquire, engage in, indulge in, carry, convey, conduct, remove, withdraw, deduct, acknowledge.

  Antonyms: Drop, reject, abandon, surrender, miss, lose, repel, refuse, decline, repulse, spurn.

- **Word:** Talent (Synonym denoting Meaning: ability)

  Other Synonyms: Gift, endowment, genius, faculty, capacity, cleverness, aptitude, forte.

Antonyms: Inability, ineptitude, incompetence, imbecility, stupidity.

- **Word:** Tangible (Synonym denoting Meaning: perceptible)

  Other Synonyms: Tactile, palpable, apprehensible, evident, manifest, clear, material, substantial, sensible, obvious.

  Antonyms: Impalpable, spiritual, intangible, incorporeal, immaterial, incomprehensible.

- **Word:** Taste (Synonym denoting Meaning: savour)

  Other Synonyms: Relish, flavour, sensibility, judgement, discernment, nicety, perception, zest, choice, elegancy, refinement.

  Antonyms: Disrelish, insipidity, ill-savour, coarseness, indelicacy, non-perception, indiscrimination.

- **Word:** Tasteful (Synonym denoting Meaning: delicate)

  Other Synonyms: Artistic, elegant, dainty, esthetic, exquisite, fastidious, fine, chaste, nice, tasty, delicious, esthetical.

  Antonyms: Coarse, rough, rude, harsh, hideous, clumsy, deformed, displeasing, fulsome, gaudy, grotesque, distasteful, horrid, inartistic, in-harmonious, meretricious, offensive, ragged, tawdry.

- **Word:** Teach (Synonym denoting Meaning: tutor)

  Other Synonyms: Discipline, instruct, tutor, school, train, educate, en-lighten, drill, inculcate, give lessons, give instructions, inform, initiate, in-still, nurture.

  Antonyms: Learn, study, practice, investigate, experiment, try, develop, receive, drink in, acquire, attain, imbibe, under- stand, glean, gather, collect.

- **Word:** Tedious (Synonym denoting Meaning: wearisome)

  Other Synonyms: Fatiguing, irksome, tiresome, prolix, dull, slow, monotonous, tiring, trying.

  Antonyms: Interesting, exciting, amusing, charming, delightful, stirring, bright, entertaining.

- **Word:** Temerity (Synonym denoting Meaning: audacity)

  Other Synonyms: Foolhardiness, rashness, presumption, recklessness, hardihood, hastiness, heedlessness, precipitation, overconfidence, precipitancy.

  Antonyms: Care, caution, hesitation, cowardice, timidity, wariness, circumspection.

- **Word:** Tendency (Synonym denoting Meaning: proneness)

  Other Synonyms: Drift, aim, disposition, direction, course, influence, inclination, leaning, bent, bias, proclivity, aptitude, propensity, liability.

  Antonyms: Aversion, repulsion, repugnance, opposition, reluctance, divergence, tangency, deviation.

- **Word:** Tender (Synonym denoting Meaning: effeminate)

  Other Synonyms: Soft, sensitive, compassionate, humane, kind, merciful, pitiful, dear, delicate, gentle, mild, susceptible.

  Antonyms: Hard, pitiless, callous, careless, rough, coarse, unkind, inhuman, unmerciful, unfeeling, hardy, strong, sturdy.

- **Word:** Tension (Synonym denoting Meaning: strain)

  Other Synonyms: Stretch, effort, stretching, tenseness, rigor, severity, harshness, stiff-ness, tightness.

  Antonyms: Relaxation, release, relief, laxity, slackness, looseness.

- **Word:** Termination (Synonym denoting Meaning: limit)

  Other Synonyms: End, conclusion, bound, result, completion, consequence, effect, fulfilment, consummation, accomplishment, achievement, finis, finality, exit, issue.

  Antonyms: Beginning, initiation, inception, commencement, rise start, origin, source, cause, process, course.

- **Word:** Terrible (Synonym denoting Meaning: terrific)

  Other Synonyms: Fearful, horrible, shocking, awful, formidable, frightful, tremendous, astounding, startling.

Antonyms: Insignificant, amusing, pleasing.

- **Word:** Theory (Synonym denoting Meaning: hypothesis)

  Other Synonyms: Speculation, doctrine, conjecture, explanation, assumption, scheme, postulate, plan, science, philosophy, exposition, rationale, supposition.

  Antonyms: fact, truth, verity, actuality.

- **Word:** Thick (Synonym denoting Meaning: dense)

  Other Synonyms: Close, compact, solid, coarse, gross, muddy, turbid, misty, crowded, abundant, indistinct, dull, numerous, inarticulate.

  Antonyms: Thin, rare, sparse, infrequent, pure, limpid, crystal-line, clear, distinct, incompact, shallow, articulate.

- **Word:** Think (Synonym denoting Meaning: cogitate)

  Other Synonyms: Contemplate, remember, reflect, muse, meditate, ponder, consider, deliberate, judge, conclude, believe, purpose, intend, design, mean, presume, venture, imagine, apprehend.

  Antonyms: Guess, hazard, dream, idle, stargaze, wander, rove.

- **Word:** Thought (Synonym denoting Meaning: imagination)

  Other Synonyms: Fancy, conceit, notion, consideration, supposition, contemplation, de-liberation, reflection, cogitation, meditation, conception, solicitude, care, concern, reasoning, idea, opinion, concept, judgement, purpose, intention, provision.

  Antonyms: Thoughtlessness, giddiness, carelessness, inconsideration, dreaminess, dullness, stupidity, rashness, impulsiveness, vacuity, dream, hallucination, aberration.

- **Word:** Thrifty (Synonym denoting Meaning: economical)

  Other Synonyms: Saving, careful, sparing, frugal, industrious, prosperous, thriving, provident, foresighted.

  Antonyms: Wasteful, prodigal, un- economical, lavish, spendthrift, extravagant, slack, improvident, unprepared.

- **Word:** Tidings (Synonym denoting Meaning: message)

  Other Synonyms: Information, intelligence, news, rumor, report, advices, announcement.

  Antonyms: Suppression, censorship, misinformation, canard.

- **Word:** Timid (Synonym denoting Meaning: fearful)

  Other Synonyms: Timorous, cowardly, afraid, pusillanimous, faint-hearted, shrinking, retiring, shy, diffident, bashful.

  Antonyms: Bold, confident, venturesome, courageous, adventurous, heedless.

- **Word:** Tolerable (Synonym denoting Meaning: endurable)

  Other Synonyms: Bearable, supportable, passable, medium, ordinary, mediocre, indifferent.

  Antonyms: Intolerable, unendurable, insufferable, unbearable, insupportable.

- **Word:** Total (Syncnym denoting Meaning: sum)

  Other Synonyms: Whole, full, absolute, complete, undivided.

  Antonyms: Partial, imperfect, incomplete, divided, fractional, sectional.

- **Word:** Tragedy (Synonym denoting Meaning: sad happening)

  Other Synonyms: Mournful drama, catastrophe, calamity, adversity, disaster, affliction.

  Antonyms: Comedy, mirthful drama, prosperity, luck, good fortune.

- **Word:** Transaction (Synonym denoting Meaning: business)

  Other Synonyms: Action, deed, proceeding, doing, affair, act, negotiation, performance.

  Antonyms: Inactivity, quiescence, rest, neglect, inaction, passivity.

- **Word:** Transient (Synonym denoting Meaning: fleeting)

  Other Synonyms: Temporary, transitory, ephemeral,

evanescent, brief, flitting, flying, momentary, passing, fugitive, short.

Antonyms: Permanent, perpetual, lasting, enduring, abiding, immortal, everlasting, unfading, undying, persistent, eternal, imperishable.

- **Word:** Transparent (Synonym denoting Meaning: translucent)

  Other Synonyms: Pellucid, clear, lucid, diaphanous, open, porous, crystalline, limpid, bright, perspicuous.

  Antonyms: Opaque, thick, turbid, mysterious, questionable, dubious.

- **Word:** Treasure (Synonym denoting Meaning: richnees)

  Other Synonyms: Wealth, aplenty, money, jewels, cash, valuables, hoard, riches, bullion, reserve.

  Antonyms: Refuse, trash, offal, dregs, trifles.

- **Word:** Trial (Synonym denoting Meaning: attempt)

  Other Synonyms: Endeavour, essay, effort, exertion, experience, proof, test, examination, experiment, criterion, ordeal, assay, temptation, trouble, affliction, distress, grief, suffering, tribulation.

  Antonyms: Non-attempt, ease, acceptance, oversight, disregard, trifle, triviality.

- **Word:** Trick (Synonym denoting Meaning: stratagem)

  Other Synonyms: Wile, fraud, cheat, juggle, finesse, sleight, deception, imposture, delusion, imposition, artifice, machination, contrivance, legerdemain.

  Antonyms: Exposure, revelation, examination, blunder, botch, bungling, fumbling, mishap, genuineness, artlessness, openhandedness.

- **Word:** Triumph (Synonym denoting Meaning: success,)

  Other Synonyms: Conquest, victory, ovation, celebration, jubilee, jubilation, exultation, achievement, attainment.

Antonyms: Defeat, failure, disappointment, discomfiture, abortion, baffling.

- **Word:** Trouble (Synonym denoting Meaning: affliction)

  Other Synonyms: Sorrow, disturbance, perplexity, vexation, molestation, annoyance, inconvenience, calamity, misfortune, adversity, misery, tribulation, distress, disaster, torment, difficulty, anxiety.

  Antonyms: Blessing, peace, composure, alleviation, appeasement, pleasure, fortune, boon, affluence, happiness, joy, success, gladness, ease, facility, amusement, recreation.

- **Word:** True (Synonym denoting Meaning: correct)

  Other Synonyms: Accurate, precise, exact, unwavering, faithful, loyal, actual, pure, real, genuine, veritable.

  Antonyms: Untrue, false, fictitious, unreliable, incorrect, inaccurate, inexact, vacillating, disloyal, faithless, counterfeit, impure, unreal, factitious, untrustworthy, adulterated, spurious, fickle, treacherous.

- **Word:** Truth (Synonym denoting Meaning: fact)

  Other Synonyms: Reality, fidelity, conformity, exactness, steadfastness, veracity, verity, accuracy, precision, faithfulness.

  Antonyms: Falsehood, falsity, lie, untruth, fabrication, fiction, fallacy, mistake, sophism.

- **Word:** Tumult (Synonym denoting Meaning: ferment)

  Other Synonyms: Disturbance, turbulence, disorder, bluster, hubbustle, brawl, riot, excitement, distraction, confusion, turmoil, noise.

  Antonyms: Peace, order, orderliness, pacification, quiet, subsidence.

- **Word:** Turn (Synonym denoting Meaning: revolution)

  Other Synonyms: Alteration, vicissitude, winding, bending, meandering, stroll, succession, alternation, chance, occasion, convenience, purpose, form, cast, shape, manner, fashion, rotation, recurrence, opportunity, deed, office, treatment, act, tendency.

Antonyms: Fixity, unchangeableness, immobility, uniformity, stability, continuity, independence, malformation, shapelessness.

- **Word:** Turn (Synonym denoting Meaning: revolve)

  Other Synonyms: Reverse, deflect, change, divert, transfer, use, employ, apply, devote, alter, metamorphose, transform, convert, shape, mold, adapt, whirl, hinge, depend, eventuate, issue, terminate.

  Antonyms: Stick, stop, remain, adhere, hold to, persist, continue, perpetuate, arrest, stereotype.

- **Word:** Twist (Synonym denoting Meaning: contort)

  Other Synonyms: Writhe, convolve, pervert, distort, wind, wreathe, insinuate, encircle.

  Antonyms: Straighten, untwist, rectify, unwind, disentangle, unravel, verify, substantiate.

- **Word:** Type (Synonym denoting Meaning: mark)

  Other Synonyms: Stamp, sign, emblem, style, semblance, representation, similitude, figure, symbol, token, character, pattern, archetype, model, norm, cast, mold, fashion.

  Antonyms: Caricature, monstrosity, abnormity, falsification, deviation, misrepresentation.

U

- **Word:** Unable (Synonym denoting Meaning: inept)

  Other Synonyms: Clumsy, helpless, hog-tied, impotent, impuissant, inadequate, incapable, incapacitated, incompetent, ineffectual, inefficacious, inefficient, inept, inoperative, no.

  Antonyms: Able, adept, adequate, adroit, alert, bright, capable, cleft, competent, cunning, dexterous, easy, effortless, endowed, equipped, facile, fitted, good, intelligent, knowing.

- **Word:** Unacceptable (Synonym denoting Meaning: unsatisfactory)

  Other Synonyms: Mickey Mouse, below par, crappy, damaged, disagreeable, displeasing, distasteful, exceptionable, half-assed, half-baked, ill-favoured, improper, inadmissible, insupportable, lemon, lousy, objectionable, obnoxious, offensive, reject, repugnant.

  Antonyms: Adequate, admissible, all right, average, big, close, common, cool, decent, delightful, ducky, fair, far out, groovy, hip, hunky-dory, ice, kosher, large, okay.

- **Word:** Unaccustomed (Synonym denoting Meaning: not prepared)

  Other Synonyms: Green, ignorant, incompetent, inexperienced, new, newcomer, novice, unacquainted, unfamiliar with, uninformed, uninstructed, unseasoned, unskilled, untaught, untrained, unused to, unversed in.

  Antonyms: Acquainted, adapted, addicted, confirmed, disciplined, exercised, familiar, given to, grooved, habituated, habituated in, inured, seasoned, settled in, trained.

- **Word:** Unadulterated (Synonym denoting Meaning: complete)

  Other Synonyms: Complete, consummate, downright, entire, flat out, free, full, infinite, outright, plenary, sheer, simple, straight out, supreme, thorough, total, unabridged, absolute, unconditional, unlimited, unqualified, unrestricted, pure, utter, without limit.

  Antonyms: Attenuated, blended, contaminated, corrupt, defiled, degraded, depreciated, deteriorated, devalued, diluted, dissolved, impaired, mixed, polluted, tainted, thinned, vitiated, watered down, weakened.

- **Word:** Unaffected (Synonym denoting Meaning: honest)

  Other Synonyms: Artless, candid, direct, folksy, forthright, frank, genuine, guileless, homey, ingenuous, modest, naive, natural, plain, simple, sincere, single, spontaneous.

Antonyms: Afflicted, altered, changed, compassionate, concerned, damaged, distressed, excited, grieved, hurt, impaired, impressed, influenced, injured, overwhelmed.

- **Word:** Unavoidable (Synonym denoting Meaning: certain)

  Other Synonyms: Certain, compulsory, fated, impending, ineluctable, ineludible, inescapable, inevasible, inevitable, inexorable, locked up, obligatory, set, sure, inescapable.

  Antonyms: Accidental, additional, avoidable, casual, causeless, chance, dispensable, excess, exorbitant, expendable, extraneous, extrinsic, fortuitous, futile, gratuitous, haphazard, inessential, irrelevant, lavish, needless, non-compulsory, nonessential.

- **Word:** Unaware (Synonym denoting Meaning: ignorant)

  Other Synonyms: Blind, careless, caught napping, daydreaming, dead to, deaf, deaf to, doped, forgetful, heedless, ignorant, inattentive, incognizant, insensible, mooning, negligent, not cognizant, oblivious, out cold, spaced out, spacey, stoned, strung out.

  Antonyms: Acquainted, aesthetic, alive to, apprised, assured, attentive, au courant, awake, aware, certain, cognizant, conversant, discerning, felt, informed, keen, knowing, known, mindful, noticing, noting, observing, on to, passable, perceiving, percipient.

- **Word:** Unbroken (Synonym denoting Meaning: continuous)

  Other Synonyms: Ceaseless, constant, deep, endless, entire, even, fast, incessant, intact, perfect, perpetual, profound, progressive, regular, solid, sound, successive, total, undisturbed.

  Antonyms: Alternate, arrested, broken, checked, cyclic, cyclical, discontinuing, discontinuous, epochal, every other, fitful, infrequent, interrupted, isochronal, iterant.

- **Word:** Uncomfortable (Synonym denoting Meaning: painful)

  Other Synonyms: Afflictive, annoying, awkward, bitter, cramped, difficult, disagreeable, distressing, dolorous, excruciating, galling, grievous, hard, harsh, ill-fitting.

Antonyms: Acceptable, accommodating, adaptable, adapted, advantageous, agreeable, aiding, appropriate, assisting, available, beneficial, comfortable, conducive, contributive, decent, favourable, fit, fitted, good, handy, opportune, proper.

- **Word:** Union (Synonym denoting Meaning: one)

  Other Synonyms: Coalition, conjunction, juncture, unification, combination, junction, oneness, unity.

  Antonyms: Analysis, disconnection, disunion, divorce, separation, contrariety, disjunction, division, schism, severance decomposition, dissociation.

- **Word:** Usual (Synonym denoting Meaning: common)

  Other Synonyms: Accustomed, everyday, general, ordinary, public, common, familiar, habitual, prevailing, regular, customary, frequent, normal, prevalent, wonted.

  Antonyms: Exceptional, infrequent, rare, strange, unparalleled, extraordinary, out-of-the-way, singular, uncommon, unusual.

- **Word:** Utility (Synonym denoting Meaning: use)

  Other Synonyms: Advantage, expediency, serviceableness, avail, profit, use, benefit, service, usefulness.

  Antonyms: Disadvantage, futility, inadequacy, inutility, uselessness, folly, inexpediency, worthlessness.

- **Word:** Ugly (Synonym denoting Meaning: one who is not beautiful)

  Other Synonyms: Loathsome, unsightly, repulsive, ill-natured, quarrelsome, unpleasant, plain, ordinary, homely, hideous, frightful, cross, vicious.

  Antonyms: Attractive, handsome, fair, pleasant, agreeable, beautiful, shapely, comely, lovely, kindly, good-natured, gentle.

- **Word:** Ultimate (Synonym denoting Meaning: final)

  Other Synonyms: Last, conclusive, farthest, extreme, most remote, elemental.

  Antonyms: Initial, nearest, beginning, primary.

- **Word:** Unction (Synonym denoting Meaning: anointing)

  Other Synonyms: Ointment, power, fervour, animation, fervency, ardor, enthusiasm, energy, spirit, emotion.

  Antonyms: tameness, coldness, lifelessness.

- **Word:** Understand (Synonym denoting Meaning: know)

  Other Synonyms: Comprehend, learn, be informed, hear, recognize, interpret, imply, assume, apprehend, discern, see, perceive, conceive, penetrate.

  Antonyms: Misunderstand, miscomprehend, misinterpret, declare, state, express, inform.

- **Word:** Understanding (Synonym denoting Meaning: sense)

  Other Synonyms: Intelligence, conception, perception, discernment, knowledge, intuition, cognition, reason, interpretation, mind, brains.

  Antonyms: Insensibility, stupidity, obtuseness, senselessness, slowness, irrationality, sluggishness, ignorance, unintelligence.

- **Word:** Undertake (Synonym denoting Meaning: engage)

  Other Synonyms: Enter, set about, attempt, covenant, contract, guarantee, promise, affirm, project, commence, stipulate.

  Antonyms: Abandon, drop, desist, discontinue, decline, complete, finish, end, terminate.

- **Word:** Undertaking (Synonym denoting Meaning: enterprise)

  Other Synonyms: Engagement, attempt, adventure, business, effort, endeavour, venture, interest, affair, matter, concern.

  Antonyms: Leisure, inactivity, recreation.

- **Word:** Undulation (Synonym denoting Meaning: waving motion)

  Other Synonyms: Vibration, wavy outline, pulsation, oscillation, swelling, wave, ripple.

  Antonyms: Equilibrium, standing, plain, table-land.

- **Word:** Uniform (Synonym denoting Meaning: unchanging)

  Other Synonyms: Equable, consistent, homogeneous, consonant, regular, constant, invariable, steady, similar, unvaried, alike.

  Antonyms: Heterogeneous, variable, varying, diverse, irregular, inconsistent, erratic, eccentric, unsymmetrical.

- **Word:** Union (Synonym denoting Meaning: unity)

  Other Synonyms: Connection, concord, combination, confederacy, alliance, coalition, conjunction, harmony, concert, agreement, league, confederation, consolidation, oneness, juncture, unification.

  Antonyms: Disconnection, separation, disjunction, disunion, divorce, severance, analysis, dissociation, contrariety, decomposition, division, schism, partition, discord, disagreement, secession, disruption, multiplication.

- **Word:** Unique (Synonym denoting Meaning: sole)

  Other Synonyms: Only, unmatched, unequalled, unparalleled, singular, peculiar, exceptional, rare.

  Antonyms: Common, universal, everyday, commonplace, ordinary, familiar, vulgar, mean.

- **Word:** Unison (Synonym denoting Meaning: harmony)

  Other Synonyms: Agreement, concord, union, accordance.

  Antonyms: Discord, variance, disagreement, divergence.

- **Word:** Unit (Synonym denoting Meaning: single)

  Other Synonyms: Oneness, unity, integral, item, individual.

  Antonyms: Sum, mass, total, aggregate, whole, collection.

- **Word:** Unite (Synonym denoting Meaning: add)

  Other Synonyms: Join, attach, combine, connect, agree, harmonise, associate, coalesce, incorporate, consolidate, amalgamate, blend, embody, merge, concur, league, confederate.

Antonyms: Disjoin, sever, separate, divide, resolve, disconnect, disintegrate, dissociate, sunder, diverge, multiply, split, disrupt.

- **Word:** Universal (Synonym denoting Meaning: common for everyone)

  Other Synonyms: General, unlimited, all-reaching, total, whole, entire, catholic, common, comprehensive, exhaustive, complete.

  Antonyms: Specific, special, individual, particular, limited, local, partial, exclusive, exceptional.

- **Word:** Upright (Synonym denoting Meaning: erect)

  Other Synonyms: Perpendicular, vertical, honest, just, honourable, conscientious, virtuous, good, faithful, true, trustworthy.

  Antonyms: Inclined, slanted, inverted, unprincipled, dishonest, unscrupulous, corrupt.

- **Word:** Uproar (Synonym denoting Meaning: tumult)

  Other Synonyms: Disturbance, confusion, bustle, clamor, commotion, turmoil, racket, noise, din.

  Antonyms: peace, calm, quiet, silence, order, tranquility.

- **Word:** Urge (Synonym denoting Meaning: animate)

  Other Synonyms: Instigate, stimulate, encourage, arouse, impel, press, drive, beseech, entreat, importune, goad, spur, incite, hasten, accelerate, expedite.

  Antonyms: Hold back, hinder, obstruct, prevent, retard, inhibit, restrain, defy, challenge, dare, oppose, object.

- **Word:** Urgent (Synonym denoting Meaning: urging)

  Other Synonyms: Pressing, importunate, immediate, important, imperative, grave, momentous, serious, cogent, solicitous, critical, emergency, necessitous.

  Antonyms: Trivial, insignificant, unimportant, immaterial, inconsiderable.

- **Word:** Use (Synonym denoting Meaning: benefit)

  Other Synonyms: Employment, application, occasion, necessity, usefulness, utility, practice, usage, custom, manner, habit, service, advantage, profit, avail, need.

  Antonyms: Uselessness, misapplication, worthlessness, disuse, non-observance, desuetude.

- **Word:** Useful (Synonym denoting Meaning: advantageous)

  Other Synonyms: Profitable, serviceable, beneficial, fruitful, effectual, suitable, effective, adapted, helpful, good, convenient, valuable, available.

  Antonyms: Useless, profitless, unprofitable, valueless, unserviceable, fruitless, ineffectual, unavailing, retarding, hindering, preventive, obstructive, cumbersome, burdensome, unusable.

- **Word:** Usual (Synonym denoting Meaning: familiar)

  Other Synonyms: Frequent, ordinary, regular, wonted, prevalent, accustomed, common, customary, everyday, general, normal, habitual, prevailing, public.

  Antonyms: Exceptional, infrequent, extraordinary, strange, unparalleled, unusual, out-of-the-way, singular, rare.

- **Word:** Utility (Synonym denoting Meaning: profit)

  Other Synonyms: Expediency, use, usefulness, avail, benefit, advantage, service.

  Antonyms: Futility, inutility, inadequacy, inexpediency, uselessness, folly, disadvantage, worthlessness.

- **Word:** Utter (Synonym denoting Meaning: issue)

  Other Synonyms: Deliver, liberate, discharge, circulate, pass, express, publish, disclose, speak, pronounce, promulgate, complete, perfect, total, entire, absolute, peremptory, unconditional, unqualified, thorough.

  Antonyms: Suppress, recall, check, stifle, hush, repress, retract, disavow incomplete, conditioned, qualified, partial.

V

- **Word:** Veracity (Synonym denoting Meaning: honesty)

  Other Synonyms: Candor, honesty, reality, truthfulness, frankness, ingenuousness, truth, verity.

  Antonyms: Deceit, duplicity, falsehood, fiction, lie, deception, error, falseness, guile, mendacity, delusion, fabrication, falsity, imposture, untruth.

- **Word:** Victory (Synonym denoting Meaning: win)

  Other Synonyms: Achievement, conquest, success, triumph advantage, mastery, supremacy.

  Antonyms: Defeat, disappointment, failure, miscarriage, retreat, destruction, disaster, frustration, overthrow, rout.

- **Word:** Vigilant (Synonym denoting Meaning: alert)

  Other Synonyms: Cautious, on the lookout, wary, awake, circumspect, sleepless, watchful, careful, on the alert, wakeful, wide-awake.

  Antonyms: Careless, heedless, inconsiderate, oblivious, drowsy, inattentive, neglectful, thoughtless, dull, incautious, negligent, unwary.

- **Word:** Virtue (Synonym denoting Meaning: chastity)

  Other Synonyms: Honesty, probity, truth, duty, honour, purity, uprightness, excellence, integrity, rectitude, virtuousness, faithfulness, justice, righteousness, worth, goodness, morality, rightness, worthiness.

  Antonyms: Evil, vice, viciousness, wickedness, wrong.

- **Word:** Vacate (Synonym denoting Meaning: empty)

  Other Synonyms: Abandon, abrogate, annul, clear, depart, discharge, dissolve, empty, evacuate, give up, go away, leave, move out, part with, quash, quit, relinquish, renounce, rescind, retract, reverse, revoke, void, withdraw.

  Antonyms: Be established, cover, dwell, ensconce, establish, fill, hold, inhabit, involve, keep, live in, maintain, own, people, permeate, pervade, populate, possess, remain, sit, stay, take up, tenant, use, utilize.

- **Word:** Vacuous (Synonym denoting Meaning: empty)

  Other Synonyms: Air-headed, bare, birdbrain, blank, clear, drained, dull, dumb, dumb bunny, dumbbell, dumdum, emptied, foolish, half-baked, inane, lamebrain, menus, nerdy, nobody home, nothing upstairs, nutty, shallow, silly, stark, stupid, superficial, uncomprehending, unfilled, unintelligent, unreasoning, vacant, void.

  Antonyms: Ablaze, aglow, alight, argent, beaming, blazing, brilliant, burning, burnished, coruscating, dazzling, effulgent, flashing, fulgent, glaring, gleaming, glistening, glittering, glossy, glowing, golden, illuminated, illumined, incandescent, intense.

- **Word:** Vague (Synonym denoting Meaning: indefinite)

  Other Synonyms: Ambiguous, amorphous, amphibological, bewildering, bleary, blurred, cloudy, dark, dim, doubtful, dreamlike, dubious, enigmatic, equivocal, faint, fuzzy, generalized, hazy, ill-defined, impalpable, imprecise, indefinite, indeterminate, indistinct.

  Antonyms: Bright, clarion, crystal, fair, fine, halcyon, light, luminous, pleasant, rainless, shining, shiny, sunny, sunshiny, unclouded.

- **Word:** Vale (Synonym denoting Meaning: hollow)

  Other Synonyms: Basin, bottom, canyon, channel, coulee, dale, dell, depression, dingle, glen, gorge, lowland, notch, plain, swale, trough, valley.

  Antonyms: Acclivity, Acropolis, ascent, bluff, bread-and-cheese, butte, cliff, climb, cradle hill, down, drift, dune, elevation, eminence, esker, fell, foothill, gradient, headland, heap, height, highland, hillock, hilltop, hummock, inclination, incline, knoll, mesa, mound, mount, pile, precipice, prominence, promontory, protuberance, range, ridge, rise, rising.

- **Word:** Valuable (Synonym denoting Meaning: priceless)

  Other Synonyms: Admired, appreciated, beneficial, cherished, collectible, costly, dear, esteemed, estimable, expensive, heirloom, held dear, helpful, high-priced, hot, hot property, important, in demand, inestimable, invaluable, of value, precious, prized.

  Antonyms: Abandoned, abject, barren, base, bogus, cheap, contemptible, counterproductive, despicable, empty, futile, good-for-nothing, ignoble, ineffective, ineffectual, inferior, insignificant, inutile, meaningless, mediocre, miserable.

- **Word:** Vanity (Synonym denoting Meaning: conceit)

  Other Synonyms: Affected way, affection, airs, arrogance, big-headedness, conceitedness, display, ego trip, egotism, narcissism, ostentation, pretension, pride, self-admiration, self-love, self-worship, show, showing off, smugness, vainglory.

  Antonyms: Abasement, bashfulness, demureness, diffidence, docility, fawning, inferiority complex, lowliness, meekness, modesty, mortification, non-resistance, obedience, obsequiousness, passiveness, reserve, resignation, self-abasement, self-abnegation.

- **Word:** Variety (Synonym denoting Meaning: difference)

  Other Synonyms: Array, assortment, change, collection, combo, conglomeration, cross-section, departure, discrepancy, disparateness, divergence, diversification, diversity, fluctuation, heterogeneity, incongruity, intermixture, many-sidedness, medley, miscellany, mishmash.

  Antonyms: Affinity, agreement, alikeness, analogousness, analogy, appearance, carbon, clone, comparableness, comparison, conformity, copy, counterpart, dead ringer, delineation, depiction, ditto, double, eequality, equivalence, facsimile, form, guise.

- **Word:** Ventilate (Synonym denoting Meaning: air out)

  Other Synonyms: Advertise, air, bring up, broach, broadcast, circulate, debate, deliberate, discourse, discuss, examine, express, free, give, go into, introduce, make known, moot, publish, put, rap, scrutinise, sift, state, take up, talk about, talk of, talk over, thresh out, vent, verbalize.

Antonyms: Banish, bar, blackball, close down, close up, curse, declare illegal, disallow, enjoin, exclude, halt, ice out, illegalize, inhibit, interdict, outlaw, pass by, pass up, prevent, prohibit, proscribe, restrict, shut out, suppress, taboo.

- **Word:** Vertical (Synonym denoting Meaning: upright)

  Other Synonyms: Bolt upright, cocked, erect, on end, perpendicular, plumb, sheer, steep, straight up, up-and-down, upward.

  Antonyms: Aligned, even, flush, level, lying, parallel, plane, recumbent, regular, smooth, straight, uniform.

- **Word:** Vacancy (Synonym denoting Meaning: job)

  Other Synonyms: Emptiness, leisure, intermission, idleness, vacuum, chasm, gap, interval, vacuity, space, void.

  Antonyms: Fullness, plethora, repletion, business, occupation, employment.

- **Word:** Vacillate (Synonym denoting Meaning: fluctuate)

  Other Synonyms: Waver, be unsteady, stagger, reel, sway, rock, hesitate, be inconstant, dubitate.

  Antonyms: Adhere, abide, determine, be steadfast, stay.

- **Word:** Vague (Synonym denoting Meaning: unsettled)

  Other Synonyms: Undetermined, indefinite, ambiguous, lax, uncertain, dim, doubtful, obscure, indistinct, unfixed, general, intangible, equivocal, pointless, unwarranted, unauthorized.

  Antonyms: Determined, limited:, strict, specific, pointed, definite, distinct, scientific, settled, clear, fixed, manifest, perspicuous.

- **Word:** Vain (Synonym denoting Meaning: futile)

  Other Synonyms: Trivial, vapid, visionary, worthless, abortive, unsatisfying, fruitless, empty, deceitful, baseless, delusive, bootless, idle, ineffectual, shadowy, trifling, unserviceable, unsubstantial, profitless, inconstant, unprofitable, null, nugatory, un-availing.

Antonyms: Adequate, solid, useful, effective, powerful, worthy, important, sufficient, service-able, potent, competent, advantageous, beneficial, efficient, ear pedient, profitable, real, sound, substantial, valid, valuable, essential, cogent, availing, satisfactory, modest.

- **Word:** Valid (Synonym denoting Meaning: sound)

  Other Synonyms: Good, justified, trustworthy, well-grounded, efficacious, weighty, powerful, efficient, conclusive, logical, solid, cogent, important, grave, substantial, sufficient.

  Antonyms: Weak, invalid, null, void, unsound, baseless, fallacious, unfounded, untrue, unavailable, inoperative, superseded.

- **Word:** Value (Synonym denoting Meaning: worth)

  Other Synonyms: Utility, desirability, importance, power, import, signification, esteem, regard, excellence, price, cost, equivalent, rate, appraise, estimate, appreciate, prize, treasure, account.

  Antonyms: Reduction, depreciation, cheapen, reduce, contemn, despise, undervalue, underestimate, disregard, disesteem.

- **Word:** Vanity (Synonym denoting Meaning: pride)

  Other Synonyms: Conceit, unreality, emptiness, hollowness, triviality, futility, falsity, egoism, self-sufficiency, show, ostentation.

  Antonyms: Reality, truth, worth, simplicity, modesty, humility, self -distrust, substance, solidity.

- **Word:** Vanquish (Synonym denoting Meaning: conquer)

  Other Synonyms: Overcome, subdue, defeat, surmount,

confute, silence, subjugate, over- throw, master, foil, discomfit, quell, disprove, confound.

Antonyms: Succumb, yield, fail.

- **Word:** Vast (Synonym denoting Meaning: wide)

  Other Synonyms: Spacious, huge, immense, great, mighty, transcendent, measureless, boundless, colossal, enormous, stupendous, prodigious, gigantic, monstrous, remarkable, extraordinary.

  Antonyms: Moderate, limited, confined, circumscribed, narrow, close, small.

- **Word:** Vehemence (Synonym denoting Meaning: impetuosity)

  Other Synonyms: Violence, fury, frenzy, ardor, fervour, fervency, warmth, zeal, enthusiasm, passion, force, intensity.,

  Antonyms: Passivity, inertia, quiescence, coldness, stoicism, indifference, unconcern, apathy, inattention.

- **Word:** Vehement (Synonym denoting Meaning: raging)

  Other Synonyms: Hot, ardent, fervid, burning, passionate, eager, violent, impetuous, furious, urgent, mighty, forcible, powerful, sanguine, enthusiastic.

  Antonyms: Cool, impassive, indifferent, feeble, mild, controlled, subdued, cold, stoical, passionless, weak, inanimate.

- **Word:** Velocity (Synonym denoting Meaning: speed)

  Other Synonyms: Celerity, fleetness, rapidity, speed, swiftness, impetus, momentum.

  Antonyms: Inertia, sluggishness, inertness, resistance, passivity, languor, inactivity.

- **Word:** Venom (Synonym denoting Meaning: virus)

  Other Synonyms: Bane, poison, Bpite, malice, malignity, hate, ill will, maliciousness, rancor, grudge, bitterness, acrimony.

  Antonyms: Medicine, remedy, benevolence, kindness, good will.

- **Word:** Veracious (Synonym denoting Meaning: true)

  Other Synonyms: Truthful, reliable, trustworthy, straightforward, honest, credible.

  Antonyms: False, deceitful, mendacious, lying, dishonest, perfidious.

- **Word:** Veracity (Synonym denoting Meaning: honesty)

  Other Synonyms: Truthfulness, reality, candor, truth, frankness, verity, exactness, correctness, accuracy.

  Antonyms: Deception, duplicity, falsehood, fiction, guile, mendacity, untruth, lie, delusion, fabrication, deceit, error, falseness, falsity, imposture.

- **Word:** Verify (Synonym denoting Meaning: prove)

  Other Synonyms: Correct, establish, confirm, authenticate, affirm, corroborate, attest, fulfil, demonstrate, warrant.

  Antonyms: Falsify, misrepresent, subvert, misstate, fail, disestablish, mistake.

- **Word:** Versatile (Synonym denoting Meaning: flexible)

  Other Synonyms: Changeable, inconsistent, variable, many-sided, capricious, erratic, fickle, unstable, mobile, plastic, ready.

  Antonyms: Fixed, uniform, immobile, immutable, unvaried.

- **Word:** Vexation (Synonym denoting Meaning: chagrin)

  Other Synonyms: Agitation, mortification, uneasiness, grief, trouble, sorrow, distress, irritation, displeasure, affliction, plague, torment.

  Antonyms: Pleasure, enjoyment, gratification, satisfaction.

- **Word:** Vice (Synonym denoting Meaning: crime)

  Other Synonyms: Sin, fault, iniquity, defect, error, blemish, imperfection, immorality, depravity, wickedness, evil, corruption.

  Antonyms: Virtue, goodness, perfection, righteousness, nobility, honour.

- **Word:** Vicious (Synonym denoting Meaning: faulty)

  Other Synonyms: Wicked, corrupt, depraved, foul, noxious, defective, unruly, spiteful, malignant, mischievous, immoral.

  Antonyms: Virtuous, pure, good, upright, noble, moral, perfect.

- **Word:** Victorious (Synonym denoting Meaning: winner)

  Other Synonyms: Conquering, triumphant, winning, successful, exultant, elated, boastful, vanquishing, subduing, prevailing, overcoming, mastering, subjugating.

  Antonyms: Defeated, worsted, humiliated, beaten, baffled, discomfited, conquered, overcome, vanquished, routed, repulsed, foiled, disconcerted.

- **Word:** View (Synonym denoting Meaning: sight)

  Other Synonyms: Look, survey, inspection, perception, examination, reach, range, scene, prospect, sketch, conception, judgement, opinion, object, aim, purpose, design, vista, perspective, picture, intention, scope, drift, estimate.

  Antonyms: Blindness, darkness, obscuration, mistiness, prejudice, misconception, misrepresentation, deception, error, delusion, aimlessness, non-intention, occultation.

- **Word:** Vigilant (Synonym denoting Meaning: alert)

  Other Synonyms: Awake, careful, on the alert, on the lookout, wary, watchful, wakeful, wide awake, sleepless, cautious, circumspect.

  Antonyms: Negligent, thoughtless, unwary, oblivious, drowsy, in- attentive, careless, dull, heedless, inconsiderate, neglectful, incautious.

- **Word:** Vigorous (Synonym denoting Meaning: full of vigour)

  Other Synonyms: Strong, lusty, robust, forcible, energetic, powerful, sturdy, hearty, thrifty, flourishing, spirited, lively.

  Antonyms: Weak, impotent, incapacitated, feeble, inactive, debilitated, powerless, effete, enervated, indolent.

- **Word:** Vile (Synonym denoting Meaning: base)

  Other Synonyms: Low, worthless, despicable, mean, depraved, impure, sinful, wicked, bad, dis-honourable, ignoble, degraded, sordid, infamous, low-minded.

  Antonyms: Noble, exalted, honourable, upright, estimable, great, worthy, eminent, liberal, free, generous, superior, dignified, sublime, stately.

- **Word:** Violence (Synonym denoting Meaning: vehemence)

  Other Synonyms: Impetuosity, fierceness, force, violation, infraction, infringement, transgression, profanation, assault, outrage.

  Antonyms: Preservation, defense, protection, mildness, self-control, gentleness, respect, obedience, conservation.

- **Word:** Virtue (Synonym denoting Meaning: energy)

  Other Synonyms: Strength, potency, efficacy, value, merit, excellence, worth, meritoriousnesa, integrity, purity, virginity, chastity, goodness, morality, uprightness, rectitude, probity, righteousness, force, power, capacity, honour, worthiness, honesty, truth, duty.

  Antonyms: Inability, weakness, impotency, inefficacy, badness, corruption, impurity, depravity, wickedness, dishonesty.

- **Word:** Visible (Synonym denoting Meaning: perceptible)

  Other Synonyms: Noticeable, apparent, open, conspicuous, obvious, manifest, evident, clear, plain, observable, palpable, discernible.

  Antonyms: Invisible, unseen, concealed, eclipsed, indistinguishable, impalpable, microscopic, indiscernible.

- **Word:** Vivacious (Synonym denoting Meaning: animated)

  Other Synonyms: Sportive, gay, jocund, light-hearted, merry, sprightly, brisk, frolic- some, spirited, cheerful, mirthful.

  Antonyms: Inanimate, dead, lifeless, spiritless, heavy, somber, melancholy, mournful, sad, inert, dull, stolid.

- **Word:** Vivid (Synonym denoting Meaning: clear)

  Other Synonyms: Lucid, striking, active, lively, quick, fresh, intense, animated, bright, strong, spirited, sprightly, brilliant, lustrous, radiant, glowing, sunny.

  Antonyms: Dull, opaque, lurid, obscure, somber, cloudy, dark, colourless, dim, pale, wan, dusky, non-luminous.

- **Word:** Volatile (Synonym denoting Meaning: light-hearted)

  Other Synonyms: Airy, changeable, fickle, lively, evaporating, vaporable, vivacious, buoyant, jocund, inconstant, flighty, whimsical, capricious, unsteady, reckless.

  Antonyms: Fixed, steady, established, determined, solid, settled, persistent, resolute, involatile, somber, demure.

- **Word:** Voluntary (Synonym denoting Meaning: spontaneous)

  Other Synonyms: Willing, un compel led, free, impulsive, unconstrained, deliberate, intentional, optional, gratuitous, by choice, discretional.

  Antonyms: Coerced, forced, involuntary, compulsory, necessitated, constrained.

- **Word:** Vulgar (Synonym denoting Meaning: low class)

  Other Synonyms: Common, general, ordinary, public, vernacular, plebeian, popular, rustic, boorish, low, coarse, base.

  Antonyms: Noble, aristocratic, patrician, high-born, refined, polite, high-bred, stylish, select, choice, cultivated, strict, scientific, philosophical, technical, accurate.

W

- **Word:** Weakness (Synonym denoting Meaning: feebleness)

  Other Synonyms: Debility, languor, imbecility, infirmity, decrepitude, faintness, frailty.

  Antonyms: Strength, vigour, tone, health, power, efficiency, nerve, spirit.

- **Word:** Wealth (Synonym denoting Meaning: rich)

  Other Synonyms: Affluence, opulence, aplenty, fortune, competence, estate, treasure, money, funds, cash, property, luxury, satiety.

  Antonyms: Poverty, scarcity, indigence, lack, want, need.

- **Word:** Wisdom (Synonym denoting Meaning: insight)

  Other Synonyms: Attainment, prudence, depth, judgement, reason, discernment, judiciousness, reasonableness, discretion, knowledge, sagacity, enlightenment, learning, sense, erudition, prescience, skill, foresight, profundity, understanding information.

  Antonyms: Absurdity, folly, imbecility, miscalculation, senselessness, error, foolishness, imprudence, misjudgement, silliness, fatuity, idiocy, indiscretion, nonsense, stupidity.

- **Word:** Wit (Synonym denoting Meaning: fun)

  Other Synonyms: Banter, joke, burlesque, humor, playfulness, waggishness, drollery, jest, pleasantry, witticism facetiousness, jocularity, raillery.

  Antonyms: Dullness, seriousness, sobriety, solemnity, stolidity, stupidity gravity.

- **Word:** Work (Synonym denoting Meaning: achievement)

  Other Synonyms: Doing, labour, product, action, drudgery, occupation, production, business, employment, performance, toil deed, exertion.

  Antonyms: Ease, leisure, recreation, relaxation, repose, rest, vacation idleness.

- **Word:** Wait (Synonym denoting Meaning: pause)

  Other Synonyms: Abide, ambush, anticipate, await, bide, cool it, dally, delay, expect, fill time, foresee, hang, hang around, hang fire, hang out, hold back, hold everything, hold on, hole.

  Antonyms: Abandon, abdicate, absent, beat it, blast off, blow, cut out, decamp, desert, disappear, emigrate, escape, evacuate, exit, get away, go, go away, go forth, make feet.

- **Word:** Wanting (Synonym denoting Meaning: lacking)

  Other Synonyms: Absent, away, bankrupt, bereft, burned out, cooked, cut off, defective, deficient, deprived, destitute, devoid, disappointing, empty, failing, faulty, gone.

  Antonyms: Able, acceptable, all right, capable, comfortable, commensurate, competent, decent, equal, fait, passable, requisite, satisfactory, sufficient, sufficing, suitable.

- **Word:** Warm (Synonym denoting Meaning: enthusiastic)

  Other Synonyms: Amorous, angry, animated, ardent, earnest, effusive, emotional, excitable, excited, fervent, fervid, glowing, gung ho, heated, hot, intense, irascible, keen, lively.

  Antonyms: Abate, allay, assuage, calm down, chill, compose, control, dampen, lessen, mitigate, moderate, quiet, reduce, rein, repress, restrain, simmer down, suppress, temper.

- **Word:** Warp (Synonym denoting Meaning: bend)

  Other Synonyms: Colour, contort, corrupt, crook, curve, debase, debauch, deform, deprave, deviate, distort, kind, misrepresent, misshape, pervert, swerve, torture, turn, twist, vitiate, wind.

  Antonyms: Align, arrange, compose, correct, even, level, make plumb, make straight, neaten, order, put perpendicular, put straight, put upright, put vertical, rectify, smarten up, spruce up, tidy, unbend, uncoil, uncurl, unfold, unravel, unsnarl, untwist.

- **Word:** Wash (Synonym denoting Meaning: clean)

  Other Synonyms: Bath, bathe, brush up, bubble, bubble dance, button chop, clean up, cleanse, dip, douse, drench, float, fresh up, freshen up, hose, imbue, immerse, lap, laund, lave.

  Antonyms: Asperse, attack, bad mouth, blot, blotch, calumniate, decry, defame, defile, denigrate, dishonour, knock, libel, malign, rip, slander, slur, smudge, stain, sully, taint, tarnish, traduce, vilify.

- **Word:** Watery (Synonym denoting Meaning: liquid)

  Other Synonyms: Adulterated, anaemic, aqueous, bloodless, colourless, damp, dilute, diluted, doused, flavourless, fluid, humid, insipid, marshy, moist, pale, runny, serous, sodden.

  Antonyms: Caked, clabbered, close, clotted, coagulated, compact, compressed, concrete, condensed, congealed, consolidated, crowded, curdled, deep, dense, firm, fixed.

- **Word:** Word (Synonym denoting Meaning: way in)

  Other Synonyms: Access, approach, avenue, door, doorway, entrance, foyer, gate, hall, ingress, ingression, inlet, lobby, opening, passage, passageway, portal, threshold, vestibule.

  Antonyms: Departure, doorway, egression, emanation, emergence, escape, exiting, exodus, issue, opening, outlet, passage, setting-out, vent, way out, withdrawal.

- **Word:** Weep (Synonym denoting Meaning: cry)

  Other Synonyms: Cry, shed tears, lament, complain, drip, be soaked, sob, bewail, bemoan, droop.

  Antonyms: Laugh, smile, rejoice, be cheerful, enjoy.

- **Word:** Weight (Synonym denoting Meaning: heavy)

  Other Synonyms: Heaviness, pressure, burden, importance, influence, consequence, moment, ponderousness, gravity, load, power, efficacy, impressiveness.

  Antonyms: Lightness, levity, volatility, insignificance, triviality, weakness, worthlessness, ease, facility.

- **Word:** Welcome (Synonym denoting Meaning: salutation)

  Other Synonyms: Greeting, reception, pleasing, gladly entertained, acceptable, agreeable, gratifying, gratuitous, free.

  Antonyms: Unwelcome, unpleasant, unacceptable.

- **Word:** Welfare (Synonym denoting Meaning: doing good for someone)

  Other Synonyms: Prosperity, happiness, well-being,

enjoyment, success, weal, advantage, benefit, profit, luck, thrift.

Antonyms: Adversity, misfortune, reverses, failure, ill luck, unhappiness.

- **Word:** Well (Synonym denoting Meaning: good)

  Other Synonyms: Desirable, fortunate, advantageous, healthy, favoured, lucky, hale, sound, Justly, rightly, abundantly, fully, adequately, thoroughly, satisfactorily, advantageously, conveniently, properly.

  Antonyms: Sickly, diseased, unwell, poorly, unlucky, unfortunate, wrongly, poorly, imperfectly, improperly, badly.

- **Word:** Wet (Synonym denoting Meaning: rainy)

  Other Synonyms: Damp, moist, rainy, humid, nasty, dank, showery, lively, interesting.

  Antonyms: Dry, parched, thirsty, arid, plain, unvarnished, shrewd, sharp, quaint.

- **Word:** Whimsical (Synonym denoting Meaning: capricious)

  Other Synonyms: Fanciful, queer, strange, freakish, quaint, fantastic.

  Antonyms: Staid, serious, softer, matter-of-fact, steady, sedate.

- **Word:** White (Synonym denoting Meaning: snowy)

  Other Synonyms: Pale, pallid, unblemished, innocent, pure, gray, hoary, fortunate, happy, favourable.

  Antonyms: Black, dark, colourless, negro, sooty, dismal, gloomy, forbidding, sullen, foreboding, impure, sullied.

- **Word:** Whole (Synonym denoting Meaning: all)

  Other Synonyms: Total, complete, entire, undivided, uninjured, unbroken, unimpaired, integral, sound, perfect, faultless, strong, well, healthy.

  Antonyms: Partial, imperfect, unsound, ill, sick, divided, fractional.

- **Word:** Wholesome (Synonym denoting Meaning: salubrious)

  Other Synonyms: Salutary, healthy, healthful, nourishing, nutritious, strengthening, invigorating, beneficial, good, fresh, sound, uncorrupt.

  Antonyms: Detrimental, deleterious, prejudicial, hurtful, pernicious, noxious.

- **Word:** Wicked (Synonym denoting Meaning: sinful)

  Other Synonyms: Criminal, guilty, immoral, ungodly, profane, un-righteous, atrocious, unholy, vicious, nefarious, heinous, abandoned, iniquitous, depraved, unprincipled, irreverent, vile, abandoned, bad, evil, unjust, ill, outrageous, monstrous.

  Antonyms: Good, righteous, just, godly, virtuous, fair, honourable, unsullied, pious, benevolent, up- right, reputable, true, excellent.

- **Word:** Wickedness (Synonym denoting Meaning: crime)

  Other Synonyms: Sin, vice, iniquity, evil, depravity, immorality, enormity, badness, vileness, corruption.

  Antonyms: Goodness, piety, godliness, righteousness, honour, virtue, benevolence.

- **Word:** Wide (Synonym denoting Meaning: broad)

  Other Synonyms: Spacious, vast, extensive, comprehensive, liberal, remote, distant, far, ample, expanded.

  Antonyms: Narrow, contracted, confined, cramped, constricted, limited, bigoted, parsimonious, close, near.

- **Word:** Wild (Synonym denoting Meaning: untamed)

  Other Synonyms: Uncultivated, undomesticated, savage, uncivilized, rude, ferocious, violent, turbulent, disorderly, crazy, ungoverned, visionary, unsheltered, exposed.

  Antonyms: Tame, domesticated, cultivated, civilised, populated, frequented, polite, gentle, refined, rational, orderly, sane, controlled, sober, collected.

- **Word:** Wile (Synonym denoting Meaning: trick)

  Other Synonyms: Snare, artifice, beguilement, allurement, stratagem, cheat, fraud, imposture, deceit, deception, contrivance, device.

  Antonyms: Artlessness, openness, candor, straightforwardness.

- **Word:** Willful (Synonym denoting Meaning: self-determined)

  Other Synonyms: Voluntary, obstinate, perverse, stubborn, refractory, self-willed, headstrong, wayward, intentional, preconceived, premeditated, designed, deliberate, purposed.

  Antonyms: Concessive, compliant, amenable, obedient, docile, manageable, adventitious, accidental.

- **Word:** Will (Synonym denoting Meaning: choice)

  Other Synonyms: Determination, preference, volition, decree, desire, command, purpose, control, disposal, testament, resolution, decision, self-reliance, force, inclination, pleasure, disposition, behest, order, direction.

  Antonyms: Indecision, vacillation, indeterminateness, indifference, sensibility, perception.

- **Word:** Win (Synonym denoting Meaning: gain)

  Other Synonyms: Get, procure, earn, be victorious, prevail, obtain, acquire, achieve, conquer, succeed, accomplish.

  Antonyms: Lose, fail of, miss, forfeit, be deprived or bereaved of.

- **Word:** Winning (Synonym denoting Meaning: charming)

  Other Synonyms: Attractive, alluring, pleasing, bewitching, winsome, fascinating, delightful, lovely, captivating, prepossessing, enchanting.

  Antonyms: Repulsive, unpleasing, repellent, disagreeable, offensive, repugnant, revolting, disgusting, odious.

- **Word:** Wise (Synonym denoting Meaning: knowing)

  Other Synonyms: Erudite, wary, learned, sagacious, crafty, judicious, discreet, skilled, intelligent, rational, sage, sensible, logical, deep, discerning, profound, philosophical.

Antonyms: Senseless, idiotic, irrational, nonsensical, imprudent, irrational, indiscreet, ridiculous, preposterous, insensate.

- **Word:** Wit (Synonym denoting Meaning: ingenuity)

  Other Synonyms: Humour, satire, sarcasm, irony, burlesque, intellect, mind, understanding, sense, man of genius or humour, penetration, discernment, in-sight, acumen facetiousness.

  Antonyms: Stupidity, inanity, obtuseness, vapidity, dullness, commonplace, matter-of-fact, irrationality, platitude, dolt, dullard, sobriety, solemnity, seriousness, gravity.

- **Word:** With (Synonym denoting Meaning: by)

  Other Synonyms: On the side of, by the help of, attending, accompanying, close, against, according to, in contrast with, upon, immediately after.

  Antonyms: Withdraw, take back, recall, retire, drawback, remove, recede, depart.

- **Word:** Witness (Synonym denoting Meaning: testimony)

  Other Synonyms: Attestation, evidence, proof, one who attests or is directly cognizant of, eye-witness, deponent, corroborator, spectator, auditor, voucher.

  Antonyms: Belief, hearsay, rumor, report, invalidation, refutation.

- **Word:** Witty (Synonym denoting Meaning: cunning)

  Other Synonyms: Acute, sharp, smart, facetious, arch, keen, amusing, humorous, satirical, taunting, ironical.

  Antonyms: Dull, stupid, obtuse, dry, prosaic, prosy, tiresome, tedious, serious.

- **Word:** Woe (Synonym denoting Meaning: grief)

  Other Synonyms: Sorrow, misery, calamity, curse, malediction, disconsolateness, tribulation, melancholy, agony, depression, unhappiness.

Antonyms: Joy, delight, pleasure, prosperity, enjoyment, bliss, felicity, welfare, cheerfulness, merriment.

- **Word:** Wonder (Synonym denoting Meaning: astonishment)

  Other Synonyms: Admiration, amazement, surprise, awe, bewilderment, curiosity, portent, miracle, prodigy, marvel, phenomenon, sight, rarity, spectacle.

  Antonyms: Expectation, anticipation, familiarity, apathy, indifference, foreknowledge, prescience, ennui, satiety, platitude, truism, commonplace.

- **Word:** Wonderful (Synonym denoting Meaning: amazing)

  Other Synonyms: Astonishing, marvelous, surprising, improbable, strange, incredulous, startling, awesome, portentous, extraordinary, prodigious, wondrous.

  Antonyms: Commonplace, familiar, expected, ordinary, wonted, hackneyed, customary, habitual.

- **Word:** Work (Synonym denoting Meaning: exertion)

  Other Synonyms: Activity, effort, toil, employment, labour, business, duty, product, fabric, production, performance, manufacture, act, deed, service, result, effect, achievement, feat, composition, structure, management, treatment, operation.

  Antonyms: Frustration, abortion, hodge-podge, failure, deficiency, defect, fault, miscarriage, rest, inertia, fruitlessness, inoperativeness, inefficiency, futility, repose, relaxation, ease, vacation, idleness, leisure.

- **Word:** World (Synonym denoting Meaning: earth)

  Other Synonyms: Universe, creation, affairs, interests, life, action, occupation, inhabitants, people, mankind, globe, cosmos, planet, nature, public, society, human race.

  Antonyms: Heaven, atom, individual.

- **Word:** Worldly (Synonym denoting Meaning: human)

  Other Synonyms: Common, secular, temporal, mundane, terrestrial, earthly, fleshly, carnal, universal, sublunary, sordid, selfish, ambitious, earth-born, groveling.

  Antonyms: Spiritual, ethereal, celestial, heavenly, lunar, solar, incorporeal, ghostly, ideal, abstract, mental, intellectual, sacred, holy, pure.

- **Word:** Worry (Synonym denoting Meaning: care)

  Other Synonyms: Anxiety, fret, solicitude, torment, vexation, trouble, annoyance, plague, perplexity, concern, fear, apprehension, uneasiness, misgiving.

  Antonyms: Trust, calm, courage, serenity, tranquility, quiet, ease of mind, resolution, dauntlessness.

- **Word:** Worship (Synonym denoting Meaning: prayer)

  Other Synonyms: Reverence, homage, adoration, submission, obsequiousness, honour, abjectness, revere, idolize, respect, defer, venerate, deify, honour, exalt.

  Antonyms: Detestation, hatred, abhorrence, loathing, disgust, antipathy, assertion, defiance, challenge, hate, disdain, abominate, contemn, loathe.

- **Word:** Worthless (Synonym denoting Meaning: undeserving)

  Other Synonyms: Useless, valueless, vile, mean, miserable, poor, wretched, abject, unworthy, ignoble, abandoned, depraved, refuse, waste.

  Antonyms: Costly, valuable, dear, high-priced, expensive, sumptuous, splendid, rich, precious, useful, excellent, estimable, virtuous, worthy.

- **Word:** Wound (Synonym denoting Meaning: injure)

  Other Synonyms: Hurt, injure, damage, harm, cut, stab, rend, lacerate, pain, annoy, mortify, offend.

  Antonyms: Heal, allay, cure, remedy, soothe, repair, appease, assuage, comfort, harmonize.

- **Word:** Wrathful (Synonym denoting Meaning: indignant)

  Other Synonyms: Furious, raging, passionate, choleric, ireful, angry, incensed, irate, wroth, mad, provoked, resentful.

  Antonyms: Calm, collected, controlled, repressed, masterly, restrained, good-tempered.

- **Word:** Wretched (Synonym denoting Meaning: miserable)

  Other Synonyms: Calamitous, afflicted, unhappy, degraded, worthless, paltry, forlorn, comfortless, distressed, shocking, deplorable, depressing, sad, contemptible, mean, pitiful, debased, humiliated.

  Antonyms: Prosperous, flourishing, fortunate, happy, enviable, felicitous, successful, thriving, valuable, honoured, noble, exalted.

- **Word:** Wrong (Synonym denoting Meaning: incorrect)

  Other Synonyms: Injurious, unjust, faulty, detrimental, unfit, improper, incorrect, mistaken, erroneous, illegal, immoral.

  Antonyms: Right, upright, lawful, equitable, fair, just, proper, suitable, appropriate, fit, correct, true, actual, real.

- **Word:** Wrought (Synonym denoting Meaning: worked)

  Other Synonyms: Elaborated, performed, done, effected, executed, produced, manufactured.

  Antonyms: Rough, crude, coarse, raw, unpolished.

- **Word:** Wry (Synonym denoting Meaning: twisted)

  Other Synonyms: Distorted, misdirected, perverted, wrested, askew, contorted, deformed, deranged, crooked, awry.

  Antonyms: Straight, rectilinear, direct, upright, erect, perpendicular, shapely, comely, symmetrical, proper, well-formed.

X

- **Word:** X Ray (Synonym denoting Meaning: Roentgen rays)

  Other Synonyms: Actinism, cathode rays, encephalogram,

fluoroscope, radioactivity, radiograph, refractometry, ultraviolet rays.

- **Word:** Xerox (Synonym denoting Meaning: archetype)

  Other Synonyms: Carbon, carbon copy, cast, clone, counterfeit, counterpart, ditto, ectype, effigy, ersatz, facsimile, forgery, hard copy, image, impersonation, impression, imprint, likeness, microfiche, mimeograph, miniature, mirror, model, offprint, parallel, pattern, photocopy, photograph, photostat, portrait, print, reflection, replica, replication, representation, reprint, reproduction, rubbings, similarity, simulacrum, simulation, study, tracing, transcript, transcription, type.

  Antonyms: Original, origination, source.

Y

- **Word:** Yawn (Synonym denoting Meaning: be eager)

  Other Synonyms: Open wide, gape, desire.

  Antonyms: Close, shut, engulf.

- **Word:** Yearly (Synonym denoting Meaning: every year)

  Other Synonyms: Annual, happening each year, per annum, every year, year by year.

  Antonyms: Perennial, everlasting, evergreen.

- **Word:** Yearn (Synonym denoting Meaning: to have eager desire for)

  Other Synonyms: Long, desire, be eager, covet, crave, hanker.

  Antonyms: Loathe, revolt, recoil, shudder at, despise.

- **Word:** Yell (Synonym denoting Meaning: outcry)

  Other Synonyms: Cry out, shriek, scream, holler.

  Antonyms: Keep silence, subdue, silence.

- **Word:** Yield (Synonym denoting Meaning: to produce)

  Other Synonyms: Furnish, produce, afford, bear, render,

relinquish, give in, let go, forego, accede, acquiesce, resign, surrender, concede, allow, grant, submit, succumb, comply, consent, agree.

Antonyms: Withdraw, withhold, retain, deny, refuse, vindicate, assert, claim, disallow, appropriate, resist, dissent, protest, struggle, strive.

- **Word:** Yielding (Synonym denoting Meaning: producing)

  Other Synonyms: Conceding, surrendering, supple, pliant, submissive, unresisting, obsequious, attentive, flexible, compliant, accommodating.

  Antonyms: Defiant, resisting, obstinate, firm, stiff, hard, perverse.

- **Word:** Yoke (Synonym denoting Meaning: bond)

  Other Synonyms: Chain, link, tie, servitude, bondage, vassalage, service, subjection, subservience.

  Antonyms: Freedom, liberty, authority, command.

- **Word:** Young (Synonym denoting Meaning: juvenile)

  Other Synonyms: Immature, inexperienced, innocent, ignorant, youthful, boyish, girlish, childlike.

  Antonyms: Old, mature, adult, experienced, knowing, senile, aged, decrepit, venerable, antique, antiquated, obsolete, superannuated.

- **Word:** Youth (Synonym denoting Meaning: adolescence)

  Other Synonyms: Childhood, infancy, youthfulness, juvenility, minority, lad, boy, girl, youngster.

  Antonyms: Age, senility, maturity.

Z

- **Word:** Zeal (Synonym denoting Meaning: energy)

  Other Synonyms: Ardour, eagerness, earnestness, fervour, enthusiasm, feeling, devotion, inpassion, spirit.

Antonyms: Apathy, indifference, coldness, carelessness, sluggishness, torpor.

- **Word:** Zealot (Synonym denoting Meaning: devotee)

  Other Synonyms: Partisan, bigot, enthusiast, fanatic, visionary, dreamer.

  Antonyms: Renegade, traitor, deserter, lukewarm person.

- **Word:** Zealous (Synonym denoting Meaning: eager)

  Other Synonyms: Ardent, anxious, earnest, enthusiastic, fervid, steadfast, keen, fervent, devoted, prompt, ready, fiery, passionate.

  Antonyms: Lukewarm, indifferent, cold, apathetic, passionless, phlegmatic.

- **Word:** Zenith (Synonym denoting Meaning: height)

  Other Synonyms: Pinnacle, acme, summit, culmination, maximum, apex, top.

  Antonyms: Nadir, lowest point, depth, minimum.

- **Word:** Zero (Synonym denoting Meaning: cypher)

  Other Synonyms: Naught, cipher, nothing.

  Antonyms: Something, existence, creation, infinity.

- **Word:** Zest (Synonym denoting Meaning: relish)

  Other Synonyms: Flavour, appetizer, pleasure, gusto, gust, enjoyment, relish, sharpener, enhancement, savour, taste, smack, sauce, appetite.

  Antonyms: Distaste, disrelish, detriment.

- **Word:** Zone (Synonym denoting Meaning: orbit)

  Other Synonyms: Girdle, belt, girth, cincture, band, baldric, region, climate, clime, circuit, circumference, zodiac.

  Antonyms: Sphere, universe.

- **Word:** Zest (Synonym denoting Meaning: energy)

  Other Synonyms: Appetite, ardour, bliss, bounce, cheer,

delectation, delight, eagerness, ecstasy, elation, enjoyment, enthusiasm, fervour, gusto, guts, happiness, keenness, moxie.

Antonyms: Aloofness, coldness, coolness, detachment, disinterest, dispassion, disregard, dullness, half-heartedness, heedlessness, indifference, insensibility.